Greg McEnnally has been teaching English in China for ten years. Prior to that he taught English in Indonesia for a year. In Australia he was a high school Maths and Science teacher and he also taught this in Papua New Guinea for three years. This background has given him some appreciation for other cultures. He loves to travel and while in China has availed himself of every opportunity to do so. This book is the result.

DEDICATION

I dedicate this book to my travelling companions, especially Bernadette, with whom I travelled most. She is expert in the details of travel, like booking flights on line, booking hotels and ordering food at restaurants. She was a most tolerant and amiable companion, even to the point of laughing at my jokes!

ACKNOWLEDGEMENTS

I would like to thank many people:
Firstly, the readers of my Jottings over the years for their comments and encouragement to put them into book form, which had not been my intention.
Secondly, my travelling companions, especially F1.
Thirdly, all those truly delightful people who offered me their friendship and hospitality, especially Erica, who treats me as her father.
Fourthly, the staff of Austin Macauley, who surprised me initially by judging that there was something here worth publishing, then with their advice and expertise.

Greg McEnnally

A TRAVELLER IN CHINA

AUSTIN MACAULEY
PUBLISHERS LTD.

ISBN 978 184963 845 6

www.austinmacauley.com

First Published (2014)
Austin Macauley Publishers Ltd.
25 Canada Square
Canary Wharf
London
E14 5LB

Printed and bound in Great Britain

Contents

Introduction — **11**

National Day 2008 — **13**

1. Kaili – 1st October 2008 — 13
2. A Kaili Wedding – 3rd October 2008 — 15
3. Kaili to Tongren – 4th October 2008 — 18

Winter Holidays 2009 — **22**

4. An Overview – February 2009 — 22
5. Tongren to Guiyang – 10th January 2009 — 24
6. Guiyang – 10th – 14th January 2009 — 26
7. Guiyang to Kunming – 14th – 15th January 2009 — 28
8. Kunming – 15th January 2009 — 30
9. More in Kunming – 16th – 17th January 2009 — 32
10. Kunming to Dali – 18th – 19th January 2009 — 34
11. Dali – 20th January 2009 — 37
12. Dali to Lijiang – 21st – 22nd January 2009 — 40
13. Yu Long Xue Shan – 23rd January 2009 — 42
14. Tiger Leaping Gorge Day 1 – 24th January 2009 — 44
15. Tiger Leaping Gorge Day 2 – 25th January 2009 — 46
16. Tiger Leaping Gorge Day 3 – 26th January 2009 — 48
17. Tiger Leaping Gorge Day 4 – 27th January 2009 — 51
18. Lijiang to Dali – 28th January 2009 — 53
19. Dali to Kunming – 29th – 30th January 2009 — 55
20. Kunming to Xiamen 31st January – 3rd February 2009 — 58
21. Hui An to Fuzhou – 4th – 6th February 2009 — 60
22. In Fuzhou – 7th – 9th February 2009 — 62
23. Fuzhou to Guiyang – 10th – 12th February 2009 — 65
24. Last Leg – Friday 13th February 2009 — 68

National Day Holidays 2009 — **71**

25. Tongren to Zhengzhou – 30th September – 2nd October 2009 — 71
26. Henan Province – 3rd October 2009 — 74
27. Kaifeng – Sunday 4th October 2009 — 76
28. Longmen Grottoes – Monday 5th October 2009 — 78
29. Shaolin Temple – Tuesday 6th October 2009 — 80
30. Final Days – 7th – 9th October 2009 — 83

Summer Holidays 2010 — **86**

31. Zhijin, Guizhou Province – 15th – 16th July 2010 — 86
32. Bijie – 17th – 18th July 2010 — 89
33. Life on a Farm – 18th – 22nd July 2010 — 91
34. Animal Farm – 18th – 22nd July 2010 — 94

35. Bijie to Guiyang – 22nd – 23rd July 2010   96
36. Guiyang to Xian, Shaanxi Province 24th – 25th July 2010   99
37. Xian – Old City Walls – 26th July 2009   101
38. Around Xian – 27th July 2010   103
39. Terracotta Warriors – 28th July 2010   105
40. Puppets and Pottery – 29th – 30 July 2010   107
41. Xian to Chengdu, Sichuan Province – 31st July – 3rd August 2010

                                                                                                                   110
42. Chengdu Opera – 3rd August 2010   112
43. Qinling Range – 5th – 8th August 2010   114
44. Jiu Zhai Gou – 6th August 2010   117
45. Luodai Ancient Town – 10th August 2010   120
46. Fenghuang, Hunan Province – 12th – 14th and 24th August 2010 122

April Excursions 2011   **125**
47. Zai Ying, Guizhou Province – 1st – 3rd April 2011   125
48. Guanzhou – Getting There – 15th April 2011   128
49. Guanzhou Teaching – 16th April 2011   130
50. Guanzhou Mountain Scenery – 16th – 17th April 2011   133

PHOTOGRAPHS   **136**

Summer Work, July 2011   **181**
51. Third Visit to Sinan – 8th – 10th July 2011   181
52. To Hong Kong – 12th – 13th July 2011   182
53. Is 8 a Lucky Number? – 7th – 14th July 2011   185
54. Hong Kong to Meitan, Guizhou Province – 15th July 2011   187
55. First Week in Meitan – 18th – 22nd July 2011   189
56. Of Swims and Tea – 24th – 30th July 2011   191
57. Meitan Culture – July 2011   193

Summer Holidays 2011   **197**
58. Tian Men Shan, Hunan Province, Part 1 – 10th – 11th August 2011

                                                                                                                   197
59. Tian Men Shan, Part 2 – 11th – 13 August 2011   199

Summer Holidays 2012 – Taiwan Series   **202**
60. Taipei – Four Sites – 6th – 10th July 2012   202
61. Taipei – The Red Line – 6th – 10th July 2012   204
62. Taichung – 8th – 11th July 2012   207
63. Shuili – 11th – 20th July 2012   209
64. Cistercian Monastery – 11th – 20th July 2012   211
65. Sun Moon Lake – 17th – 18th July 2012   214
66. Chiayi – 20th 22nd July 2012   217
67. Alishan – 22nd – 23rd July 2012   219
68. Tainan – 24th July 2012   222
69. Kenting – 25th – 27th July 2012   224

70. Taitung and Lyudao – 27th – 28th July 2012   226
71. Hualien and Taroko Gorge – 29th – 31st July 2012   229
72. Hualien to Chongqing, China – 31st July – 7th August 2012   232
73. A Point of View 23rd September 2012   235

National Day, 1st October 2012   **238**
74. Xian Nu Shan, Chongqing – 1st October 2012   238
75. Furong Dong – 2nd October 2012   241
76. Diao Yu Cheng, Chongqing – 29th December 2012   243

Spring Festival 2013   **247**
77. Songtao, Guizhou Province   247
78. Zaiying Village – 27th – 31st January 2013   249
79. Bijie City – 1st – 3rd February 2013   252
80. Country Life – 3rd – 4th February 2013   254
81. Mountain Views – 4th – 5th February 2013   256
82. Shui Ting Village – 6th February 2013   258
83. The C Household – 6th – 15th February 2013   261
84. The Inhabitants – 6th – 15th February 2013   263
85. Other Residents – 6th – 15th February 2013   265
86. Walks – 6th – 15th February 2013   267
87. Household Matters – 6th – 15th February 2013   270
88. Spring Festival – 10th February 2013   272
89. Last Days in Han Zhuang Village – 11th – 15th February 2013   274
90. Han Zhuang to Chongqing – 15th – 17th February 2013   277

Chengdu Excursion, June 2013   **280**
91. Chengdu – 21st – 22nd June 2013   280
92. Li Bing – 22nd June 2013   282

Eileen's Wedding, Xiamen, Fujian Province, July 2013   **286**
93. Eileen's Wedding – 1st July 2013   286
94. Hui An – 3rd – 4th July 2013   288
95. Fuzhou – 4th – 7th July 2013   291

Manchurian Series – the North East, July-August 2013   **295**
96. Manchuria -14th July 2013   295
97. Harbin Architecture – Hei Long Jiang Province – 14th – 18th, 21st,
26th July 2013   297
98. Two Parks in Harbin – 15th – 18th July 2013   300
99. Yabuli – 19th – 21st July 2013   303
100. Hei He – 22nd – 23rd July 2013   306
101. Oh My God! – 23rd – 25th July 2013   309
102. Harbin to Yanji, Jilin Province 26th – 27th July 2013   312
103. Yanji to Chang Bai Shan – 28th – 29th July 2013   314
104. Chang Bai Shan – Heaven Lake – 30th July 2013   316
105. Chang Bai Waterfall – 30th July 2013   318

106.   Dandong, Liaoning Province – 1st – 2nd August 2013   321
107.   Dalian – 4th – 5th August 2013   324
108.   Qingdao, Shandong Province – 6th – 8th August 2013   326
109.   Qingdao Beaches – 6th – 8th August 2013   329
110.   Qingdao; St Michael's Cathedral 7th – 8th August 2013   331
111.   Shanghai to Chongqing – 10th – 12th August 2013   334

Conclusion   **337**

Introduction

This book is based upon what I have called "China Jottings". Over the ten years that I have been in China, I have been jotting down my experiences, at the rate of roughly one a week. These I have sent off to friends around the world – personal e-mails. My objective has been firstly, to keep focused on what is happening with a view to greater understanding, and secondly to inform others. The time has now come to share these with a wider public.

It has been an amazing time, one which has witnessed unprecedented changes. Over this decade, China has grown into a giant whose economic development has been extraordinary. The world has seen nothing like it on such a scale. There have also been enormous social changes, some good some not so good. The greatest human migration ever in human history has taken place, with something like 500 million people moving from the countryside into the cities.

What I have seen I have seen and what I have experienced I have experienced, but my interpretation of these events is something else, so that the conclusions I have reached may not gel with other people's views. I have as well been informing myself through reading, and once again the conclusions I have reached may not be those of others. Feel free to disagree.

This book is concerned with my travels only, and those only between 2008 and 2013. My experiences as an English teacher may in time find themselves into another volume. One of the advantages in being a teacher is that you do have long holidays and I have of set purpose taken full advantage of this. Travel, however, is not primarily about visiting lots of places. There are many places I have not visited – obviously, since this is impossible. Even when I have visited some town, there is a lot that I have not seen. Quantity is not of prime importance; what you get out of each place is far more important. With this in mind I have endeavoured to be more of a pilgrim than a traveller. A traveller moves through the land, whereas a pilgrim allows the land to move through them and be changed by their experiences.

This is a good time to make a note about inclusive language, which I have tried to use throughout. One should not, for instance, use "man", when one is referring to women and children as well as men. There is however, a problem in that I find the use of "he/she", "him/her" and "his/hers" to be clumsy, especially when repeated. In this book I have substituted these with "shey", "shem" and "sheir", as the singular form of "they", "them" and "their". I believe it is simpler.

There are many people I would like to thank. My long suffering readers over the past ten years must come first. I am particularly grateful to those who have corrected some of what I have written. I would like to thank the people with whom I have come into contact, especially my students who have opened their hearts to me. They are truly wonderful people. Next I would like to thank my travelling companions. Sometimes I travelled alone. Sometimes I joined an organised tour. Sometimes I travelled with friends. In particular I am grateful to F1 who has been my principal companion, putting up with me on many a journey, and making these journeys so much more enjoyable. It is good to have someone who even laughs at my jokes! Her advice with regard to this book has been invaluable.

It has been a real privilege to have been here in China over this time, one that I have enjoyed immensely. I just hope this book will enable other people to share in my enjoyment and just maybe to further their understanding of China.

National Day 2008

1.   *Kaili – 1ˢᵗ October 2008*

This year, National Day, Oct. 1ˢᵗ, fell on a Wednesday. This meant that we had classes on Saturday and Sunday, making up for the classes we would miss on Monday and Tuesday. The holiday thus became seven days off, from Monday September 29ᵗʰ till Sunday October 5ᵗʰ inclusive. This gives people a chance to travel, should they so desire, and especially gives those people living away from home the opportunity to see their families; this includes migrant workers and students.

Aussie 1 and I had been invited to a wedding. The bride and groom, S and B, had been classmates and students of Aussie 1. For those of you – if any – who have been assiduously following my narrative over the years, you may recall China Jottings 99 to 102, during January 2005, when I spent some time with S, staying for some days in her house near Yichang. I had seen her on other occasions as well and had also met B. Hence I was looking forward to the wedding.

Now it just so happens that I am still working on my Z or working visa. To this end I had turned up at the local police station a couple of days earlier. The officer asked me if I was intending to travel during National Day. You can guess what is coming. So I waxed lyrical, telling him how important this wedding was for me and how much I had been looking forward to going. Upon which he said; "If you apply for your visa now you cannot go to the wedding". "I do have a photocopy of my passport," I replied. "No, you must have your passport with you." I had noticed his insertion of "if", so I said, "Oh, you are saying that I can postpone this application until after National Day?" "Yes, you still have time before your current visa expires if you apply immediately after National Day." "Thank you, officer," says I most effusively, "I will do that."

So on Wednesday October 1ˢᵗ, Aussie 1 and I boarded a bus for Kaili, some three hours away along a modern, fast expressway. This was a surprise, as I had not been expecting such a good road in this poor province. The countryside is fascinating, lush green since it appears to rain hereabouts every three days out of four. I was particularly taken by villages where all the houses seem to be the same, all dark, with black slate rooves edged in white. The contrast is striking. These are Miao villages, one of the minority peoples who nevertheless are quite numerous in these parts. Another town is also worthy of observation It is brand new, in fact still being constructed, but while it looks spick and span, there is a sameness about the buildings: all grey and all the same height, about ten storeys. And there is another oddity: it appears deserted. What is going on? Apparently it has been built for people displaced by the construction of a nearby dam, but while their houses are about to be drowned, the people do not want to move. Who can blame them?

We were met at the bus station by both S and B and it was wonderful to see them again. They conducted us to a hotel opposite, which just happens to be owned by B's father. Accommodation and meals were to cost us nothing. Wonderful, but before you all rush off to avail yourselves of such a bargain, let me introduce you to this hotel, which, of course, shall be nameless. It is dirty, with rubbish on the stairs and rubbish thrown carelessly out of windows; the view from our room over the back of the hotel is a wonder to behold, with rubbish carpeting the ground and festooning awnings. Our room was comfortable, though some westerners might not like the hard beds, and that includes the edges. The space was so cramped that I kept knocking my leg on the sharp corner of the bed in my endeavours to get past. There is a lounge chair, a TV and that is about it. So forget about a drinks cupboard, or complimentary tea and coffee. There is no en suite bathroom, not even a towel – I had to rush around to a local supermarket to buy them. Not to worry, as I needed one anyway; my apartment in Tongren did not come with a towel either. The toilet is down at the end of the corridor, consisting of six cubicles, with no distinctions for male and female. These are in the usual Chinese style of a hole in the floor, lined with tiles. Three of these cubicles are for the showers. Once the boiler is heated with coals, you can even have a hot shower, certainly hot enough. The shower head consists of a rubber hose. Now comes the tricky bit -; please try not to slip down the toilet while you are showering. Lord alone knows where you could end up. Now what rating would one give to this fair establishment? 5 star? Nah, don't think so. I think I would rate it about 1 ½.

Kaili is a pleasant town, seemingly with more to recommend it that Tongren. I really liked the bus stops. They are not just poles in the ground holding up the number of some bus route, but elaborate structures, whose roofs are built in the style of the minority peoples, either Miao or Dong. B's family – and he is the groom, should you have forgotten – is Dong. In China, of course, the majority of people are Han.

Then there is the stadium, which appears to be the major tourist attraction hereabouts and rightly so, as it is quite beautiful and unique. It is also built in Dong and Miao architectural styles, with the roofing a dark grey colour, edged with white, similar to the houses we had seen. Every so often around the stadium there is a small tower, in a pagoda-like style. The front gate is quite elaborate, sporting (!) highly decorated totem poles and crossbeams. Atop is a horned structure, presumably reflecting the buffalo, which features prominently in their culture. They even have buffalo fights. These horned roofs remind me of similar roofs I had seen in Central Sulawesi, Indonesia, also reflecting the buffalo. On either side of this main gate are bronze statues of a Dong couple on the left and a Miao couple on the right. The Dong man is playing a ukulele style musical instrument, while the Miao man has a rifle. I do not know the significance of this. On either side of the approaching plaza is an octagonal pagoda-like structure, somewhat conical, built entirely of wood, but without nails. This is a feature of Miao architecture, which – according to the display under the stadium – is "first among the world". I bet you did not know that. Again we have that obnoxious tendency to beat one's own chest to the detriment of others. Let us just say that their architectural style is unique, it is beautiful and is to be preserved – then leave it at that.

2.   *A Kaili Wedding – 3ʳᵈ October 2008*

Over the years I have attended quite a number of weddings, most of them as the celebrant. While in China I have been to just one prior to this and that ended in divorce. This would be the first time involving one of the minority groups – so I was rather looking forward to it, as indeed I had stressed to that Tongren police officer.

Naturally, we were curious as to what would happen, so in the couple of days leading up to the ceremony, we kept asking the bride (who is Han Chinese) what would happen. "I don't know" was the somewhat enigmatic reply. "What do you mean 'You don't know'? You're the bride." I was thinking of our Western model, where the bride is very much involved in the planning of her special day for months beforehand. Bear in mind too, that we of the Western World want to know everything. We hate being kept in the dark. But this is not the

Chinese way. Many are the times I have not been told that something is about to happen until just prior to the event. "We have a college dinner organized for tonight and you have been invited." Great, and I was so looking forward to my vegemite sandwich. Be that as it may, it was still a surprise that the bride herself did not know the day before what would happen.

The big day dawned. This hotel caters for weddings, so naturally we assumed that they would be doing the catering for the son of the owner. Not so. It turns out that two other weddings had been scheduled for this same evening, and our bride did not want to share her special day with any other bride. Now that rings a bell; brides the world over would agree. We slept in until called for breakfast. We assumed this would be in the hotel, where we had been eating all our meals, all of them, incidentally, being of the hot pot variety. But no, we were to go out. So we walked up the street to find a place that sells food. They brought out a table and some chairs and we sat down, or the others did, as I walked off around the corner to buy some bananas to complement our Chinese fare. It was a very nice little meal, but no sooner had we finished than the proprietor cleared the table, whipped the chairs out from under us, and stowed everything away. What is going on? Apparently it is illegal for her to serve food to customers on the footpath. Lord alone know why, as this seems to happen nearly everywhere. Police have been known to turn up with a truck in order to their confiscate tables and chairs. Apparently the previous time they had done this, there occurred the rather comical scene of the owners repossessing their property by taking them off the truck again, just as soon as the police officers turned away to confiscate another load.

The morning passed in leisurely fashion, with not much seeming to happen. We also spent time looking at the wedding photos. These were mounted in four albums of thick cardboard, showing the couple in various costumes, surrounded by slogans in English, some of which made sense. The photos had obviously been airbrushed to the extent where their individual identities were virtually lost. S looked more like Emma Peel (of the Avengers) than herself. And for this they pay some 5,000 Yuan. In my book this is a waste of money, but others evidently disagree. "Sarah, when are you going to get ready?" "Oh after lunch; there is plenty of time." Lunch was in a restaurant, about ten minutes' walk away. After lunch I went for a longer walk, both to see the sights and to get some exercise.

Late afternoon arrived and I came back from my walk to find the bride sitting on her bed – her room was two doors from ours – ready;

hair coiffured, make-up applied, white wedding dress on. Ready. Just like that. Amazing. And she looked really beautiful, so I told her that she looked better than in the photos, which she did. She looked herself. The groom was also ready – well, almost. He had yet to put on his tie. At this point, various people were helping him to do just that, as he did not know how to do it, but with little success. My services were required. I grabbed the tie and returned to my own room, where I put the tie on myself, using a Windsor knot. I like this, as the knot forms an even triangle, and is not lopsided. We slipped this over B's head and did it up. Success. As it turned out, he and I were the only ones at the reception wearing ties. People dress casually at weddings in this country; I have even seen a guest wearing shorts, thongs and T shirt! I kid you not. I like to dress formally at weddings-yes, believe it or not! There is a problem though: no one should look more handsome than the groom or more beautiful than the bride. Oh well…

After a shower (cold) and change of clothes I was ready, so we walked out to catch a taxi to the reception centre. I seemed to be having trouble with my boot. What is the matter? The matter is that at this point of time, the sole decided to part company with the uppers. Oh dear. All I could do was to lift my left leg very high so that the sole was not bent underneath. In this manner I managed to survive the evening, while providing some comedy for the assembled multitudes. I realized that I had picked up the wrong pair of boots in Sydney while packing. I do have another pair.

At the reception hotel, the bride and groom were waiting outside to welcome the guests. It is at this point that one gives them that little red envelope. I have known people here to dread being invited to a wedding, as it is expensive, the usual amount given being about 300 Yuan. One must be careful. You must not give 250 Yuan, as "250" means stupid. You must not give 400 Yuan, as "4" represents death. We then walked inside, up the stairs to the second floor, yours truly lifting his left leg roughly to chin level at each step. We found a table, sitting with the classmates of the bride and groom. Here we sat for some time, chatting.

Eventually the couple arrived, walking down to the stage at one end of the room. This was decorated with balloons, red ones shaped like a heart framing the double happiness character, flanked by pink balloons spelling out the characters for "good luck". Here the MC took the microphone and spouted forth. Why ever he bothered with the microphone at all I will never know, as he certainly did not need it. The couple were asked to perform a series of manoeuvres, bowing to each other, running into each other's arms from either end of the stage and kissing – rather perfunctorily, I might add. Aussie 1, who had taught them both, was invited to the mic to say a few words, which he did; short, to the point and very meaningful. And he did not shout.

After that it was down to business with the meal, washed down with liberal quantities of beer, not that this is a worry, as you would need to drink an awful lot of Chinese beer for it to have any effect. The formal toasts were done with rice wine, and this is a different matter: you would not want to have too much of this. The bride and groom did the rounds of the tables, eating very little but seemingly drinking huge quantities of rice wine. Actually, they didn't, as they had water in their glasses, and in any case, just sipped. I told the bride she was cheating. The meal itself was delicious. And that was that.

In due course we retired back to the hotel, where we lounged around chatting. Later the bride and groom reappeared, and I was surprised to find that the bride had divested herself of her dress, had washed off her makeup, and had even washed out her hair, being quite content to relax with her friends and family in her pyjamas. The ceremony seems a bit anticlimactic to me, even granted that it was to be repeated in her own home town and in Shenzhen where they both work, so I asked Sarah if they did not take formal vows. She replied "sort of". When they apply for their wedding license, the government attendant asks them if they want to take this man/woman for their husband/wife. They say "Yes", and that is it. This ceremony is also the one they count as the day they got married.

The next morning, Aussie 1 and I would head off to Guiyang.

3.   *Kaili to Tongren – 4th October 2008*

The following morning Aussie 1 and I were accompanied to the bus station where we boarded a bus for Guiyang, which is the capital of this province, Guizhou. On the way we witnessed the result of an accident; a car had slammed into the roadside barrier, obviously with considerable force. I do not know what happened to the occupants. The highway is excellent, surprisingly, so the state of the road can hardly be the cause of this accident. My guess would be excessive speed, possibly combined with driver fatigue, but it could be anything – overtaking, using a mobile phone etc.

It took less than three hours to reach Guiyang. This is a city of considerable size, though what that means is hard to say. In China distinctions are less clear cut than in Australia. Our towns and cities tend to end fairly abruptly and we are into the countryside. We have long distances between human settlements. In China there are many more rivers, and hence more fertile land, combined with a more mountainous terrain, so that you are no sooner out of one town or village than you are entering another. Which of the many towns surrounding Guiyang actually form part of the city? Consequently, all I can say is that the city proper would have several million inhabitants. I do have official figures, but the question remains as to what these really mean.

After I had returned to Tongren, one of my students asked me if I thought Guiyang was a beautiful city, to which I replied in all honesty that it is not, being dirty, dusty and polluted, with the buildings being somewhat drab for the most part. This did not go down too well, as this worthy comes from Guiyang. It is a curiosity here that everyone thinks their own city is particularly beautiful, yet they are constantly seeking reassurance from visitors that this is so. Of course, everyone knows that the most beautiful city is Sydney!

Shopping time. There are items we can buy in Guiyang that you cannot get in Tongren, so we had made sure we had left plenty of space in our bags to take home the loot. On the top of my list was reading matter – in English. Unfortunately I found no English language newspapers, but we were directed to a bookstore which has English language books, several of which I purchased for later reading. You may recall that I left most of my books in Sydney, due to weight restrictions. The next stop was Wal-Mart's, where we purchased such precious items as cheese, margarine, marmalade and tinned goods like tuna, baked beans and sweet corn. You can just forget about luxury items, like butter and vegemite. Tinned goods provide a welcome change to one's diet, especially if it is late, you are tired and you do not feel like cooking.

Our main reason for being here, however, was not the shopping, but to welcome our No. 2 man from Italy who was coming here with a view to the possible establishment of a more permanent presence. Our German confreres had been here from 1926 till 1951 when they were forced to leave. Some had died as a result of the treatment they had received. At the local RC centre we met the VG and a translator, before W arrived late at night from Manila, where he had been attending a conference. The next morning we headed off in a diocesan car for Shiqian, which is actually where the Germans had worked. Even by car, this is six hours away.

We left early, around 6.00 am, stopping for breakfast at 9.00am at one of the many towns which lined our route. Bear in mind that this province has an area of 174,000 square kilometres, which is considerably less than the state of Victoria, yet has a population of some 35 million, compared with 5 million for Victoria. What a contrast.

We found a restaurant consisting of a single room some 20 square metres in area, with a cement floor and furnished with a fridge, stove, table and chairs. A roller door seals it off from the street. It must be bitterly cold in winter; it was cold enough on this early October day, with light rain falling. Our meal of dumplings was nevertheless quite nice. By this time it was also necessary to visit a *cesuo*, but none was to be found. We asked the proprietor, who very kindly directed us upstairs to her own loo, as she lives over her eatery, a very common arrangement. So we trudged upstairs, interrupting a teenage son, who was draped over the lounge, watching TV. Her apartment, I noticed, was spotlessly clean and seemed quite comfortable. I had experienced similar hospitality before; the Chinese can be wonderful people.

We set off again, but had not gone too far when our translator revealed that he was feeling sick – motion sickness from all the travelling. Not to worry, as he has his own remedy. We stopped at a village so that he could purchase a bottle of the local plonk, which he then proceeded to imbibe over the next three hours. By the time we reached Shiqian there was no sign of motion sickness, but plenty of evidence of a merrier disposition. Lord only knows what his translations were like. On this leg, we witnessed three more accidents; one car in the ditch, a truck overturned spilling its load, while another truck was involved in a head-on smash. They will insist on driving on the wrong side of the road, around blind corners, so it is not surprising. It is no wonder that in excess of 110,000 people are killed on Chinese roads every year.

It was around 12.30 pm before we finally reached our destination, while I was thanking the Good Lord above that we did in fact arrive safely. I might add that our driver was very careful. We visited a church on the outskirts of the town, where our German confreres had served; it had a school and a well-made well, if I can express it in those terms. Then it was off to the centre of town to view the main church. This is in need of repair, but that is being redressed, or at least we hope work will begin soon before the winter sets in. There is a two storey building next door which used to be the convent, but was taken over by the communists as a museum; people were viewing the exhibits while we were there. In the courtyard there is another well surrounded by beautiful brickwork. There is also an orphanage here, and I had the privilege of meeting three truly lovely girls, whose education, I might add, has been funded by Aussie 1. Other funds from Kensington have been used for the construction of clean water projects in the district. We then went off to a local restaurant for a meal – a good one at that – with emphasis on the local delicacy, bacon.

By this time it was getting a bit late for me, since I needed to return to Tongren, and the bus was due to depart at 3.00 pm. By the time I got on board there were only two seats left. You can guess who took the last seat. The journey back to Tongren took another four hours, so I did plenty of travelling on this day. I really enjoyed the countryside, with the yellow of the rice just then being harvested contrasting with the green of the vegetation, especially those strips surrounding each rice paddy.

As to what our future here will be, I do not know. There are all sorts of plans afoot, aimed at establishing a more permanent presence for our group, but it is up to the powers that be, especially those in Italy. If this is what the Lord wants, then I am sure it will come about, but He tends to be full of surprises. The question arises as to my own possible role in future developments. Again I do not know, and should be prepared for surprises, but I do not think it is my scene. We will see.

Winter Holidays 2009

4.   *An Overview – February 2009*

It has been a while since I have put pen to paper; not since Christmas in fact. For most of the time since then we have been on holidays for the winter break, including Spring Festival, China's most important festival. I did a lot of travelling, mostly by train, but also by bus – both suburban and intercity – by taxi – again both suburban and intercity – by motorcycle, by pushbike and on foot. I did a lot of walking. Details of these travels will be given in later Jottings, but here I would like, by way of introduction, to point out the more salient aspects.

First, the crowds. There are more than 1.3 billion people in this country, and I reckon I have seen most of them. My first train trip was an eight hour journey to Guiyang, the capital of this province, without a seat. You can buy a place on trains here, without seat allocation. I could not even squeeze into a carriage, but was jammed with more than 30 other people between two carriages, plus luggage. Not very enjoyable.

Second, the ancient cities of Dali and Lijiang. These have real character, even though they are very touristy. I loved the cobbled streets with open waterways down the middle or to the side, with beautiful buildings featuring ancient Chinese architecture – and no cars speeding and honking.

Third, Yu Long Xie Shan (Jade Dragon Snow Mountain). A cable car takes you up to the 4,506 metre level, and from there you walk up to an altitude of 4,680 metres. Views are breathtaking, with snow around, mountain ranges retreating into the distance, and a glacier alongside. You just have to take it easy, as the lack of oxygen at this level makes the slightest exertion an effort.

Fourth, Tiger Leaping Gorge. I spent four days walking along the flanks of Bama Xie Shan, looking across the upper reaches of the Yangtze River to Yu Long Xie Shan. There is a 3,900 metre drop from the top of the mountain at 5,500 metre to the river at 1,600 metres. Awe inspiring.

Fifth, a return to Fuzhou to see some of my former students. This included a meal with the four people who came to Sydney last year for World Youth Day. Also there was a young man and his wife who do a lot of work amongst the Chinese community in Sydney. I had met him last year at World Youth Day. There are two aspects I would like to touch on here.

The first of these concerns their personal reactions. There is no doubt that the whole Australia experience, over a three month period, has had a profound impact upon them. They now know that China is not the only country in the world, and that everything that China does is not necessarily right. There is much in Australia to admire. On a faith level, it has helped them to see that they are part of a wider picture, that the Church is everywhere. I will never forget the opening Mass at Barangaroo. As we filed in, with the flags of many nations all around us, suddenly they espied the Chinese flag, and it was "China, China, China". Nothing else matters; other countries may as well not exist. Over the three months, that perception changed, so that now they have a different attitude to share with their compatriots.

The second of these concerns the U/g Church in Fuzhou. There has been a running battle between the bishop and the Vatican for many years. The former has steadfastly refused to resign, in spite of every effort, both diplomatic and otherwise. The climax really came when the Vatican sent his replacement, who soon found himself in gaol. Who told the police? So now, the Vatican has ruled that he is no longer bishop and that Fuzhou is no longer a diocese. But he is still there, at the ripe old age of 89, with some 20 of his priests supporting him; the remaining 30 do not. What a scandalous situation. In these difficult circumstances, our friends are doing their best to be neutral and bring the sides together. They are also involved in various programmes, really helping others to live out their faith.

At this point I would like to thank again those people in Randwick who generously supported these four people, either financially or with accommodation. In my opinion your contributions have been well worth it.

As you see, I had an extraordinary winter holiday. May our good and loving God bless you all.

5.   Tongren to Guiyang – 10th January 2009

Let the holidays begin. Plenty of holidays form one of the perks of being a teacher. You might work hard during semester, but make up for it at the end. Well, I did say "might".

I was off to Guiyang, the capital of this here province. There are several ways of getting there. You could fly, if you are prepared to fork out the 500 Yuan air fare. I was not. There were no flights anyway, due to snow. Or you could take a bus and travel in air conditioned luxury, getting there in about 5 hours for 125 Yuan. Still too expensive. Or you could take the train at only 51 Yuan for a seat. Unfortunately, by the time I came to buy my ticket there were no seats; standing room only. Ok, that will do, and it is only 30 Yuan.

There is one slight problem; you cannot get the train from Tongren, but must travel to another town called Yuping. Tongren is a marvellous place, but centre of the world it ain't. I thought I would just catch a bus, paying some 22 Yuan, but at the front gate I met some students who were going and had hired a taxi. These are not your green and white taxis which whiz around Tongren streets with a great blaring of horns. No way. These are special blue taxis which shuttle between towns with an even greater blaring of horns. The cost is 100 Yuan, but when you divide that amongst the four passengers, it is not much more than the bus. And you save 5 Yuan anyway in getting a local taxi to take you to the bus station.

So in we piled, four of us plus luggage, including a bag of food that my students gave me as I got in. We left at 7.45 am and took almost two hours to get to Yuping, partly because of the conditions, and partly because the driver got lost. Conditions included fog, with some ice and snow, and a very crowded market in Yuping, which took us twenty minutes to negotiate. As we travelled the sun came up and a beautiful sight it was, with its pale orb partially obscured by a brindled salmon coloured sky, peeping shyly between conical limestone hills.

We got to the station not before time to find a multitude of people had beaten us. Oddly enough there was actually the semblance of a queue as people lined the platform at the expected entry ports. Somehow I made it onto one of the carriages – well, sort of. I did not quite make it into the seating section, but onto the end section where two carriages join. Each carriage seats some 120 people; Westerners that is. Lord alone knows how many Chinese squeeze in. At my end of the carriage there were more than thirty people, plus heaps of luggage, jammed in wherever anyone could corner a little space. This train must have been pulling in excess of 3,000 people, so with this overload, off we went.

Stations along our route created something of a headache for the train staff as it was difficult to get the doors open, the press of people being so great. Where can they go? Somehow, the impossible would happen at each station, the door would be opened, and then there would be a surge of people struggling to get out, being met by an equal surge of people trying to get in, with muggsy in the middle. Fun? Well it depends upon your definition. Welcome to the holidays.

Now this next bit you will not believe, but I declare and avow it to be true, that the train staff still serve meals, pushing their trolleys up and down the aisles and from one carriage to next. In their way – wedged in tighter than a goog in its shell – was me. The train attendant is saying something to me in Chinese, a rough translation of which probably goes something like: "Get out of the b... way you imperialist running dog", but my Chinese is not the best, so it may have been: "Excuse me sir, but would you mind awfully just moving a little bit, so that I can feed the hungry hordes?" "But I have nowhere to go," pleads I. Well, somehow, it happened. I would pass my backpack to someone, lift my other bag and place it on top of the food (truly), then pull in my ample girth and somehow she would get by. Moses parting of the Red Sea had nothing on this manoeuvre. On one occasion, the train lady reached over with her key and opened a tiny compartment reserved for staff. In tumbled a lady plus me plus our luggage, till the train lady could get past. Wonderful here; out of the press, and it even has a seat. I could stay here. No chance, as we were summarily ordered out and the door once more secured. Oh well.

When I could, I would squat down on my bag, close my eyes and attempt to rest. Four hours into the journey, when I was in this position, I thought I heard, "Teacher, Teacher". Is that me? I opened my eyes to find one of my students calling me. We have a seat. "A seat?" A real seat? One which is off the floor and has a back rest? Oh bliss, Oh joy! Somehow I managed to squeeze into the carriage with my luggage to find a group of students together. They had brought some small plastic stools, thus freeing a seat for me. "We saw you earlier", they explained, "but thought you were Chinese"! Must be the blue eyes. Needless to say, the rest of the journey was considerably more comfortable as we chatted away.

We had almost reached Guiyang, when a young man close to our group opened the window while the train had come to a temporary halt, and jumped out. He did not have ticket. I hear you say; "With so many people around he would have a good chance of getting away with it." Not on your nelly. In this country the authorities keep a sharp eye on everybody, including yours truly, which is why I do need to be careful to watch my Ps and Qs. Later, at another train station, I saw one man being tackled by the station police. Oh boy, they meant business; they just slammed him, without a thought for the milling crowds.

We got into Guiyang around 4.30 pm, by which time the train was in a shambles with rubbish strewn from one end to the other. The spot where I had been crammed for the first half of the trip would have been looked down upon disdainfully by any self-respecting pig. As for my bag, it was simply filthy. Later I gave it a wash and the dirt which came off it could have filled your average pig sty.

The students very graciously helped me to get a taxi to my hotel, where I just wanted to vegetate. In fact the next day I did just that: a nothing day, with me feeling as flat as a pancake. Now they say that the population of China is in excess of 1.3 billion people. Well let me tell you that in my opinion, that figure is a vast under estimation. Anybody feel like joining me for the next train trip in China? No? You don't know what you're missing, and at only 30 Yuan a ticket, it's a steal.

6.   *Guiyang – 10th – 14th January 2009*

At the end of the previous Jotting, I stated that the day following my arrival was a non-day. Well it wasn't the only one, as I found that after the semester's work, I really needed to relax and do nothing. I can be pretty good at doing nothing. I would go so far as to say, at the risk of putting tickets on myself, that I do nothing well. Hence Guiyang became a rest interlude.

One of the ways in which I like to explore a strange city is to use public transport. You simply hop on a bus – any bus – and stay on till it comes to the end of its route. Then you come back again. It is cheap too. When I was in London, for instance, it was then costing eight pounds to take the red open air double decker tourist bus, or you could use the normal suburban bus for 1 pound, which is what I did.

While doing this, sitting in bus 44, I discovered the city's main park. This looks interesting, so let's get off and explore. It is small, measuring only 171,000 square metres, or just over 400 metres per side. Compare this with Sydney's Centennial Park, which has an area of 2.2 square km, or about 1.5 km per side. This one is called He Bin Gong Yuan. On a small hillock there is a Ferris wheel, not that you would get much of a view from the top. I decided that I did not really need a ride. On another grassy knoll there are many birds in small cages, twittering away, possibly to each other. Trees. Shrubs and flowers abound, so it is quite pretty. The lower path, furthest from the road, follows the river, along which it is very pleasant to ramble. Throughout the park are practising musicians, seemingly oblivious to each other. Some are using a variety of instruments, some are singing, while one man was singing into a microphone accompanied by two *erhus* and a saxophone; there's a meeting of East and West. Vendors are not going to miss a chance, so by the river they are selling tofu, and by the road balloons. The tofu is sliced thinly into small squares, which are then roasted over hot coals; rather tasteless, actually, unless combined with *lajiao* – ground, spicy red pepper. The balloons certainly add a splash of colour.

There is another major park in the city, a flat area with paths, flowers etc., and some grass. In this area people fly kites, hold art exhibitions or just stroll and chatter. The main feature is two glass pyramids, but these are not for decorative purposes only, nor do they mark the entrance to The Louvre, but they do mark the entrance and exit points for a vast underground Wal-Mart's store. I have shopped here before, as I can buy goods here that cannot be bought in Tongren; cheese for instance.

Near our hotel is a tiny park, with no grass, but plenty of steps, and built like a fortress. At the top a stone slope had been polished to make it slippery, so down this slope were kids sliding higgledy piggledy, really having fun. I might add that the kids were not the only ones who were enjoying this slide.

The city is a little grotty, though the look is being improved as more modern buildings are erected. The traffic consists mainly of cars, taxis and buses. There is no suburban rail network and surprisingly few bikes and few trucks.

One favourite past time was to sample the local cuisine, both Western and Chinese. The former includes KFC and Jazzy Pizza, but not McDonald's. Probably the best was a roadside meal. By day, you have a footpath, but by 7.00 pm, you have a tent erected, a gas stove in action, tables and chairs out and various foods on display. You select what you want. You can buy skewers of meat or prawns for one Yuan each. The soup was delicious. All in all it was a great meal, costing only 10 Yuan each (about $2), including the beer.

After four days of recuperation in Guiyang, it was time to pull up stakes and head off for Kunming in the neighbouring province of Yunnan. Come along for the ride.

7.   *Guiyang to Kunming – 14th – 15th January 2009*

To get from Guiyang to Kunming, I opted for an overnight train, and at this time of the year when the hordes are moving, was very fortunate to obtain a hard sleeper for 150 Yuan. This is a good price, bearing in mind that it not only conveys you to your destination, but also provides a night's accommodation. A soft sleeper has four bunks to a compartment – a double bunk on each side – and a door which can be closed. This hard sleeper had six bunks to a compartment, three on each side, and no door. I had a top bunk, which could be accessed via a ladder on the side of the train's corridor. Once on top, one can lie quite comfortably, but there is not enough room to sit up. In the soft sleeper one can sit up and read with a degree of comfort.

I arrived at Guiyang train station at 6.30 pm, in plenty of time. The waiting room was so packed there were no more seats, so I stood. This waiting room was like a dark seascape, with everyone (myself being the lone exception) with black hair. As well, nearly everyone wears dark clothing in this country; I have no idea why. So we had a seething, drab coloured mass, reminding me of the waves of a deep sea. And then there is the luggage. I never cease to be amazed at what people carry. As well as your regular bags, there were boxes, huge bags, bags of rice, seats and even a bathtub. Truly.

And then they were off. In this country there is always a race for any doorway. Passengers for our train were in four lines, which the rail attendants – wisely in my opinion – decided to stagger. As the line next to ours was moving, a woman in our line began leaping over the seats to join it. A piercing whistle rent the air and she was summarily ordered back to where she had been. She went. When our turn to move came, we made it all the way to the gate, when the barrier was closed with me next in line. That's OK, I can wait; we will all get there eventually, and the train will not leave without us. But then the official took one look at my long nose, blue eyes and generally handsome visage, and opened the gate. As a result, I did manage to get to my carriage (5) and bunk (18) before most of the other passengers. Actually this did afford one advantage, in that I was able to store my bag on the overhead rack before it became completely filled. The bunk is really quite comfortable and comes equipped with a pillow and doona.

The compartment lights went out at about 11.00 pm – or at least I think they did, as I was in the land of Nod long before then. I slept well, too, getting up around 5.00 am to use the toilet and washroom before the hordes descended. I only just made it. The former consists of a hole in the floor and not much more. As I have mentioned before it is locked prior to coming into a station, for obvious reasons, and if the staff forget to lock the door, there is the sign outside to remind passengers; "Do not use while train is stabilizing". I do not know if you knew before that trains stabilize at stations, but you learn something every day. The washroom consists of three stainless steel sinks and a mirror.

It was still early when we arrived, but I got a taxi to our hotel anyway, arriving there at 7.30 am. At the station I also noted the bus numbers, so that we could compare this with buses which go past our hotel, and yes, I found that the No. 83 does, so that when it comes time to leave, I need not get a taxi. It was way too early to book into the hotel; the staff told me to return at 10.00 am. Not a problem, as long as they can mind my bags, which they promised they would do.

This was breakfast time, so I wandered next door to a restaurant and ordered *guoqiao mixian* or "across the bridge noodles", which is a Kunming specialty, though I did not know this at the time. You are served a dish of hot water, with a thin layer of oil on top, into which the waiter puts pork slivers, spring onions, some chicken and noodles. This restaurant has its own security guard, dressed in a police uniform, and he was having his breakfast at the same time. They love uniforms in this country.

With two hours to kill, I wandered around the neighbourhood, especially the nearby canal, bordered by narrow parkland on each side. In an open area, people were getting their morning exercise. About a dozen ladies were performing a fan dance. Another group of about 30, mostly middle aged to elderly women, were doing a slow dance with more or less grace. With some physiques, being graceful is just that little bit harder, especially when the age factor is added. A third group of elderly people – both men and women this time – were doing a sword dance, with much ritualistic thrusting and parrying. All the while other individuals were doing their own brand of tai chi. One of the features of China is that it is common to see people exercising in one way or another in the early morning. No, I did not take part, though I did enjoy watching them.

The weather, I might add, was not cold. In fact Kunming is called the Spring City, due to its mild climate, not cold in winter, except at night and not too hot in summer. Its altitude of 1895 metres is partly responsible for this. The temperature range is not unlike Sydney's.

At 10.00 am I duly returned to the hotel to book in.

8.　　Kunming – 15th January 2009

Having settled into the hotel, (another "7 Days") it was time to put the feet up for a while before exploring this city further. After a rest, some laundry and a light lunch, it was time to sally forth once more, it being now about 2.00 pm. I was particularly keen to find the house of Zhu Di, which I knew was not far from our hotel, but it took a while to find it. That we did so was by dint of following brown signs, which I could not read, but seemed to indicate something of importance, and by asking. Here an historical interlude is in order.

It is interesting that the Mongols conquered this region, defeating the Dao kingdom as early as 1274, which is five years before the fall of the Southern Song Dynasty. By 1368 the Yuan Dynasty had run its race, being succeeded by the Ming Dynasty. Yet certain strongholds still held out, the last of these being Kunming. In 1381 an expedition was sent to reduce this, under the command of Zhu Di, the emperor's son, who was born in 1360. A 12 year old Mongol boy, Zheng He, was captured and castrated – wonderfully enlightened times, these – later becoming one of Zhu Di's servants. He grew to be a giant of a man at 1.87m tall. He was chosen to lead China's vast fleets during Zhu Di's reign as the third Ming emperor (AD 1402 – 1424), being sent out on seven major expeditions. It was Zhu Di who built the Forbidden City in Beijing. He also built those sections of the Great Wall most seen by visitors today. He also reconstructed the Grand Canal. He was one of China's greatest ever emperors, which did not stop him from being a tyrant, summarily killing off anybody who looked as if he just might at some time in the future think about the possibility of life being better under someone else. He would also kill off entire families and anybody remotely connected with the thought of revolt. Great guy. In the process, he antagonized his southern-most province, which against all odds did succeed in achieving independence. It is now known as Vietnam. Of all the lands conquered by the Chinese (Han), it is the only one to date which has succeeded in its quest for independence.

I found Zhu Di's house, and although very nice is still quite simple, with rooms surrounding a central courtyard, an architectural style very common throughout China. Next door a fellow was writing a large sign on a wall in ancient Chinese characters, not the ones used today. It seemed fitting.

Next I sallied forth to find Cui Hu, or Green Lake, which I did find eventually, after some searching. This is really nice, so much so that I would return here several more times. It is not large, being only 21 ha in size. One end abounds in seagulls. I do not think I have seen so many in such a small area before. Next we came upon a monument, also featuring seagulls, which had been donated by Wagga Wagga, a city in the Riverina District of NSW. It appears that Wagga Wagga and Kunming are sister cities. I am always a little bemused by this, as there is such a discrepancy in size. Wagga Wagga probably has about 50,000 people, where Kunming would have about a hundred times that population.

This park, too, is a place for people to practise their music. One group of five men were playing the Radesky March on trumpets and saxophones, attracting attention from the passers-by. It is such a rousing piece. Others were practising tai chi, including the same group we had seen in the morning. Haven't they got it right yet? Some of the minority people, dressed in their traditional costume, were also playing and dancing. The park is a collection of ponds, isolated by walkways, grassed areas, shrubs, trees and flowers, set off beautifully by pavilions and stone bridges. We found one shop here which sells delicious doughnuts.

Having walked through Cui Hu, you can find the beautiful campus of Yunnan University, so I walked through here as well, looking for an English bookstore. Sadly, I did not find it, but I did find a language school for overseas students who are learning Chinese. Maybe I should enrol. To date, some 15,000 students have graduated, but I do not know when the school opened. The university itself began in 1923. Interestingly, the buildings are very Western in their architecture.

That was enough for one afternoon, so I headed back to the hotel for an hour's rest, before heading off again to eat. I found a small family restaurant which served good, inexpensive food. Unfortunately, I dipped into the *lajiao,* and the pot was not real hygienic, giving me a touch of diarrhoea. Not to worry, as I brought with me a packet on Imodium Never leave home without it. I also bought an ice-cream, which I thoroughly enjoyed as you cannot get them in Tongren during the cold months of the year.

I had done enough for one day, having walked about 15 km, so had just a short stroll after the evening meal before retiring back to our temporary home. I do a lot of walking when on holidays: probably not everyone's cup of tea.

9.   *More in Kunming – 16th – 17th January 2009*

Next morning I was not exactly up at the crack of dawn ready for the next great adventure. It was more like 9.00 am when the first eye opened, but I was still too sleepy to note which eye. Even though I have been living in China for five years now, I still like a Western breakfast. And when I travel I like to take it with me; cereal, milk, banana, orange and coffee. Pity hotel rooms do not have a toaster.

Having sustained the inner man, it was back to the railway to buy a ticket for the next leg, on to Dali. I managed to get another overnight hard sleeper for 90 Yuan for the following Sunday: really good value. While there, I had lunch; didn't I just have breakfast? Hungry work this, buying tickets.

The No. 83 bus got me to the railway station, so it was assumed that the No.83 bus would also get me back. While this is more or less true, one discovered that the outward and inward journeys do not always follow the same route. I wanted to connect with the No.73 bus which ran out to Dianchi Hu, a rather large lake, in fact the 6th largest in China, close to the city. After some little while and a few false leads, I made it. The lake is named for the Dian people who used to live here. Not much was known about them until 1955 when one of their burial mounds was discovered. It turns out that they formed quite a sophisticated agrarian bronze-age society, living around this lake and three other lakes in the district. They flourished particularly during the Warring States Period (376 – 221 BC) and early Han (AD 206 BC – 225). It is claimed that they invented the bronze drum; it might even be true. They were a settled people, battling with nomadic peoples for much of their history. Hence many of their implements are of a military nature, such as swords, shields, armour and helmets. But they also made ploughs, pots and pans, statues, decorations and rather elaborate belt buckles. However they were no match for the invading Han Chinese armies, and disappeared from history.

On the bus I noticed a young couple wearing identical clothes; same shirts, same vest, same trousers, even the same shoes. I guess they are making a statement.

I got off at a minority village, where the entrance fee was 75 Yuan. I declined. I have been burnt before at a minority village in Hainan. Instead I paid a more modest 8 Yuan to enter Haigen Park bordering the lake. This is really nice. I came across a eucalyptus grove, featuring trees imported from Australia back in 1897. Whenever you bring something in from outside, you have to be so careful. So much damage has been done in Australia by introduced species which do not belong: the rabbits, foxes, cats, cane toads, ants etc. and amongst the plants, hyacinths, cactuses, lantana etc. Travelling around China I have seen so many eucalyptus trees, mainly gums. It seems they are taking over. Eucalyptus oil is a poison, so not many animals can feed from these leaves. The koala is one, and it is very fussy. Even here, the animal is affected by the poison, so it is drowsy most of the time, sleeping some 20 hours per day. China does not have many koalas, or other animals to eat the eucalyptus leaves, with the result that these trees could take over, pushing the native vegetation out. It is happening. There is a headline for you: CHINA TAKEN OVER BY AUSTRALIANS.

One section of this lake features many seagulls, being fed by some people and being photographed by others, who looked very professional. I took photos of them, silhouetted against the lake. There is a toilet here with a sign outside declaring; "Zoology Water Closet". Possibly it is an animal toilet, but more likely the waste material is broken down by bacteria (not animals), then reused locally. So it is environmentally friendly.

This is a lovely area to wander around, and I did so happily for a couple of hours, before heading back for a 7.30 pm meal. I found a place which specializes in *jiaozi* or dumplings. It was quite nice but I could have done with a few more vegetables, a deficit I made up at lunch the following day.

The next day I wanted to visit Kunming museum, as these institutions often provide an excellent way of finding out about a place. I decided to go by bus, but the first bus only went one block before turning off the intended route. So I caught a second bus, with the same result. Let's walk; it was only three kilometres anyway. At present there is not much in this museum, but they are renovating, so probably preparing for a new exhibit. The first room features a 6.6 m high Buddhist sutra stone coming from the time when this region was part of the Kingdom of Dali (937 – 1253 AD). Another room features four species of dinosaurs found in Yunnan, three of them carnivores and only one a herbivore, which is strange, since herbivores always outnumber carnivores, for obvious reasons. A third room displays photos of the city from the 1980s to the present, revealing its metamorphosis from traditional Chinese style buildings to modern high rise, much the same as most other cities in this world of ours.

And that is about it. I sat outside in the warm sunshine eating strawberries which were expensive, but so sweet, before hoofing it again to Kunming's central square. This area is dominated by two large ornate gates, which are very beautiful, and is not dominated by traffic, which is even more wonderful. I love malls, and would return here later. There are many stalls selling handicrafts, jewellery, spices, clothing etc. I actually bought some gifts. From here I strolled through a market area, before finding a place for a meal – choosing McDonald's, believe it or not, then home.

As a footnote, I tried to find out via the internet what caused the demise of the Kingdom of Dali, but only found Chinese sites. You needed a user name and password to access, which I provided. On the next page one was again asked for user name and password, again I duly provided. On the third page one was again asked for user name and password – not provided. I could be doing this at Christmas. What is going on? Possibly the authorities have blocked access, and if this is the case, why would they do so? Was the kingdom overthrown by Chinese armies? But this is not new; it is the way China has always acquired its territories. Mystery.

10.   *Kunming to Dali – 18th – 19th January 2009*

Sunday 18th was a rest day, as indeed Sundays are meant to be. I hopped on a bus to visit a horticultural exhibition. Upon arrival I found that the entrance ticket was 100 Yuan, which I deemed to be a little steep, so declined. Apparently there was an international horticultural exhibition here in 1999 and the city fathers are still trying to make money out of it ten years on. There is an impressive array of flags outside, doubtless representing the countries which took part, but coming to the end of their lives; they were looking decidedly tattered.

Come the afternoon, I returned to Cui Hu, Green Lake, which is becoming something of a favourite. It is so soothing to the spirit to be in a beautiful place where other people are relaxing, enjoying life. It is good to be alive. Here I sat and watched the sun set, enveloping the lake in a reddish glow. Then it was off to find somewhere to eat. Finally I went to McDonald's for an ice-cream and a read, while waiting till the time came to leave, then a stroll back to the hotel to pick up my bags and a walk to the bus stop to catch the No.83 bus to the railway station.

There was no trouble boarding the train, but I was surprised to find that it was a double decker. Whereas before we had six bunks to a compartment, here we had only four, but with another four on the level above us, there were thus eight altogether. Once again I had the upper bunk, which I prefer, as it gives one a little more privacy – and it is also cheaper – though I ended up swapping my berth with someone else so that a family could be together.

After a conversation with three students, I turned in around 11.30 pm, and slept soundly till the lights came on at around 6.00 am. On this train, they did turn the overhead lights off at night, which is not always the case. It is good to travel with eyeshades. This early rise gave me time to get cleaned up and have some breakfast before our 7.00 am arrival. From Kunming to Dali is only about 340 km.

I walked outside with luggage on this cold and windy morning, planning the next step. I needed somewhere to stay and wanted to go to Dali. Immediately I was beset by local taxi drivers. One in particular was very persistent. He kept telling me that this is not Dali, but another city called Xiaguan. You cannot get a bus to Dali; there are only taxis, and he would take us for 50 Yuan. After some time patiently bearing this harassment, I headed off. I thought that I would just hop on the first bus and see where it goes, noting possible hotels along the route. As I wandered off, I was approached by an elderly lady selling tourist maps. This I would need, so bought one for 5 Yuan, and it did indeed prove to be invaluable. I caught the No. 8, and as luck would have it, it went to Dali, some 15 km away, for the cost of only 1.5 Yuan per person. That taxi driver was a liar. You can see why I do not have a lot of respect for taxi drivers.

The Old City of Dali is really beautiful; for me it was love at first sight. I hopped off in the main street right outside a hotel, so we went in. It offered a very nice room, with a great view and at a reasonable price, so took it. Later I did check out others, but this was the best. The only problem was that small boys were playing in an area out the back. Now why should that be a problem? Ordinarily not, but with Spring Festival around the corner, they were letting off fire crackers intermittently every day and a large part of the night. Bang. Somehow, I could – bang – never get used to it, or – bang – anticipate when the next – bang – would go off. Now while each bang costs so little, only about I Mao (or Jiao), which is less than 2 cents, there were just so many of them that it must have cost their parents a small fortune. As for their urinating outside my window, well we won't worry about that.

I spent the rest of the day exploring the town, walking outside the old walls to the Three Pagodas, about a kilometre to the northwest. It is one of the major draw-cards hereabouts. I did not go in as the entrance fee of 120 Yuan is simply too steep, but you could see them quite plainly from outside the compound in which they are located. The tallest one in the middle rises to 17 storeys (pagodas always have an uneven number of storeys) or nearly 70 metres, with the other two being nine storeys each or 43 metres and 70 metres from the main pagoda. They were built between 823 AD and 859 AD, so were built well, having survived both time and earthquakes. They are octagonal in shape, so maybe this helps. No doubt the landscaping around them is superb, but I have seen this elsewhere.

Just a note here about finances: travel can be expensive – very expensive – but it does not have to be. You do not have to travel first class. You do not have to stay in 5 star hotels. You do not have to pay a lot of money to enter some sites. You do not have to see everything. What is important is appreciating what you do see.

The houses outside the Old City are quite beautiful, all built in the same style, with white walls and grey rooves with upturned eaves. Doors tend to be red. The outsides are decorated with tiles illustrating plants, scenes or Chinese characters. Dragons and phoenixes feature prominently. The streets in this part of town are barred to cars. They are narrow, with plants down the centre together with street lights and paved with stone. They look really attractive.

As to the Old City itself, it is built on a grid pattern, so you are unlikely to get lost. It is surrounded by a wall some 7.5 m high, with one or more large gates on each side. It is built at the foot of Cang Shan (Cang Mountain) to the west, with Erhai Lake a couple of kilometres away to the east. The town is now very touristy, with most shops selling knick knacks and with plenty of restaurants. I learnt not to eat along the main drag, but to find a family style place off the beaten track. The food is considerably cheaper. So this first day in Dali was a very happy one, in which a lot was achieved.

11.   Dali – 20th January 2009

Dali is beautiful and is a nice place to be. Holidays and travel should not, in my opinion, be primarily about going and doing, but about being. I know someone who is an inveterate traveller – and at this point I hear you say; "There you go, talking about yourself again" – but actually I am thinking of someone else, who, I feel sure, has made a list of every city in the world, being determined to see them all before he dies, not in order to gain anything from them, but simply in order to say, "I have been there". To my way of thinking, it is not my presence in some location that is important, as much as the presence of that location within me. With Dali, it is not what you do there that is important, so much as just being there, enjoying it and learning from it, being changed in some way.

While it is true that we have here no abiding city, why cannot we make our cities as idyllic as possible? Why cannot we live in peace, surrounded by cleanliness and beauty? It can be done. I am sure God did not mean us to live in squalid poverty. Dali can be both a model and a spur for us to clean up our ghettos worldwide.

The Old City is actually mostly new, but the buildings are consistent with the original structures first erected in AD 1382 (early Ming Dynasty). The city is square, each side being about 3 km, and surrounded by a stone wall 7.5 m high and 6 m thick. There is a major gate on each side with a two storey structure above each with the upturned eaves typical of Chinese architecture. At night, when lit up, they look even more beautiful. The streets form a grid pattern running east-west and north-south. Vehicles are only allowed on one major through street, meaning most of the city is a giant mall, people friendly, where you can stroll around without the honking of speeding taxis, trucks and cars.

Most of the shops are for tourists, selling wall hangings, clothing, jewellery, etc. Many are restaurants. One whole street is given over to Western style goods and food, where you can buy a sandwich, an Australian steak, a pizza or a cheesecake. Wonderful. Appropriately it is called Xi Jie, or West Street. Open drains run down the side or centre of these streets and this clean, running water adds to the appeal. Sometimes there are added features, such as a water wheel, or statues, or rocks or small bridges. The road surface is mostly paving stones.

On the Tuesday, I caught the No. 20 bus to Dali University, only about 10 minutes away to the south-west on the lower slopes of Cang Shan. I tell you this is the most beautiful campus I have seen anywhere. To the west runs snow-capped Cang Shan range and to the north-east the Old City and further away to the east Erhai Lake. Since the university is built on sloping ground, you ascend level by level, each connected by a series of steps, so I imagine that both students and staff would be pretty fit. Nobody was there at this time, however, it being the winter holidays, so we had the place to ourselves. There are something like 400 steps from the lowest to the highest level.

The forecourt is imposing, featuring a series of ponds, an upward soaring sculpture and ten stone pillars, five on each side. The five northern ones feature famous Chinese historical people, while the five southern ones feature Western people. The pillars are dedicated to Philosophy, Science, Literature and Art. On each is carved in base relief the person and his/her dates. Westerners include Aristotle, Plato, Socrates, Galileo, Newton, Einstein, Marie Curie, Dante, Shakespeare and Da Vinci. The Chinese side tends to be a little more political. An inscription in the centre urges students to emulate these great people from the past, so that just as they forged our present, we should strive to forge the future. I might add that there is still room on these pillars for more names to be added – waiting for me?

The full text of the inscription, for those interested, reads (sic): "History becomes so resplendent because of them and they are immortal because of their brilliance. To commemorate these great men, we must not only to remember their achievements and contributions, but more to bear in mind their courage and tenacity to shoulder historical responsibilities. To emulate these great men, we are not only to learn from their knowledge and wisdom, but more to learn from their personalities and virtue to create the human civilization. Accept your mission and create the future." It could be written better, but the sentiments are to be taken note of.

The design of the buildings is really pleasing, with curves extending in both the vertical and horizontal dimensions, reminding me of Parliament House in Canberra, though I doubt if they contain the same symbolism. Actually it is a bit stronger than a doubt; the concept of the people being over the government is completely foreign here. Basically the faculty buildings occupy three distinct levels, with the English Department being at the top. Is that symbolic? To the north-west is a park, with a lake, pavilion, bridge, paths and plants. It is good to be alive. Near here is another open area. I did not see any outdoor sports facility; no tennis courts, no basketball courts, no swimming pool, no oval, but these may have been to the south-west, an area I did not explore, though I did notice student accommodation in this direction.

On this bright, sunny day I had my sandwich lunch sitting down on some steps looking out over this wonderful vista. A cool breeze was blowing, but the weather was very pleasant indeed, in spite of the fact that this is winter and we are at an altitude of some 2,000 metres.

In the afternoon, by accident more than by design, I found the Catholic church. I was surprised to see this built in the Chinese style. Too often around the world I have seen churches built in European style architecture and this gives the wrong message. While this is fine for Europe, the Church is supposed to be catholic. It is not Islam, which tends to be quite mono-cultural – Arabic. Here in China it is particularly important to present the Christian message within Chinese culture, as in the past Christianity – and particularly Protestantism – was associated closely with invading European armies. Here the architecture and art reflects not just Chinese, but local Bai style. The enclosed photo shows this church.

French missionaries brought Christianity to this part of the world in the 1860s. It is a diocese, covering some 200,000 square kilometres. Prior to the communist take-over the Church was doing well, but fell on hard times with the expulsion of missionaries and the appropriation of church property. In 1983 the government returned Dali church. There is now a seminary, but at present only three priests are working in the diocese, so the emphasis is being placed upon the training of lay catechists. If anyone would like more details you can consult their website at; www.catholicdl.org/. There is also an e-mail address; dalicatholicchurch@gmail.com. By the time I wandered in it was late afternoon, yet they very kindly opened up for me to have a look and receive some information.

That night I was able to watch an English language movie on CCTV 6. Each Tuesday at 10.00 pm this channel has an English movie, and when in Fuzhou I would watch it from time to time. But I cannot do this in Tongren since I do not have TV. Hence I really enjoyed this one. Furthermore, these movies are generally of excellent quality.

12.   Dali to Lijiang – 21st – 22nd January 2009

The next day my companion and I hired bikes so that we could travel further than is possible by foot. In particular we wanted to ride down to Erhai Lake. It is not easy to get to, as there are not many roads leading down. We did get there down one road, but found that the edge of the lake is marshland. We thought there might be a path around the lake, but if there is, we did not find it. I noticed a man pushing his heavily laden bike up an incline on one of the sandy roads, but it was too much for him, so I gave him a hand. Effusive thanks. "*Bu yong xie*". (Don't mention it.) It had been some time since I had straddled the saddle. I was not in good condition, so it is just as well we did not ride too far, maybe 25 km. The cost was only 10 Yuan per day: eminently reasonable.

Our lunch was a sandwich on the road, but for my evening meal I went to a pizza place, being managed by a personable young Canadian lady. I finished off with a cheesecake, all up 42 Yuan.

One can stay in Dali reasonably cheaply if you do not join organized trips. I could have visited a village of the minority Bai peoples. I could have taken a road tour around the lake. I could have hopped on a boat to visit one or more of the islands. All of the above are hugely expensive, so I chose not to.

The Bai people, incidentally, have been in this neck of the woods for nigh on 3,000 years, well before the Han people arrived. In fact the first time a Chinese army was sent against them, during the Tang Dynasty (about 8th century AD), the Bai won. It is not often that Chinese armies were defeated by local peoples. The Bai then set up their own kingdom which survived for another 300 years.

The following day, Thursday, I caught a morning bus and headed off to Lijiang, about 200 km away, along the way seeing some beautiful countryside – and lots of eucalypts. Lijiang too has its Ancient Town, built during the late Song and early Yuan dynasties (AD 1250 – 1300), but at only 1.4 square kilometres it is considerably smaller than Dali. Nor does it have a wall around it. But it does have similar shops and architecture, in Naxi, Han, Bai and Tibetan styles. It also features cobbled streets, made of red breccia and granite, and open waterways. The planning of the latter must have taken a degree of ingenuity, as the streets do not form a grid pattern, as in Dali, but wind hither and yon, so that it is easier to get lost. Furthermore, the town is hillier than Dali which tends to have a uniform slope from west to east. Five major streets radiate from a central square. The Yu (Jade) River splits into many streams in order to crisscross the city. This Ancient City (also called Dayan) is separated from the new town by a hill, known as Lion Mountain.

Our travel Bible, also known as Lonely Planet (Never leave home without it!) recommended Mama Naxi's as the place to stay, a guest house in Dayan. The bus, however, dropped us off at the new town. How do you get there? – especially considering the fact that there are no cars in Dayan, and there are at least three Mama Naxi's. There were two of us on the bus intending to stay there, so we rang them, and were told that a driver would pick us up at the bus station. Wow! – that is service. He duly arrived, deposited us just outside Dayan in a parking lot, then we followed as he led the way. Yes, it would not be hard to get lost here, as we weaved our way around several bends. At the correct Mama Naxi's we met our hostess, Xiao Han. The room is only 25 Yuan (about $4) a night, on the second floor, after you have negotiated the steepest staircase you ever did see, with an unsteady banister to boot. The toilet/shower is downstairs. They also provide meals. The evening meal is huge, featuring five or six dishes and as much rice as you can eat, all for only 10 Yuan. I made sure I ate here each night.

I spent the remainder of the day walking around the winding streets, looking at shops, appreciating the beauty and trying not to get lost. Would you believe I did miss the correct turn-off, but got back safely anyhow, largely due to the clear sky, so I could keep an eye on the stars and also on Jupiter. The air is so clear here, helped largely by the altitude of 2,400 metres. Yet though this is winter the weather is cool but not cold.

There are two large water wheels, the main purpose of which appears to be as a tourist attraction, as every man and his dog seems to want to be photographed in front of them. You almost have to purchase tickets in advance. Maybe the authorities will do that next year, as they are past masters at charging fees, as we have seen. There is an open area not far away where men in traditional garb await with horses, for anyone who wants to go for a ride. Many of the shopkeepers here, belonging as they do to a minority group, either Naxi or Dongba, wear their traditional dress. One young lady was sitting in front of her loom, ostensibly weaving a wall hanging in what could well have been the Tang Dynasty, except that she was chatting on her mobile phone. Didn't know they had them back in AD 800. We also found a bookshop selling titles in English, and they were stocked with many good books. I would

41

love to have bought quite a few, but they are heavy to carry, and there is only so much room in my bag.

Lijiang is really nice, but what I really wanted was to climb Yu Long Xue Shan. This will be something very special indeed.

13.　　*Yu Long Xue Shan – 23rd January 2009*

Some years ago, Aussie 1 ascended this mountain and was so taken by it that it now features as his screen saver on his computer. He also boasts that he did it without oxygen. Well, anything he can do, I can do … though maybe not better.

Yu Long Xue Shan literally means "Jade Dragon Snow Mountain". It ascends to a height of 5,500 metres and with the aid of a cable car, you can ascend almost to the top. It also has a glacier, so I really wanted to go up. I checked out the tourist agents in Lijiang and found that it could cost 480 Yuan; very expensive. I thought I could do it more cheaply if I went on my own. Accordingly I asked advice from Xiao Han who told me what to do. She also told us it was worth it. She was right.

Next morning I and another person staying at this guest house walked about 20 minutes to a hotel where we boarded a minibus, No. 7, which was already almost full. There were a couple of seats down the back and a couple down the front. The back also had a man smoking, so I opted for the front. Many more people jammed aboard, sitting in the aisle, sitting on the engine cowling, plus luggage. One gentleman had two mattresses with him Extraordinary. My backpack was unceremoniously shoved out of the way, buried under the mattresses and upturned, resulting in the loss of my water bottle, though I did not realize this till afterwards. Oh well, one can always buy another water bottle. I paid 10 Yuan for the bus, on what proved to be a two hour trip out of town to the foot of the mountain.

The bus dropped us off at a major service centre, featuring the ticket office, shops, a waiting room, landscaped surrounds and even an eagle sitting on a perch keeping a watchful eye on us visitors. We paid 80 Yuan park maintenance fee, another 80 Yuan entrance fee (How clever; it is a bit like airlines charging extra for fuel surcharge.) and a whopping 174 Yuan to ascend in the cable car. We also paid another 40 Yuan for an oxygen bottle – just in case. I have suffered from altitude sickness before, when in Papua New Guinea, a group of us decided to climb 5,010 m high Mt. Wilhelm, so I did not want a repeat. On that occasion, we went up too fast – all on foot though; no cable car there.

We boarded a large bus to be ferried to the cable car, and then took our turn, as each car takes a maximum of six people. The ride up ascends from the 3,050 metre level to 4,506 metre level in about 30 minutes. The views are absolutely spectacular. Having ascended so high, so quickly, I knew from my previous experience that we would have to take it easy. You could certainly feel the effects of the scarcity of oxygen. Every step required a little more effort. I deemed it prudent to remain at this level for some time, to get us used to the thin air. In any case, the views warranted a longer stay. One could also buy a cup of hot coffee, and boy, did that go down well!

We stayed for nearly an hour at this 4,506 m level before we began climbing the 500 or so steps to the 4,680 m level. It took us over an hour, arriving at the top just after 12.00 noon. We climbed very slowly. After each flight of stairs, I would rest on the balustrade for a short while. Numbers of people fell by the wayside. One young woman collapsed right next to us. But, intrepid travellers that we are, we made it, and I have photographs to prove it. Up the top we found an enterprising gentleman selling medallions inscribed with the date and your name. And it costs only 40 Yuan! Boy, is he making a killing. Even granted it costs him around 10 Yuan for each piece of metal plus engraving equipment etc., he must be clearing at least 30 Yuan each, or probably more than 3,000 Yuan per day, when the average worker here gets about 800 Yuan per month. No, I did not buy one. Nor did I need oxygen to reach here; Aussie 1 please note!

The top of the mountain still towers above us, but this is as far as we can go. There is a glacier right next to us, maybe 100 metres across, though it is not very long. At the bottom, I had noticed glacial striations on some rock, so in the past the glacier extended into the valley below us, but not now. Incidentally, they said that this is the closest glacier to the equator; it is not. That honour belongs to Kilimanjaro on the border between Tanzania and Kenya. There is a platform here, decorated with some Tibetan totem poles, as this whole area has always been Naxi and Tibetan.

I took so many photos from up here, all of them great, as this place is truly awesome. I have one of mountain ridge upon mountain ridge, mist covered, fading into the distance, much like depictions in traditional Chinese paintings. Is it any wonder that mountains have long been considered the abode of the gods, and that many theophanies have taken place on mountain tops, whether Sinai or Tabor or wherever? For the ancient Greeks, Mt. Olympus was the abode of their gods, but here in China it is the abode of the dragon. I wonder what this says about how the Chinese really see this mythical beast. On mountain tops it is as if one is half way between heaven and earth, and is thus the meeting place between the divine and the human. Certainly on top one can experience a great sense of God's presence.

Wonderful as it is, we do not live on mountain tops, so the time came for us to descend, rather reluctantly in my case. It took us only half the time to get back to the 4,506 m level. In the cable car I had faced uphill when going up. Now I faced downhill on the return journey, just a little scary as the mountain side dropped away below. Back down in the valley, it took a little while to find a bus back to Lijiang, but when it dropped us off, we were in an unfamiliar part of town. It took some time, with the aid of a map and a tongue, to find the No. 8 bus to take us back to our now familiar water wheels. We got back to our guest house just in time for the evening meal.

What a day. I would recommend it to anyone. God is good.

14.   Tiger Leaping Gorge Day 1 – 24th January 2009

I had told Xiao Han that I wanted to go to Tiger Leaping Gorge. On Saturday morning, the day after ascending Yu Long Xue Shan, I was awoken by her asking if I was still interested. Indeed, and in fact was intending to catch a bus that afternoon. She replied that there isn't any, that there was only one bus going that day, that there would be no more for some time because of Spring Festival, and that the bus was leaving at 9.00 am. Yikes. It was now 8.40 am. I moved. She asked if I wanted breakfast. Yes indeed, if only because the driver would also be eating, so would not leave without us. Besides, a large tomato and egg pancake, plus a Yunnan coffee sounds pretty good.

In point of fact, we did not leave till 9.30 am, just two of us from the guest house. We had not got far when the driver's mobile phone rang. It appears that two other people wanted to join us, so we rendezvoused with them. B is from Brazil, so speaks Portuguese; he studied in the U.S. so speaks excellent English, and is learning Italian. Why? Because his girlfriend, S is Italian, so naturally speaks Italian; she also speaks excellent English, and for the past two years has been studying Chinese here In China, so her Chinese is excellent. Wow. So in the minibus, we had five people from five different countries, who speak between them five different languages. How do I know they were boyfriend-girlfriend? Without going into details, let us just say that they were all over each other, so let us leave it at that, and you will have to trust my excellent intuition.

At around 1.00 pm we arrived at Qiatou, some 75 km from Lijiang, and at a somewhat lower altitude of about 1800 metres. Here we had descended into a deep valley separated by two mountains; Yu Long Xue Shan we have met; the other is Bama Xue Shan, which peaks at 5,396 m. We stopped at Jane's Guest House, which isn't actually run by Jane, but another lady, M, who – surprise, surprise – hails from Clovelly Rd., Randwick, my bailiwick. It is indeed a small world. She was very worried about our safety, as there had been a knife wielding attack on two tourists the day before, so wanted us to travel in numbers. In consequence we were joined by J and his girlfriend P, both Aussies. It turns out that J's mother is a paediatrician at Sydney Children's Hospital, where I worked for nine years. The world is getting even smaller or maybe you just find Australians everywhere.

Some were keen to start hiking, like right now, so after hastily buying some snacks for lunch, off we went. Now this is winter – or is supposed to be – but this day was bright, sunny and hot. I was definitely overdressed, as I had come prepared for mountain winter conditions. Not to worry. So I became adept at wrapping my jumper around my waist and tying my coat by its sleeves to my backpack. Thank goodness I did not bring long johns.

The climb was very dusty, but somewhat humorous. I do assure you that what I am about to tell you is true. We were followed by horses. Yes, horses, plus their handlers. Now these guys wanted us – for a reasonable fee, of course – to ride their sturdy beasts. Hey, I came for a walk. They just followed every metre of the way. Talk about vultures, waiting for their prey, ready to pounce should anyone falter. It reminded me of climbing Mt. Sinai to the accompaniment of camels, where their handlers, too, were trying to coax us to get aboard – all for a reasonable fee, of course. I remember a cameleer telling me at one point that it was still a long way to the top. "How far?" I asked. "Two hours", was the reply, to which I remarked; "What? Only two hours? Is that all? Oh that is nothing!" Needless to say he was astonished, and never pestered me again. These horses, however, just plodded along behind.

Meanwhile, we were admiring the scenery and the farms we were passing through. They appeared to be growing rice, corn, barley (*da mei*) and also wheat (*xiao mei*). Terraces slope down to the river below, which hereabouts is known as the Jinsha, but forms part of the upper reaches of the Chang Jiang, otherwise known as the Yangtze. In the distance looms the mighty Yu Long Xue Shan, which we had ascended yesterday from the other side to this. Here we were on the slopes of Bama Xue Shan. It is so pretty, especially with bright yellow flowers sparkling in the sun.

We trudged on. The vultures hovered. Nobody had died yet, though P was sick from something she had eaten the previous night. She did vomit into a ditch. That's better. We were stopping more frequently for rests and for drinks of water. I was glad that I had replaced that lost bottle from yesterday. We took turns leading, just to throw the vultures off the track. It is certainly a testing climb.

At 3.10 pm, almost exactly two hours after leaving Jane's, we arrived at Naxi Guest House. We sat down for a well-earned rest. B and S had a full lunch. I munched on some dry biscuits with a refreshing drink of mint tea. After half an hour, it was out onto a kind of terrace to take photos of our group, as, sadly our fellowship was about to break up. The two Aussies were pushing on to the next guest house, while B and S were heading back; I would be staying here for the night, resuming the climb next day.

It was time to relax, do some laundry, check the internet, and watch the shadows creep up the mountain side. The air was clean, clear and crisp. After a wonderful meal, I watched the stars, shining brilliantly, with Orion almost at the zenith. From many parts of China you only read about stars in books. But yes, they are real. It is good to be alive. So please feel free to join us as we climb higher up this mountain on the morrow. Sweet dreams.

15.   Tiger Leaping Gorge Day 2 – 25th January 2009

It was around 8.30 when I surfaced next morning. Breakfast was a mixture of cereals which I had brought with us, plus fruit and a boiled egg from the guest house.

By 10.00 am we was once more on the trail, taking in the wonderful scenery. This next section, I knew, would be the toughest as it included "the 28 bends", which, as the name suggests, has 28 hairpin bends", as the trail zigzags back and forth gaining altitude so that it could cross over a saddle. By 11.30 am we had reached the top at an altitude of 2, 670 m, so we have climbed about 1,000 m from the river.

At this point I rested under a crude awning, wondering which way to go, as the trail forked, with one path leading up and the other down, so I rang Naxi Guest House just to be sure. I did not like the look of the downward path. Sure enough, going up was correct. Actually there was not far to go before the trail starting going down. Descents can be more difficult than ascents in that you put more pressure on your knees and there is more danger of slipping. Most of the time, however, the descent here is not steep and is incredibly enjoyable, with the sound of the river below, rushing through the gorge, and at times one could see it, snaking around bends, while above towered the mountain.

Picture, if you can the vastness of this scene: the top of the mountain (Yu Long Xue Shan) is at 5,500 metres, while the river is at 1,600 metres at the northern end of the gorge, meaning that the vertical drop is some 3,900 metres. On the slope of Bama Mt. we were looking up and looking down.

One of the most memorable nights of my life was sleeping at the bottom of the Grand Canyon in the United States, walking down the South Kaibab trail from the south rim then walking back up the Bright Angel trail. Now the south rim has an altitude of 2,100 metres, while the Colorado River is at 400 metres, so that we have a vertical drop of 1,700 metres. But here at Tiger Leaping Gorge, the drop is more than twice that. In the South Island of New Zealand, the drop from the top of the mountain to the water in Milford Sound is around 3,000 metres, so it is also greater than that.

I could see far below a large boulder in the river, thus constricting the flow, so increasing velocity and sound. This is Upper Tiger Leaping Gorge. Apparently a tiger used this boulder to leap across the river; either that or it was someone's imagination that did the leaping. They do love flowery expressions in this country. What I particularly loved was the solitude: no honking traffic here, no crowds of people, in fact no people at all; glorious.

By 1.15 pm we had reached Tea Horse Guest House, where we stopped for lunch. I thoroughly enjoyed a cup of tea (naturally), some yoghurt and a Naxi sandwich. The latter consisted of four layers of unleavened bread, with a paste of some sort, an onion, a tomato then a fried egg on top. It is better, I think, to put the egg inside the sandwich. It was most welcome. And it cost only 8 Yuan. I would have expected everything to be so much dearer up here. The menu is written on pieces of bamboo, tied together, which is the way books were written before the invention of paper. It added a nice touch. I took some great photos here as well.

At 2.45 pm we set forth once more. Over this next section I was a little worried, as this was where those two robbers had struck just two days ago. Consequently, I walked somewhat warily, scanning the trail both ahead and behind, forming a plan should anything happen. Thankfully nothing did and subsequently I found out that the police had arrested them.

Along this section, at places where the incline is not too steep, there are small farming communities. What a place to live. I just could not get enough of this scenery. We did see some locals and some goats, but no other hikers and no robbers. I cannot understand this weather, however, as it is so balmy, yet it is supposed to be winter. Certainly at times it is windy, especially on exposed spurs on the trail. You really have to grab hold of your hat. Mine did blow off on one occasion.

At 4.15 pm we arrived at Halfway Guest House, at an altitude of around 2,300 metres, where we planned to stay the night. The first thing we did, however, was to sit down to a well-earned cup of tea. This guest house advertises itself as having the toilet with the best view, and they are not wrong. The outside wall only comes waist high, so while one is doing other things one can also take in this extraordinary scenery, looking out at the steep sided mountain opposite up to its snow-capped peak and down to the river below. The dining room too provided great views, so I sat here for some time writing as the sun set.

Accommodation is dormitory style. I found I was sharing the room with a couple of Frenchmen. We got along quite well. I did not have a late night, as I had done a lot of walking today, so could do with a good night's rest. See you in the morning.

16.   Tiger Leaping Gorge Day 3 – 26th January 2009

Today is Australia Day, which – for those of you who are not Australian – commemorates the landing of the First Fleet with its load of convicts on this day in 1788. I heard a joke recently about an Englishman intending to come to Australia. Bureaucracy demands that the paper work be done, so as he was filling it in and answering the questions he came to one which asked; "Have you ever had a criminal record?" – to which he replied; "I did not know that was still a requirement". Later I was to find that this actually happened, and that the bureaucrats were not amused. Oh for a sense of humour.

Today is also Spring Festival this year, so being up here in the mountains is a good place to be, away from the noise of exploding firecrackers and away from the crowds. The timing has been perfect, getting the last bus to take us here before the festival and the first bus to run after the festival.

Last night I even watched a little TV, and viewed part of the annual nation-wide Spring Festival concert, which most Chinese watch. Each year, it seems, the acts are much the same, with some singing, dancing, comedians and opera. The latter was on show while I was watching, so I did not watch for long. I know the Chinese culture is long and rich, but I have never warmed to this aspect. I find the drums annoyingly discordant.

Once again I had a good night's sleep; not hard to do here. I fetched some hot water for breakfast, which I had while sitting on the verandah looking at the superb view. It is so vast, both horizontally along the gorge and vertically seeing more than 3,000 metres at a glance. I realised that the green dots on the mountainside opposite were actually trees. By 9.30 am we were ready to leave. One of the Frenchman then gave me the key to his room in the next guest house to which we were headed; he had forgotten to return it. It would be no trouble to return it for him.

The first hour of the walk was easy going. It is a little cooler today; definitely a two layer day. After a while I saw that I had company; a young lady with a baby on her back was herding a flock of goats. They kept up a good pace too. They followed along for quite some time before they headed off the track to graze a section of the mountain side which was not quite so steep – the goats, that is, not the woman! She stayed on the track to keep an eye on them for a while, before she turned back the way she had come. No doubt she would return in the evening to take them home for the night. It was wonderful to see just how sure footed these animals are on these steep slopes.

At 10.30 am it was time for a break, just as the sun was rising. This requires some explanation, but you need to picture the scene. We are walking north around the slopes of Mt. Bama, which is therefore to the west. Down below is the Yangtze River, on the other side of which, to the east, is Mt. Yulong. Hence the sun rises over this mountain, which is not only high, but long, being some 35 km in length; hence the late sunrise. As we continued to walk, we kept in the sunshine, but watched as the shadow crept below us down the mountain side. The river itself would only see the sun briefly around noon, while some sections on the northern side of bends would never see the sun. It was interesting, too, to note that there is more vegetation on north facing slopes than there is on south facing slopes. Why this should be remains a mystery to me, unless it be that the south facing slopes experience a greater temperature range, hence harsher conditions and possibly more erosion.

For the second hour the track became a lot steeper, with small waterfalls tumbling down the gullies. One was a little bigger and looked spectacular. In wet weather it could be a little hazardous, as it splashes right across the track, so one needed to take extra care. One could slip – and it is a long way to the bottom.

We arrived at Tina's Guest House just before noon, so stopped here for lunch. Once again I ordered a Naxi sandwich, but this one was different from yesterday's, in that it consisted of two (not three) layers of unleavened bread, round and about 20 cm across. The bread was thinner, too, and not unlike pita bread. Inside were spring onions, tomato and egg, but cooked, not cold. I liked it better. It cost a little more at 10 Yuan, compared with 8 Yuan yesterday.

We had now reached the road which runs alongside the gorge. Tina's is built very close to the edge of another smaller gorge on the slopes of Mt. Bama. A bridge spans this, from which you can look straight down at least 200 metres, and watch the water join the Yangtze. From here one can walk down to Middle Tiger Leaping Gorge, which means another boulder in the path of the river. It also means paying more money. It is about a two hour hike.

We headed off down the road for about three more kilometres. This time I am not going to mention the name of the guest house, for good reason. I asked the proprietor where I could get a geology map of the region, as this is an interest of mine. I could see at a glance that the river is cutting through a fault zone, but you need intensive geological mapping of the entire region to see just what has happened. I was told that you cannot get one. Why on earth not? – Classified information. Why? It appears that all of this area has traditionally for thousands of years been occupied by the Naxi and Tibetan peoples not the Han. Tibetan architecture is in evidence. I met a Tibetan man who found it difficult to hide his hatred of the Han people for invading his country and taking it over by military force. He talked of imprisonment of his people, the torture and deaths, the attempts to destroy Tibetan culture and religion and the policy of driving Tibetan people from their land to replace them with Han people, while all the while telling the world how good China has been to them, "liberating" them from feudalism. Enough, but I thought it important to pass on this person's views.

This guest house is quite comfortable, though again the toilet-shower is in a separate building. I found too that the floor of the latter to be always wet. There are other guests here, too, from different countries. It seems this whole walking venture is popular with people from other countries, but we met no Chinese doing it. The closest is an American whose parents were born in China. Now that we are back in "civilization" the fire crackers are once again piercing the otherwise quiet air. We have now reached the northern end of this remarkable gorge.

I had a good meal here, followed by a good night's sleep, ready for some more walking tomorrow.

17.   Tiger Leaping Gorge Day 4 – 27th January 2009

In the morning I asked for and got the necessary ingredients for a good Western breakfast, my style: mandarins, banana and hot water, to go with my cereal and coffee, though the water was not very hot and not very plentiful either. The water in the shower was also not hot.

Now you might remember that I had brought back the key which our French friend, J, had taken with him. As it transpired I found myself in the same room. While it was OK, it could have been better if the sheets had have been changed. When it came to settle our account, I was told that I still owed them 5 Yuan. The room itself had been paid for in advance, but there was also a 40 Yuan deposit on the key, plus last night's meal, which was expensive, and the breakfast this morning. Bear in mind that they had gained 40 Yuan from the deposit not collected by J, so they were ahead, but did not offer me anything for returning their key. I gently pointed this out, and stated that I had no intention of paying them the extra 5 Yuan. Let's call it quits. They agreed and we parted amicably. All in all this is not a place I would recommend.

This is the furthest I would go on this holiday; it was now time to head for home, apart from a side trip to Fuzhou. This being Spring Festival, however, the bus back to Lijiang would not be leaving till the afternoon. Five of us decided to walk to Qiatou, which I thought was about 16 km. There would be two Filipinas, one American, one Irishman and yours truly. Two of us went ahead to Tina's Guest House where we had an early lunch. The other three joined us later. By 12.30 pm we were ready to hit the road – for road it would be, not a mountain track.

The walking was easy, gently undulating for the most part, with the river not far below us, perhaps 200 m at the start. Bear in mind that the river falls some 230 m from the southern to the northern end, so really the road ascends as much as it descends, while the river rises to meet us. From here one can see that the river is noticeably green in colour, and again I would like to know why; maybe copper. Most of the rock I noticed is limestone, with some shales and schists, the latter due to contact metamorphism along this fault line.

This is a truly wonderful walk, full of beauty and not difficult, just a little long. As the afternoon wore on people were getting tired, though it was difficult to find a suitable place to sit down for a rest. We passed Middle Tiger Leaping Gorge and later we passed Upper Tiger Leaping Gorge. This latter is very touristy, with a car park on the road filled with cars and buses. On the other side of the river a bridge straddles a smaller gorge on the side of Yu Long Xue Shan. This links with a walking track cut into the side of the cliff face, and stretching back about two kilometres to a car park on that side of the river. The boulder is directly below us at this point, with the river rushing around both sides. I might add that white water rafting has been banned here as being too dangerous.

Further on there is a five star hotel and it truly looks lavish. Pillars out in front are made from loose rock held together by wire shaped like a wine glass; it is really a gabion. At this point I was making every effort to divert people's attention from the walk as the kilometres rolled by. We reached the 16 km mark, and no sign of the end. It must be close. The 17, 18 and 19 km posts slipped by – or maybe stagger by – and we have still not reached Qiatou. I was in the lead, trying to keep the others going, next came the American, then the two Filipinas, with the Irishman bringing up the rear; we were strung out like Brown's cows.

After 21 km, someone had had enough and flagged down a passing van. The driver refused to take her unless she paid 5 Yuan. She agreed. Then the second Filipina joined her, and then the other two, with me left alone. Then I too made a mistake. I really wanted to finish this walk, so I asked the driver how far it was. "More than four kilometres", was the answer. This would take me the best part of an hour, so to avoid holding the others up, I too got on board. Would you believe, Qiatou was just around the next corner, less than two kilometres further on. For the sake of money, the driver was a liar, not the first time on this trip I had experienced this. The one who was absolutely ropeable was R, our Irishman. He really let fly, telling the driver what he thought of him stating that he could not even give a lift to some tired walkers without making money, something that would not happen in Ireland. Certainly on this occasion, the Chinese did not exactly cover themselves in glory.

As luck would have it we had only just arrived in Qiatou when our bus also arrived, so we climbed on board straight away. I would have liked to have spent a bit of time with M, the owner of Jane's Guest House, who, as you may remember, comes from Randwick, but this was not possible. The ride back to Lijiang cost 50 Yuan. By that evening we were back, with the driver dropping us off close to those two large water wheels. From here we knew our way back to Mama Naxi's Guest House, just in time for their filling and inexpensive meal. In fact on this night they outdid themselves possibly because I had brought extra guests, providing no fewer than seven dishes for five people. There was a little bit of controversy when it turned out than one person, being Seventh Day Adventist, does not eat pork. This caused some hassles; is this really necessary? I asked her if she believes in the Bible, and she said; "Yes". Well, if you read chap. 10 of Acts you will find it stated quite explicitly that all foods are acceptable. It is not for us to call unclean what God has made.

This time I had a different room from last time, this one being on the ground floor and having an en-suite. It was a little more expensive, but still cheap at only 40 Yuan. After the meal I did some much needed laundry, though it was difficult to find enough space for it to dry.

There was no need for us to stay in Lijiang any longer, so the decision was made to leave the following day and head back to Dali.

18.   Lijiang to Dali – 28ᵗʰ January 2009

By the following morning, the laundry was mostly dry. Breakfast was according to my usual Western style. I spent the morning packing up and checking the internet. I had an early lunch here at 11.30 am, consisting of a dinner-plate sized Naxi bread, with tomato and two fried eggs on top. That will do nicely, thank you.

Since our hostess, Xiao Han, had been so helpful, I gave her a small koala toy by way of saying "Thank you". I also settled the account. I had to tell her about the laundry because she had not included the 5 Yuan charge for use of the washing machine. Before we left, she rang up the bus company asking them to pick me up, and then asked the cook to take me there. This worthy young man then set out on his bike, carrying my bag, whilst I followed in his wake. As well as that, Xiao Han gave me a bag of mandarins. People can be so generous, yet others – like that driver in Qiatou – are so mean-spirited.

In due course the bus arrived, after some time waiting. It was a minibus, but with only four people aboard. We had a good two hour trip back to Dali, passing more eucalyptus trees and even the odd wattle out in bloom. Crikey, I could be back in Aus. Just outside of Dali, we stopped, and it was "everyone out". Goodness, what is going on? We were told to climb aboard another larger bus coming behind us. This I did, after paying the 35 Yuan for the fare to the driver of the first bus, who handed this over to the conductress on the second bus, who then gave him the change, which he then gave to me. Confused? – And why the rigmarole? – Who knows; must be China.

The strange thing is that we only went a very short distance before we arrived outside the Old City of Dali, and told to get off again. Ok, but we are still a long way from the guest house where I had planned to spend the night. There was nothing for it but to hail a taxi. This driver did not know where "Friends Hostel" was so we spent a little time looking for it. Having got there I found that the 40 Yuan tariff was now 100 Yuan (around $18). What! How come? Festival, that's how come. As it turned out, the room was down a spiral staircase, directly below the front office, so one could hear every footfall; as well the water was tepid and there was no toilet paper. Not to worry. At least I got a thermos of hot water.

Having checked in, the next priority was to get a train ticket to Kunming, so I dumped the bags and walked through the city to catch the No. 8 bus into Xiaguan. I came by overnight train, so this time I wanted to travel by day and see the sights. The ticket cost 45 Yuan for the six hour journey. I could have gone by bus in only five hours, but I prefer the train – well normally. It is also cheaper, the bus fare being 85 Yuan or 120 Yuan, depending on the type of bus.

With ticket thus clutched firmly in hand, it was time for the evening meal. A strolled along a group of stalls close to the train station, thus providing a number of options, finally settling for a family restaurant, others being rejected on the grounds of being either too dirty, or too full, or the food being too stale. For 20 Yuan I had cauliflower, a couple of green veggies, rice and a soup. The owners appear to be an elderly couple, being assisted by their daughter and married son, plus his wife. I noticed a new car out the front, so they must be doing well. Later a large tourist bus drove up and parked outside, which they proceeded to clean, so I gather this too belongs to them. They are doing very well. I might add that the father did nothing; it was the women who did most of the work.

Back in Dali, I had an ice-cream as I strolled around. There are many more people here now than there were before Spring Festival. I think I came at the right time. It is not quite as peaceful either, as – BANG – those fire crackers keep going off – BANG – when you are not expecting them, like – BANG – now.

The next sight was really nice. People had a Kunming (or paper) lantern, measuring about 40 cm high by about 30 cm across. They were just lighting the candle at the bottom. Soon the lantern rose majestically and slowly into the air. Mind you it did not go far, coming to rest in a nearby tree, but it looked great while it lasted.

Back at the hostel, I was soon in bed and slept like a top. The next thing I knew was the alarm going off at 6.30 am. This gave plenty of time to check out, though I was a little bit early for members of the staff, who were still asleep. I had breakfast and headed off at 7.45 am, carrying my bag about 1.5 km to the bus stop. There were few people about at this hour, with some shop keepers just beginning to open up. There were, however, three Chinese tourist groups, with 20 to 30 people in each and the respective leaders holding aloft the obligatory flag.

As the early morning sun touched the top of the mountain range (Cang Shan) I noticed there was more snow there now than at the beginning of last week, glowing pink in the early light. Soon the now familiar No. 8 bus arrived in plenty of time for the 40 minute trip back to Xiaguan to catch the 9.40 train to Kunming. Join me aboard.

19.   Dali to Kunming – 29th – 30th January 2009

Once aboard, I found that I was sharing the compartment with a family, some members of which were ensconced in the next compartment, so that there was plenty of to-ing and fro-ing. On one occasion, about 11.30 am, I noticed no fewer than five children playing games more or less harmoniously, so this was obviously a more extended family. One father was sitting opposite me; most of the time he slept, but even when awake had little to say. As for managing the children, that was Mum's job. And it was a job. At one point we had no fewer than ten people in our compartment.

All of this, plus the past few weeks, got me thinking about travel. Gregory the Great tells us to use the things of this world but to desire the things of the next. Wise words indeed; he was a wise man, and possibly the greatest pope the Church has had. All life is a journey and the wise traveller travels light. Many things are useful as we travel, even essential, but only for part of the journey. You cannot board this train, for instance, without a train ticket. It is essential. But once we have arrived at our destination, it is no longer needed. Indeed it may become an unnecessary burden. We could keep it as a memento, which is fine, but there is a danger that the present will become bogged down in the past, making it difficult to move into the future. We cannot live in the past. Old age begins when our primary gaze shifts backward rather than forward. Then we cease living in the now.

I am returning to Fuzhou, the city I lived in for four years, to see some of my former students. I know the city will be different, and so will my students. Indeed, I am different. Part of the excitement is to see how they have grown. Paul tells us that the world as we know it is coming to an end. What fades cannot have lasting value. The only things worth having are really the things of the next world, such as complete relationships and perfect peace – in other words, love, centred in God.

While musing thus, I was also gazing out the window, admiring the beautiful countryside, especially with the yellow flowered *tai cai* in full bloom, set against the green of other crops, all in neat rows or curves. The white walled, grey roofed houses complement this. Farm houses are also often made of brick or mud brick. The towns tend to feature white tiles on the outside of buildings, colourfully decorated. Once again I noticed many eucalyptus trees, including many saplings, so they are thriving.

By 12.30 pm, two of the children had flaked out, one snoring loudly, while another was playing games on his phone, which was making boring noises, seemingly being repeated endlessly. Meanwhile I noticed that our journey was taking us through many a tunnel. China is such a mountainous land that this is a commonplace. I estimated that something like 100 km of this present trip alone is inside tunnels, the longest of which is close to 10 km.

By late afternoon we were back in Kunming. The first thing to do was to book a ticket to Fuzhou, but was very surprised to be told that there weren't any. When I was in Fuzhou I knew that the Fuzhou to Kunming run was common, but no, definitely not. I could go to Xiamen, so I opted for this. From Xiamen to Fuzhou is about 4 hours by bus. The ticket was for the following Sunday, February 1st, giving me a couple of days back here in Kunming.

This time I thought I would try another hotel, the Camellia, recommended by Lonely Planet. Not knowing how to get there necessitated getting a taxi – no problems here. And it is a very nice hotel at a reasonable price. On my bed I found a sign, to wit; "For economizing on resources, reducing water contamination and protecting our environment for existence, the cleaning of cotton fabrics in the hotel will be changed to once cleaning for one guest." Get it? When I checked in I was given a meal ticket for breakfast, which is included. Wow! That is the first time on this trip that that has happened.

For the rest of the day I wandered around the area. When time to eat, I just went into KFC, almost opposite the hotel: very convenient.

The next morning, Friday 30th, I duly presented my ticket for breakfast to find that it is indeed a lavish spread, smorgasbord style. Need I tell you that I made full use of it; porridge, toast, egg plus various other cooked foods, fruit juice, coffee... It was a feast. It is also an international hotel with people here from many different countries. I got to chat with many of them, including Australians, and, hey, you do find them anywhere. Here is an interesting tit-bit: one lady decided to check out a Versace handbag. Now I would reckon that if you need to ask the price of these luxury goods, then you cannot afford them. How true in this case; it was 23,700 Yuan, or about AUD 5,000. Just to put your lipstick in? Unbelievable. What it does say is that there is plenty of money in this town.

After breakfast I went to check out the Provincial Museum, which I did not get to when I was here before. The building is an imposing structure in Greek architectural style. Here I found out more about the Dian people. Their clothing was rather simple, not much more than a tunic. They do not seem to have worn shoes. Central to their culture was the buffalo, used for ploughing, for food, for worship and even for entertainment in the form of bull fights. It also featured prominently in their bronze-ware. It seems strange to me that I saw no evidence of earthenware vessels. Their jewellery consisted of jade, amethyst and agate, probably obtained through trading. For coins they used cowrie shells. Dance and music were important to them, using percussion and wind instruments but, curiously, no string instruments. They appeared to be involved in fairly constant fighting with their nomadic neighbours. Captives were either kept as slaves, or beheaded, or fed to pythons; charming. In AD 190, like many other peoples in this part of the world, they were conquered by the Han army, becoming subject to the Chinese Empire. Their culture managed to survive for another couple of centuries, but now they are no more. Perhaps there is a lesson here.

20.   *Kunming to Xiamen 31ˢᵗ January – 3ʳᵈ February 2009*

The two days spent back in this city gave me a chance to revisit some of my favourite places, such the central square and Green Park. It was also a chance to relax without rushing around. After this I would have a long train trip, so I wanted to be ready. It gave me a chance, too, to visit Wal-Mart's to buy supplies – yoghurt for instance – and to use the internet, for which they charge 6 Yuan for 30 minutes, or 10 Yuan for an hour. For evening meal I used a restaurant in a back street which is both inexpensive and good quality.

On Sunday, February 1ˢᵗ, I checked out but left the bags at the hotel, before wandering off to do some shopping. I had lunch in a McDonald's then read for a little while till it was time to leave. I walked back to the hotel, collected the bags and hailed a taxi, it now being about 3.30 pm. About 400 m from the railway station, it was clear that this traffic was going nowhere fast, as there had been an accident involving a bus and a truck, so I got out, deciding to walk the rest of the way.

By 4.40 pm we were off. I must say that the trains have been excellent in keeping to the timetable. The countryside is limestone, dotted with pillars up to 4 m high, with the fluted sides (rillen karen) characteristic of karst topography. The soil is reddish. I was a little surprised to see that this land is still given over to cultivation and not pasture, as the stony ground makes it difficult to tend. It is not a problem for sheep, for instance, which simply graze around the stones. I did see one flock of goats, but that was it.

The sun set at about 7.00 pm, which is quite late for this time of the year, but remember that we are still some distance to the west of Beijing, to the tune of some 14 degrees of longitude (or one hour sun time) and in China, everything is dominated by Beijing, so that instead of four time zones, there is only one. For this trip I have a soft sleeper, top bunk. There was no hard sleeper to be had, and I was lucky to get this, but it is very expensive, at more than 700 Yuan. Oh well, it is not my money. The university does not pay me unless I specifically ask, then gives me the minimum, so that I did not have enough money for this holiday. I borrowed from Aussie 1: great bloke.

During the night I got up to stretch my legs and look out the window. While you cannot see much of the countryside, you can see the lights from the train windows falling on the dark ground, like beads strung along the string of night.

Next morning, I was preparing to eat my usual breakfast which I had brought with me, when one of the other travellers suggested we go to the dining car. I told her I cannot do that, as I would not be buying anything. She insisted, so off we went, with me hopping into my cereal when we were presented with the menu. I stalled for time – so that I could finish – by ordering Western food, which I knew they would not have. "Muesli, thanks, then a couple of bangers with fried egg and hash browns. Oh, and coffee." It worked. We were still ordered out (told you so!), but I did get to finish my cereal. Gosh I'm terrible.

This journey is really something, with the route taking us from Kunming in Yunnan Province, east into Guizhou Province, then south east into Guanxi Province, north a little around Nanning, before heading almost due south to Maoming in Guangdong Province, then north east to Guangzhou, before winding considerably but heading more or less north east to Xiamen in Fujian Province. All in all we would be on the train for more than 40 hours, including two nights. As I said; quite a journey.

I had brought with me some instant noodles for one night's meal, but for the second night I thought it would be good to try the dining car. So I did. They can't kick me out now, as I am buying food. But no sooner was the last mouthful swallowed than I was told to leave. Goodness: is this a record? – being kicked out of the dining car on a train twice, in the same day! It is a pity, really, that the dining staff was so inhospitable; they really spoiled the trip. The food was OK; it was the staff which left the sour taste in the mouth.

On Tuesday 9.15 am we arrived in Xiamen. The first thing I did was to take a suburban bus to the intercity bus terminal to buy a ticket for Hui An and to store my bags. My bus was due to depart at 2.00 pm, giving me plenty of time. I like Xiamen, and have been here several times before. It holds happy memories for me, not just because it is clean and modern, but primarily because of the people I have been with. Having spent so long on the train, it was so pleasant wandering around and stretching the legs. I found a lovely, modern, underground shopping plaza, an ideal place for lunch.

By 4.00 pm I was in Hui An, where I was due to meet Tina, a former student of mine from ACC (Anglo Chinese College), Fuzhou. I arrived, but no sign of her. I rang her. "Where are you?" she asked. "At the bus station," says I. "Yes, but which one?" "You mean there is more than one? Dammed if I know." I found a young man called, Michael, who spoke excellent English, and passed my phone to him, so that he could tell her. It transpired that there are four bus stations. Soon after,

Tina arrived. It was good to see her again after 18 months. I had taught her for 3 ½ years and we had become quite close.

She took me to a hotel, clean and inexpensive, with Western toilet and hot water. Great, as the first thing I did was to shower and change clothes, having been in the same clothes for two days. Being now a little more respectable I met Jojo, one of Tina's colleagues and a girl called Su – Miss Su, that is. Everyone in her village has the same surname. Interesting. They hired a car to go to a seaside town called Chong Wu, which I had actually visited before, and to go to a seafood restaurant. They gave us too much, and one dish was so spicy I could not eat it – but nor could the others. Apart from that it was very nice. So we strolled and chatted. It was good to catch up again. Next we hired another car and whizzed off to a KTV, where we were joined by several other young people. I stayed about an hour, before leaving them to it. Outside we got a motorcycle to take me back to my hotel. Here I actually watched a bit of tele before turning off the light.

21.   Hui An to Fuzhou – 4th – 6th February 2009

The next morning Tina turned up with the other Miss Su. Later her younger brother joined us. He had left school after junior secondary to go to work, because his family could not afford to keep him. What a pity. This happens not infrequently in this country, but it is generally the girl who has to forgo her education in favour of her brother. There were now four of us and two motorcycles, so the two girls rode together, while I hopped up behind the brother. No helmets are required, at least not by law. The girls were soon way ahead, as my driver was so careful. I also noticed that when we came to hills, his bike was struggling: not many revs here. As we travelled I kept an eye on the farms and their workers. Most seemed to be hoeing the ground, though I did see one lady ploughing with the aid of a buffalo, probably in the same time-honoured way her forebears had done for thousands of years.

In due course we arrived at their village, or rather at the village where Tina had spent a lot of her time. It seems that from the age of twelve she was taken under the wing of a rich uncle, since her own family is poor. She lived with his family and he paid for her education until she graduated from college. Now she is on her own. She has a job, but is looking for another. The house of her uncle is lavish; it has four storeys with colourfully decorated tiling. He is rich alright, and in fact is a businessman working from Shenzhen, a city about 600 km to the south west. We had lunch here: meat with potatoes and peanuts, thus using the local products. Next door is their former house, which has only one level, built around an open courtyard, plus a flat roof.

In the afternoon we hopped back on the bikes to go to another village nearby where Tina's family live and where she had spent her early years. Her parents are currently adding several floors to their house as it was too small and the roof leaked. They cannot afford this, so have borrowed from friends. I met Tina's mother, but not her Dad, who was busy in a nearby house, playing cards.

A group of us then strolled around the village and out to a nearby dam. While this is small, it is the biggest thing around here; the local tourist attraction. It was built around 1960 and holds back a pretty lake, which makes a nice backdrop to this village. I noticed more eucalypts here and also casuarinas, another Australian tree. As we walked it gave me a chance to talk more with Tina.

Soon, however, it was time to say goodbye, so it was back on the bike to my hotel to pick up my bags then head to the bus station – a different one this time – to catch a bus to Fuzhou. Tina gave me instructions as to where to get off and what suburban bus to get once I had reached Fuzhou – No .30. Fine, except that having waited for half an hour it occurred to me that maybe this bus does not run after certain hours, and it was now getting a little late. So I had to get another bus and then a taxi to get to my destination. I would be staying in my old apartment. This would bring back memories.

The next day, Thursday, was a time to rest and phone around, letting people know that I was in town, so that I could meet some of them. It also gave me an opportunity to go for a walk and note any changes that had taken place. This included looking at the cathedral. While this has not changed, the open area in front of it has gone, being replaced by a highway. The old presbytery, all 600 tonnes of it, was lifted up and transported to the other side of the cathedral; what an undertaking! In the evening I watched a video, something I do rarely, as I do not have a video player in Tongren.

On Friday, the fun started. At 10.00 am I met some of my former students at Wu Yi Square. It was really good to see them and chat, as we wandered around, taking heaps of photos. There was Angela, who had been the princess in Sleeping Beauty, and Hugh (aka The Frog) who had been the frog in the same play, Sunny, Serena and Maurice. Afterwards we had lunch at a restaurant near Dong Jie Kou, off Jintai Lu, a little out of the way. After lunch, we walked to what is Old

Fuzhou. This is a very old area of the city, near Dong Jie Kou, one which I have visited previously and photographed extensively. I am glad I did, since it has now all been pulled down and rebuilt in the old style. To me though, it has lost something. Now, instead of being a living community of people, it has been turned into a tourist attraction, with shops selling the usual touristy things. I would like to see them turn it back to a community of how people lived centuries ago. Soon it was time to say goodbye to A, F, S, S and M, as I was meeting someone else at 3.00 pm.

I did not have far to go, as I met Cathy at McDonald's, though there was some confusion as there are two of these establishments, and we were waiting at different ones. She is a teacher whom I had got to know at ACC, and has proved herself to be a good friend over the years. She is married with a baby, so could not spend too long away from home. We had a meal too; lots of eating on this trip.

At 7.00 pm I met another of my former students. I wanted to meet her because she had given me an expensive coat – my thick, warm coat – for my birthday two years ago, so I had a small gift for her. We met at a bookstore, so I could buy something to read, which would save me from going to a bookstore in Guiyang. Would you believe it, she presented me with yet another coat! Oh dear, this is not why I met her. Obviously, I cannot let this continue.

After chatting a while, we said our goodbyes and I caught a bus to Shi Da, leaving me a 20 minute walk back to my apartment. What a day. It was wonderful to see these people again. This is why I returned to Fuzhou. Let us see what tomorrow brings. Zaijian.

22.   *In Fuzhou – 7th – 9th February 2009*

On Saturday morning I saw Grace, another former teacher from Anglo Chinese College, who came to the apartment, bringing along her daughter, who is now about four years old. Grace now teaches at the No.1 middle school, a rather prestigious institution which I have described before. She is a lovely person, always most helpful.

In the afternoon, around 3.30 pm, Jy arrived, another of my former students, who has also featured in some of my previous Jottings. He is an outstanding young man. He has the distinction of having represented Fujian Province in the CCTV 9 Cup, a nation-wide English speaking competition, in which he did very well indeed. Currently he is teaching at a university, plus a middle school, while also holding down a weekly

TV programme; a busy man. It was good to catch up. We have a mutual friend, IJ, another of my former students, who is presently studying for her masters in the U.S. and is an amazing young lady. We rang her, because – coincidentally – today is her birthday.

Next, of course, we went out for the obligatory meal, this time to a new restaurant in Tai Jiang, just over Rainbow Bridge. One of the waiters had this knack of lengthening noodles prior to cooking, by swinging them around his head every whichway quite skilfully. I was not the only one intrigued either, as a little girl from the next table was watching goggle-eyed at each performance. After the meal it was time for photographs – also obligatory – before strolling back home. En route we watched paper (Kunming) lanterns take to the sky, as we are getting close to Lantern Festival.

Jy is the kindest hearted man you would ever come across, though not the world's greatest communicator, so to be able to spend quality time with him, finding out how his life is unfolding, his successes and disappointments, his hopes and dreams, is precious time indeed.

On Sunday morning, F1 and I walked across Rainbow Bridge to attend 8.00 am Mass at the Sacred Heart, as we had done many times in the past, when I was teaching at ACC, while she was teaching either at the middle school or at Hwa Nan. Now she is at ACC while I have moved to Tongren.

After Mass, I caught the No. 20 bus to Wu Yi Square, to meet another of my former students, Mary, my consort. Not long after I arrived in Fuzhou in 2002, Jy and Mary invited me to climb Gu Shan with them, which I did for the very first time; I made other ascents later. At one point, I dressed up as an emperor, while Mary dressed as my consort and we had our photos taken. So she is for evermore my consort. She is also a lovely person, so I was delighted to be able to catch up with her and her doings. She is now teaching small children. Naturally, we shared a meal. She asked me where I would like to go, but – in typical Chinese style – she had already decided on a place, where we had a Western style steak; wonderful.

Later I spent some time in Oceanworld Bookstore, close by, to buy a book to read on the return train trip. As I have said before, you cannot get English books in Tongren. I had intended to visit a bookstore in Guiyang, so this would actually save me time later. I bought "Oliver Twist", which I finished on the journey. I like Dickens, though his characters and scene depictions are both a little black and white. I suppose, though, that he is making a strong social statement, which in his day needed to be made, and indeed, still does. The book I was reading at the time was "My Feudal Lord", another social commentary, in this case a damming indictment of Islam and the way it treats its women. I would recommend it – the book, that is, not Islam.

Later that day, I accompanied F1 to the railway station, as she was going to Nanchang in Jiangxi Province to stay with a friend of hers, but I am grateful for her hospitality, because I am using her apartment while she is away. Yes, it is her apartment now, but for four years it was mine.

On Monday morning I spent some time collecting teaching material in preparation for the semester ahead. I met Mary again plus Olivia for lunch. Olivia, another of my former students, is also involved in the teaching of small children, so they have much in common. In fact for a lot of the time, they were going hammer and tongs in Chinese, while I listened. Olivia, unfortunately, is not well. She had actually rung me some time ago in Tongren, asking if I would be interested in returning to Fuzhou to teach small children. While I am flattered by the offer, this is really not my scene. I think I will stick with university and college students.

At 5.00 pm I was picked up by Sulin in her uncle's car and driven to their place to celebrate the Lantern Festival (*Yuanxiao Jie*). I could not have got there on my own, partly because it is not on a public transport route, partly because of my faulty memory, but mainly because the city has changed so much. Several entire building blocks in front of their place have now been demolished. This family is U/g RC. I know about them and they know about me. Three years ago, F1, Aussie 3 and I were invited by this wonderful family to celebrate Spring Festival. Sulin is now studying in Chongqing and is managing quite well. She is a smart girl. Her little cousin, M, is no longer a little girl, but is growing into a beautiful looking young woman, and in fact has already landed some acting roles. I might also add that Sulin's cousin (1st cousin, once removed) has been a good friend for some years. Quite recently she married an Italian gentleman, so is living in Italy. There she does not have to worry about being persecuted because of her Catholic beliefs.

As usual, the women prepared the meal though beforehand the uncle performed the tea ceremony. It was a seafood meal, with crab, various kinds of molluscs, fish, prawns and a soup. We also had wine, but as is usually the case with Chinese wines, the quality leaves a bit to be desired. I would love to see Australian wines readily available here at affordable prices.

All the while, the air is being rent with the sounds of exploding firecrackers, so after the meal, the family decided to join in. Outside we went, led by the uncle, in order to set off their own variety. This consisted of metre-long tubes with a wick at one end. After this was lit, you had to be careful to point the tube away from you and away from everybody else, best achieved by pointing it into the sky. At intervals of about 15 seconds, there would be a whoosh as a small rocket whizzed out, exploding in colourful sparks about 20 metres away. There were about ten of these to a tube. Great fun was had by all, as the whole city was similarly engaged in exploding fireworks of different kinds, in a cacophony of sound and a myriad of lights. As well, upwards of a dozen Kunming lanterns could be seen floating gently across the sky, some close to the full moon, which of course this festival is celebrating; it is the first full moon of the lunar New Year. Later that night, after I had returned home, I stood on the roof of the apartment building to watch these lanterns and fireworks light up the sky, and together with the lights of the city, reflect off the waters of the Min Jiang. Beautiful.

What a great day this has been. God is good.

23.   Fuzhou to Guiyang – 10th – 12th February 2009

Tuesday was largely a quiet day. I made sure everything was packed for my departure tomorrow, watched a video then went for a walk. I walked around the hill, as I had done many times before, but this was a little different, as I remembered previous walks. I must be getting maudlin in my old age. I also caught up with the news of the horrific bush fires in Victoria, with much loss of property and considerable loss of life.

In the evening I walked to Shi Da and at 6.45 pm met V, her cousin, F, and her boyfriend, and S, who was in the same class at ACC. It was wonderful to see them again. From here we took a taxi to a restaurant in a part of town I am not familiar with, where we joined up with S, MW, J and his wife, T. It was quite a gathering. To put you in the picture, Vicky, Fiona, Susan and Mandy W came to Sydney last year for World Youth Day, largely on the back of generous donors. I was therefore very keen to find out how they were doing and in particular, what effect WYD is having on their lives now and on the lives of others. During our meal I was able to elicit a degree of information. It transpires that they have been affected, not only by WYD itself, but also by the whole Australia experience. As well, they are influencing others. In a previous writing (Jotting 228) I outlined what is happening to the U/g (underground) church in Fuzhou, so I will not repeat that here: maybe in another place.

Once more I was to enjoy a wonderful meal, of spicy fish, beef, soup, and beer. There were also pig's trotters, but I must confess that I have never warmed to eating feet, whether pigs or chooks or anyone else's. J works with the Chinese Church in Sydney, so is familiar with our food and drinks. He remarked that he really likes Australian beer, as it has body, whereas the Chinese beer is as weak as water. He is right too. To this, V and F agreed. After the meal we went to the apartment of a relative for further discussion and tea. I can report, therefore, that all is well with them, and to thank again those people who generously sponsored these people while they were in Sydney.

Next morning, Wednesday, after breakfast, I locked F1's apartment behind me and headed off to the local bus stop to catch the 953, though only for a couple of stops. It meant I did not have to carry my bag for some 1 ½ km. From Liu Yi Nan Lu I caught the No. 17 bus to the railway station, where I was due to meet Mary and Olivia. I was in plenty of time, but had to wait. The area, I might add, was really filthy, in spite of the efforts of a cleaner who came along. People do tend to spit as well as drop rubbish. Then along came a woman who decided to vomit onto the pavement next to me. Oh the joys of travel.

Eventually Olivia turned up, with us trying to find each other via our mobile phones. It still seems odd to me to be using a phone to talk to someone who is only a few metres away. But where is Mary? She will come later, so the two of us went inside and found the correct waiting room. People were already boarding. Where is Mary? She turned up eventually, running to meet us. So we had time to say hello, take a photo, then say goodbye. It was really great of them, however, to take the time to see me off. I really appreciate it. They are wonderful people. I had noticed that when I was teaching Olivia at ACC, she would be helping others who were struggling. On one occasion I had failed a particular student, if I can put it that way. Actually teachers do not fail students; they fail themselves. Teachers judge their standard – amongst other tasks. Olivia took some trouble to bring him along to me for a retest. Subsequently I found out that he is in fact her boyfriend.

Onto the train I went for yet another long trip, this one about 28 hours to Guiyang. I found that I had my back to the direction we were travelling. During the night, however, at a place called Lou Di, the train reversed direction, so that in the morning I was able to see what was coming. I prefer it this way.

Along the way the countryside is looking beautiful, though patches are looking a little dry, as there has not been much rain for a while. Rice paddies are still showing the stubble from the autumn harvest. The yellow flowers of *cai tai* complement the greens and browns, while terracing makes use of every square metre.

I could have got off at Kaili, which would make the trip about six hours shorter, but I wanted to go to Guiyang, where I arrived at 2.00 pm. The next priority was to get my ticket for Yu Ping for the following day. I met a gentleman on the train who decided he wanted to be my friend, so elected to help me buy my ticket. Where is the ticket window? "No", he says, "not those; it is over here". This meant walking for some distance, carrying my heavy bag, along a barrier, then around it to where about 30 temporary windows were open to cater for the extra crowds. I was about 20ᵗʰ in line. When it was my turn, she suddenly closed her window. She is off duty. Thanks, lady. So I had no choice but to queue up somewhere else, this time with only about six people ahead of me. As we got closer, I noticed that the lady in the next cubicle also shut up shop. Goodness. When it came to my turn, this lady too closed her window. I just can't take a trick.

There was nothing for it now but to go back to the main ticket windows where I had been heading in the first place. So back the way I had come we trudged, first away from the station, around the barrier, back to the station, to join yet another long queue. This time I did not even get to the front, as the helpful gentleman got in before me. After all of this, he told me that there is no train to Tongren. I know that. I want a ticket to Yu Ping. This met with the same result; no ticket. What? You have to be joking! I may have to get the bus.

Enough, so I bid farewell to helpful gentleman and hailed a taxi to my hotel, the same "7 Days" I had stayed in before. Then I rang Echo, to tell her I was in town and what had happened at the railway station. It was now well after 3.00 pm. I knew she was teaching until 3.30 pm, but should meet me here at about 4.00 pm. So I waited…and waited. 5.00 pm came and went. I did not want to go out in case I should miss her. At 6.00 pm she arrived. Where had she been? She had been to the railway station, where she did in fact buy a ticket for me for the following day. Echo trumps helpful gentleman. It cost 51 Yuan. I have a seat. You may remember that for the outward journey I could not get a seat, so … well…. We talked for a while and I gave her a present. Then we went out for a walk. She showed me the bus stop I needed to take in order to get to Wal-Mart, as I needed to do some shopping. Here we said goodbye. She is a great lady. She has a little baby to look after and several jobs to hold down as she struggles to make ends meet.

It is only two stops to Wal-Mart, so not far. There is a KFC here, so I had my evening meal before doing my shopping. Here I bought goods I cannot get in Tongren. like some cereals, tinned goods and cheese. Outside I watched a paper lantern rise gracefully into the air, though it did not go far before descending and falling into the river. It was a lovely, balmy night, so I walked back to my hotel. It is not that far, only about 25 minutes. It was time to turn in, before I return to Tongren tomorrow.

24.   Last Leg – Friday 13th February 2009

Friday 13th. Goodness: is that ominous? Actually, no; this date is no more ominous than any other. The rest is superstition.

I had asked the hotel to give me a wake-up call at 6.00 am, which they duly did. It was time to head back to Tongren. I had breakfast in my hotel room as per usual custom and checked the little bit of laundry I had done last night; it was dry. At 7.00 am I checked out, then retraced my steps from last night when I was with Echo. There is an interesting underpass to negotiate. It descends below a major intersection and is quite large, having quite a few shops within it. The steps going down, however take a bend, so that you are not sure which direction you are facing. On a previous occasion I had emerged again to find that I had taken a wrong turn. This time, however, I had been careful to memorize our route from last night.

Back on the street I took the correct turn to the bus stop, put my bags down and waited for the 253. By 7.50 am I was at the train station; it was so, so crowded, which should come as no surprise to those of you who have borne with me in my journeys thus far. In due course I found the correct waiting room, then train, then carriage and finally the correct seat. I sat down put my book (Oliver Twist) on the table as I proceeded to get out my paper and pen to do some writing. Immediately a man grabbed my book. No, he was not trying to steal it; he was just curious. When he found it was in English, he did deign to put it back again, remarking, *"Wo kan bu dong"* ("I can't read it"). I know you can't, mate, but thanks for returning it. There is very little sense of personal privacy in this country.

Meanwhile I was getting out my biro. Now where is that biro? I had brought five with me on this trip. Of these two ran out, one did not work and one I lost, so that I was now down to my last one. It should last the distance. So I began writing. You can probably predict what happened next; the other passengers were leaning over to read what I was writing. They still could not read. Hey, half the time I cannot even read my own writing. I could see, however, that they were really taken with the speed I was able to write in this strange script. Again, of course, there is no sense of privacy. This goes part way to explaining why it is that the government pries into every aspect of people's lives here. It is just the way they are.

This train is just so crowded. However Echo did manage to get me a seat – bless her little heart. As we pulled up at Kaili (once more), many people got off, but so many others piled aboard. There were vendors on the platform selling food and drink. These were simply passed through the window; there was no hope of getting out in order to buy something. As usual, train personnel were going through the carriages selling socks, toys and other knick knacks, complete with demonstrations of these worthy products.

Once again the countryside is so mountainous, with the train passing through tunnel after tunnel. While reading my book, the light was changing dramatically, as we dipped in and out of these tunnels, which makes it a little difficult to focus, since it takes time for the pupils to dilate or decrease. In between, in the valleys, one can see lush, fertile land. Rice paddies occupy the smallest pieces of arable land, many of them now filled with water prior to spring planting. The rock type is sedimentary, mainly sandstones but with shales and limestones.

By mid-afternoon we had reached Yu Ping. I got out and looked for a taxi, one of those blue intercity ones. As usual I was accosted by many drivers hoping to get my fare. One fellow wanted me to have his taxi all to myself, which would mean my paying 120 Yuan. Yes, it is Spring Festival time so the price has gone up. Normally it is 100 Yuan. I carry my bag a little further and find other people about to hop into one of these taxis; there are three of them, so they are looking for another passenger. I agree to join them.

In we get and off we roar. This guy must think he is a racing driver, and that is exactly what he turned out to be. At a temporary halt, another blue taxi came in from the left and shot passed us. Then it was on. We raced along doing 140 kph. In towns he would barely slow down, but honk his horn and roar through. It really does appear that there are no road rules in this country. Overtaking slower vehicles on blind turns is a commonplace. We won. We beat the other taxi. And we survived. We got to Tongren in one hour, whereas you may remember that on the outward journey it took us two hours.

I staggered out of the taxi near the intercity bus station, placed my bags on the footpath and hailed a local taxi to take me back to the university. I am home again, or what passes for home in this point of my life.

What a marathon this has been. And I hear you say, "What a marathon reading about it" – those of you, that is, who have survived the ordeal. Indeed. I have written no fewer than twenty one Jottings on this holiday, totalling in excess of 23,000 words. But this five week holiday has been the longest and best holiday I have ever had in China. It has truly been an amazing experience and I consider myself to be so fortunate as to be able to do this. God is indeed good.

As I type this into my computer we have only a few more days before classes resume, and I am fully aware that I have a mountain of work to do. It is unfortunate that Aussie 1 will not be back for some time, so I have volunteered to take his classes. I will be a busy boy. Perhaps I really needed that holiday. So no more train trips for a while, no more struggling crowds, no more mountain vistas. It is back to work.

National Day Holidays 2009

25.   Tongren to Zhengzhou – 30th September – 2nd October 2009

National Day in China falls on 1st October, because on that day the Communist Party took over the country's governance. Curiously, when I ask my students what the day means, they say it is China's birthday, thus dismissing in a sweep, so it seems, 5,000 years of history. So let us say it marks the beginning of the current dynasty, and since this took place in 1949, we are now celebrating 60 years of this rule. Now 60 years is a very important celebration here, as it marks five completed 12 year cycles, five being another important number. The Chinese, for instance, thought there were five basic elements.

All this adds up to massive celebrations, especially in Beijing. This is probably not the best time to travel, especially to Beijing, which is precisely what a friend of mine did. Now while I am not that stupid (Did I say "friend"? – probably ex-friend on the basis of what I just wrote) I did travel, first to Chongqing and thence to Zhengzhou. I did a lot of travelling, but we had the time, as this year the holiday was especially long. As well as the four days for National Day, there was a fifth for Mid-autumn festival. Add to that the fact that my Fridays are free, throw in the weekend, and hey presto, I got eight days. And while I am gallivanting around the countryside, I am still getting paid. Hey, who's complaining? Actually I have not yet been paid for this semester. The university is not very good in paying me.

I have a very good friend in Aus. who was born in China, leaving the country – coincidentally – in 1949. Her family was having a reunion; the first time in 25 years that the six children had gathered together. It was a very important occasion. I am honoured to have been invited to join them. To this end, I left Tongren Wed night 9.40 pm on a crowded train heading for Chongqing, and without a seat. In this town you cannot buy a train ticket until a couple of days beforehand. This is because priority is given to those passengers joining the train at its point of departure- Shenzhen in this case. In between it is pot luck. I got lucky, as I managed to get a seat only a couple of hours into the journey, not that I got much sleep.

At the uncivilized hour of 5.15 am, we arrived at Chongqing North Station – there are two. I was being met by a lovely young lady, Sulin, whom I had known in Fuzhou and whom I have mentioned before. She is now studying law at one of the universities and is doing very well; she is a bright, practical girl who knows what she wants. She was due to arrive at the train station at about 9.00 am, leaving me four hours to kill; not a problem. I found a suitable, reasonably uncrowded spot to read, pray and have breakfast which I had brought with me. After her arrival we spent the entire day at the station, walking, talking, and eating. It was a wonderful day: doing little, being everything.

We had a coffee in McDonald's and later lunch, actually sitting there for some hours, with the parade through Tiananmen Square being shown on TV, so I saw most of it. For those benighted souls who missed the spectacle it was highly militaristic, with precise battalions representing the army, navy and air force, together with a display of military hardware. On any day of the week, you can watch military films on TV. There is even a military channel. Later, my students were boasting to me about the power of China's military muscle. This is a highly militaristic country, and yes, it is very powerful. One might ask, for what purpose?

At 7.50 pm I caught the slow train to Zhengzhou, but this time I had a sleeper. There were many stops, not always at stations. Sometimes it stopped to let other train go by. Goods trains seem to have priority as do express passenger trains. At two stations we remained for about 45 minutes each, while the engine was uncoupled from one end and another attached at the other, so that we reversed direction. This procedure is not uncommon. However the train was comfortable and I slept well. There were six in my compartment, but most got off early in the morning, apart from one taciturn young man, who alighted later in the morning, leaving me to myself for the rest of the trip. What a surprise that was. Piped music, occasionally pleasant, permeated the train.

Apart from reading "Jane Eyre", doing puzzles and even praying, I took notice of the countryside. Over this flat land the fields are large, not like the small rice paddies we find in the mountainous south. As well as some rice, there was a lot of corn being grown, plus other crops, possibly millet. As I watched workers were gathering the harvest. It is important to have the crop in before the onset of winter; chilly nights can damage your crops, and in these northern climes winter can come quickly. One place has already had a light dusting of snow. From this one can see why the full moon is so important, enabling one to work during the night until the harvest has been gathered. In a month's time, at the next full moon, it will be too late. So this mid-autumn festival is parallel to the European Harvest Moon, only Europe does not have moon cakes. These can be expensive, too, with elaborate boxes of six small cakes costing up to 300 Yuan. The moon is not larger at this time, by the way, except maybe a little elongation due to atmospheric refraction. It is just that one notices it more, especially when it is actually rising.

What a fascinating time this is to be in China, as this country develops at a pace. I saw groups of workers, sickle in hand, bending over, cutting the stalks, then beating the grain out against a screen so that the grain falls into a trough. I also saw mechanical harvesters at work, doing large tracts of land very quickly. Some farmers were ploughing and I noticed four distinct methods, indicative of stages in China's development. 1) Three men would have ropes over their shoulders as they pulled the plough through the soil, with a fourth man guiding it. 2) One man would pull a large wheel, behind which was a second man with the plough, thus cutting human labour by half. 3) Oxen were pulling the ploughs, that is, one ox per plough. This has the distinct advantage of using less human labour. This too is a time honoured method which I have seen used extensively in other parts of China, and indeed in other countries. 4) Modern tractors, mostly small in size, are now coming into vogue. It was as if in this one day I was looking at a thousand years of farming.

There is something else I noticed which speaks volumes about the cohesiveness of this society. In towns you will find like shops clustered together, e.g. six tea shops in a row. In these farming areas we passed through, each district was doing the same thing. In one area, everyone was harvesting. In another everyone was ploughing. Some were also planting, by simply broadcasting the seed, which presumably, would lie fallow in the cold ground over winter, till they germinated in the spring thaw. In another district, everyone was burning off the stubble, so that the atmosphere was thick with smoke, which was being blown in parallel plumes in the same direction, before layering, not far above the ground.

At Zhengzhou I was met, eventually, by M, her nephew and his girlfriend. Unbeknown to me, there are two exits from the station, both of which debouch onto an open plaza, but I came out the south end, while they were waiting at the north end. We did meet, after a period of time and a degree of confusion, but all ended well. I was then driven to my very comfortable hotel, the Zhongtian Guesthouse, where I spent the next six nights. As to what happened in the interval, watch this space.

26.   Henan Province – 3ʳᵈ October 2009

On Saturday I slept in until 8.00. I had breakfast in the hotel dining room, available from 7.00 till 9.00 am. This is part of the tariff and offers a variety of Chinese food, mostly cooked. There is a chef on duty who will cook an egg for you. I made the most of it, as for the next three days I would be getting my own. M's niece and family are staying in this same hotel, so I joined them. For the next few days I would be seeing some of the local sights, joined by two or three of the family members, the guard changing each day. I mean, golly, somebody has to keep an eye on me.

At 9.00 am we drove to the Henan Provincial Museum. The central building is pyramidal in shape, with the top flaring out in a most pleasing manner. We entered another building on the left hand side, housing artefacts from periods in China's history, mostly from the Warring States period (475 BC – 221 BC), then the Han (206 BC – AD 220), Tang (AD 618 – 907) and Northern Song (AD 960 – 1127) dynasties. There is a lot of pottery and some later bronze works, some quite intricate; these craftsmen were very skilled. There is as well a little porcelain and gold from the Qing dynasty (AD 1644 – 1911). These were located on the right hand side. The left hand side featured paintings which had previously not been on display. They are all water colours, as they did not have oil paintings. They featured the usual themes; horses, tigers, chooks, flowers and landscape scenes, often mountains and water, (*shan shui hua* paintings, literally mountain, water, flowers).

At 10.30 am we went upstairs to the second floor for a half hour concert. There were four items featuring some 15 musicians in all, playing a variety of instruments; pipa, *erhu*, 2 *gu zhengs*, 2 kinds of drums, 2 kinds of flutes and 3 sets of bells from small to large. These are all traditional Chinese instruments, although the pipa actually came from Iran, while the *erhu* came from East Turkistan. The musicians too were dressed in traditional Chinese style, with long flowing robes – no trousers. Nowadays both sexes wear trousers for everyday use. There were four items, all traditional music, one of these being a song.

After this we visited the building on the right hand side for yet more artefacts, including a large bronze container, which had been reserved for the exclusive use of the king. I think it was his beer mug. Now that's living. In this mode we went to a great restaurant for lunch, serving Western style meals. For the first time in China I had lamb chops. Mind you, they were a trifle underdone, but still very nice. M, our host, works in this same building.

The afternoon was rest time, also giving me a chance to reflect upon this region. This province is called Henan, boasting a population of close to 100 million people, which is about three times the size of an average country. It can truly be called the cradle of Chinese civilization, as this is where it all began, with Henan being the centre of the nine original regions. This is where urbanization began. Many of the early dynasties had their capitals here, in Anyang, Kaifeng or Luoyang.

"He nan" literally means "south of the river", the river being the mighty Huang He, or Yellow River, called the Mother of Chinese civilization. It is the river which has made the soil fertile, as it periodically overflows its banks spreading its yellow soil over the flat plains, in the process, of course, also flooding the towns. An interesting natural phenomenon this, when the same process which brings destruction, also brings prosperity. Volcanoes have a similar affect. The soil is loess, wind-blown from further west then compacted into soft layers. Erosion tends to create steep sided gullies.

West of Zhengzhou is Song Shan, a mountain which I will talk about later. This was considered to be **the** central mountain, not just of Henan, not just of China, but of the world. Furthermore, it was considered central not only in the horizontal dimension, but also in the vertical, linking Heaven and earth. Well we all have a sense of my own person as being the centre, at least of my world, and society is an extension of the individual. But here the people have this idea down to a fine art. Indubitably it is from here that this country got its notion of China as being Zhong Guo or Middle Territory. Everybody else, every other country is but a satellite. In Chinese the word for "yes" is "*shi de*". But here people say "*zhong*" – "middle". Wow!

In the evening I walked to the family apartment, following the directions I had been given, about 4 to 5 km from my hotel. I got there OK, but there the map was a little inaccurate, so I needed help to find their actual building. In due course I was met, after a succession of "Where-are-you?"'s. Here I met all the family, and quite a mob it was, about 20 in all, half of them being Australian. I bought some moon cakes along the way as my humble contribution to the repast, but they already had plenty. It was good to meet them all, and an honour to have been invited to this great occasion, the first time in 25 years that the original six children had come together. Afterwards, I was driven back to the hotel, so no need to walk.

27.   Kaifeng – Sunday 4th October 2009

The next morning, Sunday, I was up at the crack of dawn, having asked the receptionist the previous night for a wake-up call. Not only was the call on time, but it was also in English. After a bite of breakfast in my hotel room, I walked the three kilometres or so to the Henan hotel, a comfortable 40 minutes' walk, where I met my travelling companions for the day. Our bus was a little late, meaning we did not leave till around 7.50 am. Mary and her sister were there having also brought some breakfast for me.

Off we went, driving out of the city onto a broad eight lane highway for the 50 km run to Kaifeng. This new road is first class, with a smooth surface and arrow straight. This is quite a large city, but without the soaring skyscrapers of most Chinese cities; these have been forbidden. The reason is that deep foundations would destroy much of the city lying some eight metres beneath the surface. This is an ancient city, but periodic flooding from the nearby Huang He (Yellow River), every couple of years or so, has covered it with silt, thus progressively raising the level of the city. Eventually it may be above the level of most floods.

The first place we visited is the former residence of a Song dynasty judge, named Bao Zheng, who lived from AD 999 to 1062, just prior to the Norman conquest of England. This residence has now become a national shrine, and it is truly imposing, being quite spacious, beautiful and situated on the shore of Baogong Lake. There are statues of cranes, a fountain, a large rockery a pavilion and running water. This is because this man is highly venerated. Why? He was an incorruptible judge, renowned for his fair judgements without fear or favour. I find this fascinating. Here is a country where bribery and corruption are a way of life, yet this man is honoured. Evidently the people are well aware of the ideal; they know what is right, even if they do not observe it. It is still an ideal.

Our second stop was to what is called the Iron Pagoda. This impressive 15 storey structure stands 55 metres tall, but in spite of its name, is not made of iron, but of brick. The outside, however, is faced with dark coloured tiles, so that it does look a little like iron. It has a long history, too, dating from the 11th century. It is surrounded by very spacious grounds, with a lake, lawns, shrubs and pavilions. There are many souvenir sellers as well, but I did not buy anything, as they can be bought cheaper elsewhere.

One member of our group stood out. She was a lady in her forties, on her own, but dressed to kill, with plenty of make-up on and wearing a figure hugging black dress, the entire bodice being a bright floral pattern in purple green and white. This was crowned with a large white, broad-brimmed hat. It appears she was on her own and lonely, so M asked her to join us for lunch. She was delighted. She has one child, an 18 year old daughter who is a student. Her husband has an important job, so we gathered they are rather wealthy. She was good company and insisted on paying for the meal. She even bought me a small present, an intriguing puzzle devised by the tutors of the young Qianlong, who was emperor in the Ching dynasty at the end of the 18th century.

In the afternoon we went to Ching Ming Shan He, a large tourist park, covering an area of some 40 hectares and commemorating the achievements of the Northern Song dynasty (AD 960 – 1127) when Kaifeng was the imperial capital. It is a wonderful place to wander around, and watch people dressed in period costumes, while others are plying trades which are centuries old. I would have liked to have seen more of this. There is a sizeable body of water, winding through the park, one section featuring a couple of warships dating from the 12th century. There was even a mock naval battle, one ship being Chinese and the other some enemy. It was real goodies and baddies style. Naturally the goodies won, much to the delight of the numerous spectators. I must say the cannon fire was impressive, shooting up great spouts of water, or flames if the shot "hit" the land. This battle was supposed to have taken place in AD 1105. However, I can find no reference to any naval battle at that time, when the Northern Song dynasty was under threat from the Junchen. These northern peoples eventually succeeded in capturing both the city and the royal family in 1127, thus putting an end to the Northern Song dynasty. One family member did escape to set up the Southern Song dynasty, making Nan Jing (southern capital) the centre. This dynasty lasted until AD 1279, when it fell to another northern people, the Mongols.

One great feature of this park is the shopping, so I took the opportunity to buy gifts for people back home. Does anybody want a silk housedress or a silk scarf, or hangings? I have them, plus sundry other goods. I really liked this park and could have spent more time here, getting back to life in the 12th century.

At 5.15 pm we were back on the bus heading down the expressway back to Zhengzhou, arriving not long after 6.00 pm. There is a central intersection in the city, with pedestrian overpass and five roads leading off. It was here Mary, her sister L and I had our evening meal. I then walked the 20 minutes back to my hotel, up Hua Yuan Lu, right into Hua He Lu, then left. This route is becoming familiar. Before retiring I did my laundry for the day, which I did each night. It was a really good day. I wonder what the morrow will bring… Wait.

28. *Longmen Grottoes – Monday 5th October 2009*

For the second morning I got my early wake up call. Again I had breakfast in my hotel room, before walking the 3 kilometres to the Henan hotel to meet our tour group for the day, including M's sisters M and HL. Around 8.00 am we were off to Luoyang which had been the capital for a number of dynasties. One of these was the Northern Wei, which moved here in AD 494. Buddhists followed, and in AD 593, they began carving into the cliffs on either side of the Yi River about 16 km from the city. These carvings continued for around a thousand years till the 16th century, though most of the carvings, some 100,000, were done in the first 200 years. In the 19th century Western souvenir hunters damaged some of them, by removing parts, especially heads, which are now in Western museums. A lot more damage was done by the Red Guards under Mao Zedong between 1966 and 1976. These latter did not remove heads; they just smashed them.

So what are these carvings? Most of them are figures of Buddha or Buddhist saints and most are bas-reliefs. Some of the grottoes are natural, but most have been carved out of the rock to form niches, inside of which the figures have been carved. Many of the figures are quite small, only a few centimetres high, but some are large to the point of being massive. I was standing at the base of the largest of them, which is about 20 metres high, jotting down some notes, using a fence as a table – no seats here – when a curious gentleman came over and tried to read what I was writing. There is not much sense of privacy or personal space in this country, as I have remarked before. Mind you he had no hope. Goodness, I can't read my own writing half the time, so what hope has he got? "Wo kan bu dong", he said. "I can't understand it". "No, mate, you are not supposed to".

I was next addressed by another gentleman in excellent English. "Where did you learn your English?" It turns out he is Nepalese. There are four of them here, all doctors, all doing post graduate studies – in English. That was a surprise. I asked him if he thought China was any threat to his country, but he thinks not. He thinks this country is suffering from indigestion, having swallowed so much territory belonging to others that it is finding it difficult to administer it all. He also thinks the geography is too difficult. Certainly geography played a large part in China's failure to conquer Korea, in spite of many attempts, and also in China's failure to conquer Myanma. He may have a point.

One of the questions I was asking myself is; why are people here? This is a Buddhist site. Are the people Buddhist? Well some are, but most are not. This place has now become a national shrine, simply because of the existence of so many carvings and their history, not because of their meaning. This country is bursting with people and there is also a lot of money around, so if you were to put a thimble on a mountain top, people would go to have a look. Where one person goes, thousands are sure to follow. Having said this let me assure you that these carvings are amazing.

Having walked along one side of the Yi He, we crossed a bridge to the other, where there are more carvings. High on the hill overlooking the river there is a temple complex, called Xiangshan. It is here that Chiang Kai-Shek and his wife Mei Ling had a summer residence. There is a lovely view from here looking across the river to the grottoes opposite. The grounds of this complex include a cemetery for a Tang dynasty poet, Bai Ju Yi (AD 772 – 846) and his family. It is wonderful that poets are so honoured in this culture.

Small electric buses were available to transport people back to our bigger buses, but I preferred a pleasant walk, crossing the Yi River via a bridge, then through gardens. We had lunch here, before heading off to the next attraction, Bai Ma Si, or White Horse Temple. This marks the site of China's first Buddhist temple. According to one legend, during the Han dynasty (206 BC – AD 220) Emperor Ming (AD 58 – 75) had a vision of a tall golden man (Buddha?), so sent envoys to look for him. In AD 67, these brought back two Indian monks, carrying Buddhist scriptures on the backs of white horses. Even if the authenticity of this is dubious, the facts remain that Buddhism did come to China around this time, adapting to native beliefs to mould a distinctly Chinese form. It is also a fact that this temple is called Bai Ma Si. It has the usual architectural layout of four shrines down the centre, with living quarters on each side. There were lots of people here, some few burning incense and bowing, most just wandering around. Some monks will tell your future – for a fee – and I saw one of them with a thick wad of 100 Yuan notes; lucrative business indeed. No I did not contribute to the pile. My God is a God of surprises and I prefer it that way.

We spent just over an hour here, from 3.45 to 5.00 pm. Then it was back into the bus for our return journey to Zhengzhou. Once again we found a restaurant to have our evening meal, before I headed back to my hotel. Now tomorrow will be special.

29.   Shaolin Temple – Tuesday 6th October 2009

For the third morning running I was up early, my trusty wake-up call not letting me down. I had my usual breakfast in my hotel room, before walking to Henan hotel to meet the bus and companions for the day. We left around 7.50 am, arriving at Shaolin Temple around 9.30 am. This is the famed centre of Chinese martial arts, especially Kung Fu. It is a Buddhist monastery of the Mahayana sect, founded in AD 497. Today the town boasts many Kung Fu academies, teaching some 50,000 Bruce Lee wannabees, the largest of them has some 20,000 students. Like so many things in China, this is huge. Not all of the students are from China, of course, since Kung Fu now has an international following. Between the academies and the tourist industry, this town is very prosperous. One question I have concerns the present day link between Buddhism and Kung Fu. I plead ignorance on this point, but my suspicion is that in our modern era the link is tenuous. Perhaps a parallel may lie with other centres of learning. Universities grew out of the Catholic Church, yet you do not have to be a Catholic today to attend university.

Having arrived at the imposing gateway we paused for the obligatory photographs, together with millions (well, almost) of other people, before proceeding to a marshalling yard, looking distinctly like races for sheep. Perhaps we are in for a dip, but no, we were being funnelled onto a line of electric vehicles which would take us – for a further 10 Yuan – to another part of the complex. They certainly know how to shift masses of people. They know how to make masses of money, too. So on we got, being deposited some two kilometres later at what is called the Pagoda Forest.

This is an area containing some 228 pagodas or stupas, which contain the ashes of notable Shaolin monks from the Tang dynasty (AD

608 – 907) till the present. The oldest has been dated at AD 791. In size they range from three to eight metres high, from one storey for your average guy to seven storeys if you were very special, like the latest addition constructed in AD 2002 for the then head monk, who was reputed to have had more than 3,000 students. The pagodas have different architectural styles, reflecting the period in which each was built. Some are square, some are hexagonal, while others are round. Some are made from brick, others of stone. The oldest have an open doorway near the bottom.

From here some of us opted to go up the local mountain, Song Shan. It used to be called Zhong Shan, the central mountain, not only of China, but of the world, during the Eastern Zhou dynasty (770 – 221 BC), though the people in that far off time had a very narrow view of the extent of the world. It is still considered one of the five sacred mountains in China. We took an Austrian designed cable car to San Huang Zhai, which is not the summit, but a ridge, thus providing views on two sides. If you want details, the ride covers 2,860 metres ascending 453 vertical metres, taking about 15 minutes. Up here we had something to eat. I do not know our altitude, but were still some distance from the 1,512 metre summit.

With many other people we followed a path around the side of the mountain. In places, this path had not been cut into the rock, as is the usual practice, but had been set against the rock, resting on supports. When it comes to mountain paths and steps, these people are amazing. The drop is sheer and long. Now I am not going to bore you with details, but there is another reason I was amazed – the geology. Some of this rock is really old, dating back some 2.5 billion years, whereas most of the rock in this country is much more recent. There were, it seems, three Precambrian orogenies (mountain building episodes); the Songyang Movement, 2,500 million years ago, the Zhongyue Movement, 1,800 million years ago, and the Shaolin Movement, 600 million years ago. I am absolutely amazed at these dates, to the point where I would really like some confirmation. I have not been able to get hold of a geology map, as these seem to be categorized as state secrets, and certainly not one in English.

I would have liked to have continued walking much further along this path, but unfortunately we had to get back down to rejoin the rest of our group. Some of us got into a van which took us a short distance to a village where we had lunch – noodles. We were driven back again too. From here we went to yet another Buddhist temple, Shifang, the site of the original Shaolin monastery, and once again there were more photos than prayers. There is a large stele here donated by another ancient Shaolin monastery, in Fujian province, where I used to live. It was founded by monks escaping from here during a time of destruction. There were a few of these over the course of history. There is a lesson here.

From here we walked about 1.5 km back towards the entrance where there is indoor theatre, in which there would be a martial arts display. Unfortunately, by the time we got there it was full. Not to worry; there would be an outdoor display close by, so that is where we headed, with me not expecting to see much because of the crowds. I was pleasantly surprised therefore, to find some front seats unoccupied. Wow! – Ringside seats. Soon I learnt why. Performances were being held on top of a stage at least 3 m high, so that for most of the time we were looking up at the top half of people's bodies. That is why those in the audience who knew had chosen seats further back.

These performances were extraordinary. They included the expected running, summersaults, shouting and thrusting with weapons – and then there were the other acts. One young man proceeded to break some pieces of steel (?) over his head. Don't try this on someone else's head. A young boy, exhibiting extraordinary agility, was able to bend over so that his mouth was on his foot, then pick up his foot in his mouth, before resuming his upright position. I bet you cannot even touch your toes with your hands! Another young man thought it was more comfortable to be held aloft, lying on spear points. Ouch! Now I would not recommend that you try these at home, but there was one act you might like to have a go at. Take a pane of glass. Have someone hold a blown up balloon on the other side. Now take a needle and throw it through the glass so that it bursts the balloon. The glass, of course, must be unaffected. Is this fair dinkum? One wonders.

From here it was back on the bus to be taken to the obligatory tourist shop. This one was efficiency plus. A walkway, a la airport mode, zigzagged across the shop from entrance to check-out, exposing potential customers to a maximum array of goods. As you entered you were given a tag, which was dropped in a box at the exit. Thus the shop owners know how many people each tour guide brings in, so can work out his commission. These people sure know how to sell. Most of the goods appeared to be packaged foods of some sort. I was not all that interested. Near here there is an ancient astronomical observatory, dating from AD 1276, during the Yuan dynasty. I would have been more interested in seeing that.

From here it was back on our bus for the journey home to Zhengzhou, where we had another delicious evening meal. What a great day. How many Kung Fu aficionados would give their right arm to come here, yet I get the opportunity, and I have not even perfected my yell. The ways of the Lord are strange. Nevertheless, I really appreciated being here. Many thanks. After three hectic days, tomorrow would be a rest day – and I could sleep in. Good.

30.   Final Days – 7th – 9th October 2009

My morning was free, so I sampled the hotel breakfast for only the second time. Each night the staff had been leaving my tickets in my room, but I had not been using them. It is mostly Chinese fare of course. Later in the morning I went for a fairly extensive walk, up the main road as far as the zoo, then winding my way back through lesser streets. I did not go into the zoo, so I cannot comment on it. The weather has changed, with some light drizzle and decidedly cooler. I am glad we had fine weather for our tours, when I was wearing shorts and T-shirt.

In the afternoon, M fetched me to take me to the Henan Geological Museum, where he does some work, so I think our entrance was free. We hired a cassette so that I could follow some English commentary. They do have a geology map, but in Chinese. There is a good dinosaur section and some great fossils. I was enjoying myself, as my long forgotten Geology started to come back; after all, it is nearly 30 years since I graduated from university. The museum also featured a 3D film of ancient life, which was quite well done. At one point the front seats even drop down, scaring the hell out of the children and probably more so for their mothers. Since this is holiday time, there are a lot of children here. Outside there is a very good rock collection, featuring large samples in the form of boulders. When at university we would collect our own rock samples, mostly rather small in size – say fist size – but one girl used to collect much larger samples. I wonder how she transported them all. This museum I liked. Unfortunately they closed their doors at the early hour of 4.00 pm, so we were booted out

M then took us for a tour of newer parts of the city, and very impressive it is. There is a cultural centre, consisting of five futuristic buildings like large elongated balls – a bit like bike helmets, rounded up front, narrowing towards the back. Each ball has a different function; opera, concert, plays, art and dance. Nearby is a convention centre, the whole complex grouped around a man-made lake: very impressive. We also visited a new apartment complex modelled on Canadian architecture, being shown around by a salesman who must have thought I was a rich businessman. Little did he know. At 10,000 Yuan per square metre, these do not come cheap. There is a lot of money here. There is a lot of money in China.

From here we repaired to a restaurant for a family meal. Some 20 people gathered, half of them Australians, including N, from the former Yugoslavia (his father being Croatian and his mother Serbian), who is married to one of the girls of this Chinese family. Since he was never really accepted as being either Serb or Croat, he is now Australian. This was also an engagement party for M, who had been chauffeuring us around, and MM. There are lots of "Ms" in this family. The Coogee M (Mary) gave the engagement ring, a beautiful ruby centred ring, with small diamonds clustered around. The meal was delicious, featuring Peking duck, befitting such an important occasion.

The following day, Thursday, I chatted for a while in the restaurant with some of the delightful children from this Aussie Chinese mix, before packing and relaxing. At 11.30 am I checked out, the bellhop carrying my bag to the corner where we caught a bus, returning to the family apartment, where I left my bag. M and I then had lunch, wonderful lamb chops, such a rarity in my normal diet. There has been lots of eating on this trip. Close by is Wal-Mart where we went shopping. I wanted to buy goods which cannot be procured in Tongren, such as cheese and butter. Aussie 1 wanted Mozzarella cheese for pizzas, but they did not have any. Just outside, however, sample pizzas were being given away and they were willing to sell me some of their cheese. Wonderful. Then it was back to the apartment for goodbyes, before walking to the train station, my bag balanced on a brand new bike. Here M had a special pass; he seems to have special passes to everywhere, but this one comes from his fiancée who works for the railways. With this I was able to go to the VIP lounge – no crowds. Furthermore, I was the first to board, before the cleaners had quite finished, and so was also the first into my compartment. This had never happened before. Wow.

After we got started at 5.30 pm, the attendants came around not only checking tickets but IDs. Where is my passport? You cannot just wander around in this country. The authorities have to know exactly where everybody is at any time. There is tight control from on top. Actually, the attendants were less interested in my passport than in my Foreign Expert's Certificate. As usual a token was given in exchange for my ticket. This allows the attendants to know when you are getting off. They return your ticket before you come to your station. It does have an advantage if you do not know how far it is to your destination. I generally ask, as an added security, the time of arrival. I did this here, but found the train was an hour late in arriving. I was packed up, waiting.

It was a good trip. In fact I enjoy train travel, well, usually. I woke at around 7.00 am, and just lay there in my bunk thinking of the wonderful time I had been blessed to enjoy. I also watched the scenery roll by. It was especially beautiful on one section as we followed a green coloured river, with cliffs on the other side. We passed through many tunnels; I estimated at least 100 km in all. My sole companion got off at 9.15 am, leaving me alone in my compartment. How rare is that! At 5.00 pm Friday we finally pulled in to Yuping. I found a taxi, already occupied by one of my students, who was returning late. Classes resumed today, though I am fortunate in having Fridays free. Tomorrow, even though it is Saturday we have Wednesday classes, and on Sunday we have Thursday classes. That is how it works.

Thanks for staying with me on this great holiday.

Summer Holidays 2010

31.   Zhijin, Guizhou Province – 15th – 16th July 2010

Normally I return to Australia at this time, but this year it would be different. In fact this would be my first full summer in China, meaning that I will be skipping most of the winters. This is a change, since I generally skip most of the summers.

We left Tongren on July 15th by bus, bound for Guiyang. The "we" includes F1, who had dropped in for a few days from Fuzhou, via Beijing, and two of my students, Erica and Cindy. It is a six hour trip along a good, fairly new expressway. Actually, it is already breaking up, due to the very heavy loads that trucks carry; they are vastly overloaded. We left around 9.00 am, and I enjoyed watching the scenery. Corn and rice are ripening nicely, due for harvesting in late September. Many sunflowers are out in bloom, deliberately planted next to the corn in order to protect the corn; the birds will go for the sunflower seeds first. It does make for a colourful scene. We brought lunch with us to eat on the bus, or most of us did, as Erica eats less than the average sparrow.

There is a new bus station in Guiyang, so we went there immediately by taxi; it is a long way out of town – about 7 km. This side of the city is witnessing a lot of development, with perhaps 100 high rise apartment blocks all going up at the same time, enough to house at least 50,000 people. We were very lucky to get a connecting bus to Zhijin, where we were headed. Before boarding, quite by accident, we ran into A, who has just graduated from our college in Tongren. She is now looking for a job, and is quite dejected both because of the tough competition, and because she now finds herself out on her own, away from the comforting supports of college life. I hope she finds her niche.

This second bus we were on for the day is smaller, holding about 20 people, and considerably older. The gears have seen better days, as the driver did more grinding than a barista. There was nothing wrong with the horn, however, which the driver proceeded to blast any time he saw

86

another vehicle, or indeed, another person. We climbed into some lovely mountainous terrain. We had one humorous incident at a toilet. We climbed aboard and took off, only to find that we had left one passenger behind. Did the bus driver go back for her? No way, so the poor woman took off up the incline. We had just negotiated a hairpin bend, so she climbed straight up the embankment, somewhat out of breath, as you might imagine. Later, at around 7.00 pm, it was wonderful to watch the sunset in these mountains.

We arrived in Zhijin, some 1350 metres above sea level, about 8.40 pm, being met at the bus station by Tracey, one of our first year students. She had organized accommodation for us at a hotel run by her uncle, with a meal in a nearby restaurant. It was good to meet her family. Zhijin has a population of around 500,000, and they are lively. Even though we were tired, and it was after 11.00 pm by the time we got to bed, there were nearby fireworks to ensure that we did not get to sleep just yet. Throughout the night, young guys on the street outside our window kept shouting in loud voices. Add to this the constant noise from horns, and you might gather that we did not get much sleep.

At 9.00 am we met the others and went off to the local bus station. Here we hopped onto an 11 seater, paying the princely sum of 7 Yuan, but the system is curious. You get in without a ticket. After a couple of kilometres, a woman gets on, and you pay her. She gives you the ticket. 20 minutes later another woman gets on and collects your ticket. I have no idea why they use this system. As I said, it is curious.

We were here in order to visit a local cave. Yes, it is limestone country. The entrance is impressive, with a large open space and clean modern buildings, and not a souvenir seller in sight. Apparently they used to be here, but were cleared away. Entrance is expensive, at 140 Yuan. I tell you, this government is the world expert in making money. It is a large cave, the largest that I have been in, and that includes Wee Jasper, near Canberra. We were conducted through by our tour guide, who was rush, rush, rush. I am sorry now that we listened to her, as all of us would much have preferred a leisurely stroll, even if it took three hours, rather than racing through in two hours. She was dressed in the costume of one of the minority peoples, but, rather incongruously, was wearing sneakers.

This cave is up to 175 metres wide and 150 metres high! How on earth does the roof stay up? – although in places it has in fact fallen in. One can see new stalagmites, up to 50 cm high, forming on the fallen sections, meaning that this cave-in occurred about 50,000 years ago. The rock itself was laid down some 65 million years ago, which is relatively young as rocks go. Cave formation did not begin until the limestone was uplifted to form land some 2.5 million years ago. Much of China is so young. Explored sections extend for 12 km, though we did not go this far. There are five large chambers, featuring the usual stalagmites and stalactites. There are also many mysteries, more than I have seen anywhere else, and some are quite delicate, as they stick out at up to 90 degrees. To refresh your memory, the stalagmites start from the ground, while the stalactites hang from the ceiling; the mysteries jut out at an angle, probably due to airflow.

Our route took us up and own many steps; we climbed around 600 altogether, so it is quite extensive. Strategic lighting of course highlights the more amazing features. There are actually toilets inside the cave, and this was a surprise. There are also photographers willing to snap away at 20 Yuan a pop. No thank you; we brought our own cameras, and in fact took many a photo. There were six in our party, including Tracey's brother, who asked for an English name, so I obliged. "His name is John." His Chinese name is Huan, pronounced the same as Juan (or John) in Spanish. We were told that it would be cold inside, "so bring something warm". Accordingly, I brought a winter shirt and a track suit top (for F1). We needed them. Inside it is a cool 15 degrees, which seems cold when the outside temperature is 30 (as it was on this day), but seems warm in the middle of winter, when the outside temperature is zero degrees.

The entrance into the cave is quite small, as is the exit. Just outside is a shop —naturally – where the girls spent some time – again, naturally. They did have some very good wares. Not far away is a Buddhist shrine, where – for a mere 800 Yuan – you can have your fortune told. These monks sure know how to charge, a fact I have discovered elsewhere. There are people selling food here as well, and if you so much as glance in their direction, the women start chattering away like a flock of birds. We had, however, brought our own light repast, much to their disappointment.

Back on the bus, we sped back to town, with no possibility of photographing the wonderful scenery, as we careened around corners, or on the wrong side of the road at a great rate of knots. We made it safely. China's guardian angels really must work hard. In the arvo I even had a short nap, in spite of an incessant cry from a melon seller in the street, blaring out "*fenzi gua*" about once every six seconds. I was tired.

At 6.30 pm we shared evening meal. My contribution was the beer, but my opener was back in my hotel room. Not to worry, as Tracey's female cousin opened the bottles – with her teeth. Ouch! Anyone know a good dentist? I was particularly surprised to see a girl do this, rather than some macho male. Then it was back to the hotel for shower and bed. Tomorrow we would be bussing out.

32.   Bijie – 17th – 18th July 2010

Our hotel room does not have an en suite bathroom, meaning one lines up outside waiting. On this morning, I waited 40 minutes before I could get in. We were pushing it to get to the foyer by 8.30 am to meet the others. We said goodbye to Tracey and John and caught a taxi to the bus station. By 9.30 am we were off to Bijie, in a 20 seater bus, heading north east for a three hour journey; the ticket was a reasonable 50 Yuan.

Once again I enjoyed the mountain scenery, with fields of rice, corn, sunflower and tobacco. One of the girls asked if West Lake was beautiful, in Hanzhou. I said it was okay, but vastly over-rated, and that I had seen many more beautiful lakes. Just then we crossed over one such lake – cf the attached photo. Surprisingly, this time we had a good driver. Bijie is both a county, having a population of 7 million, or about the same as NSW, and a city of about 200,000.

We were met at the bus station by Andrea, who is in the same class as Cindy and Erica. She had her boyfriend with her, whose name is Joe, because his Chinese name is Zhou (same pronunciation) – and boy, are they in love! We were to see much evidence of this. I hope he knows what he is doing. Andrea, you see, is a very beautiful young lady, but tough as nails. I think I know who will be wearing the pants. We walked some 20 minutes to our hotel, the Hong Du Holiday Hotel, which was a little expensive at 218 Yuan per night, but very nice. We could have booked the villa, which would have been a mere 9,000 Yuan per night! No thanks, we will leave that for the Communist Party officials.

For lunch we wandered around the corner for noodles, which were edible, but very spicy. In fact they were so spicy that for one member of our party they were inedible. Too much spicy food has some nasty effects, both short term – runny nose, catching at the back of your throat making breathing difficult, teary eyes, smoke out of the ears and fire out the mouth… – and, also, long term, necessitating more frequent visits to the toilet. After lunch, clutching a handful of tissues, we walked to a beautiful local park, featuring a small lake with a pavilion in the middle. We spent some time here, chatting, both amongst ourselves and with some of the locals, including a little girl, about ten years old. She was extraordinary, sitting on her own, listening. When we included her in our conversation, she was well able to participate in English, displaying a charming personality. Erica's elder sister also joined us. You can tell they are sisters, and in fact Erica's passport declares they have the same birth date; the One Child Policy comes into play here.

For our evening meal we went to the house of a friend, a very good friend, as I learnt later, as he and Erica form an item. They are lovely people, but very poor. Three people live in two very small rooms. One can only describe conditions as being squalid, both inside and outside. The meal itself, prepared by Cindy and Erica's sister, was really good. It is amazing what people can do, even in adverse situations. We were honoured to be invited. After dinner, we strolled around town, watching people relax. In a public square, children were playing with toys, especially those which can be thrown into the air, spinning back to earth in a display of lights, while other children were learning how to roller skate. It is great to see people enjoying themselves.

The next morning I was amused by some of the signs in the bathroom. One admonishes "carefully slide". Whoopee! – sounds like fun. It also sported a "Houdini hearter". I am sure that famous escapologist would be thrilled. We had a late getaway, as Erica was delayed, but eventually she turned up and we took a taxi to the bus station, but not the one we had arrived at. This one is something to behold. It is small, muddy and unkempt. It has a toilet of the same standard, cesuo rating 2 (where toilets are rated on a 1 to 5 scale).

Around 11.00 am we left for a ride of something over an hour of lurching and jolting, swaying and bumping over a narrow road of pot holes and mud. Isn't life exciting? And I was perched up front to get the best views of it all. We stopped briefly at the house of Erica's grandmother, so that the two could meet; we had a most obliging driver, who did not mind waiting. By around 12.15 pm, we found ourselves in a village, where we were conducted into the back room of a small building and asked to wait. In the front room, women were making a kind of rice biscuit, which one little lad was eating. After a while we went to a small restaurant for a meal. Out back, it too had a toilet, cesuo rating -1; the corn field was better.

Later we piled into a car, which had been especially hired to take us to Erica's farm. This was a surprise to me, as I was expecting to walk, which would have taken about an hour. Instead, we got there in about 20 minutes, again jolting, swaying etc. over a narrow, pot-holey, muddy road. The car dropped us at a small hamlet, comprising only a few houses, and from here we had a walk of about 5 minutes to Erica's house. The track was mostly mud, so that it was difficult for us to find a foothold, especially as we were carrying our luggage.

This is mountain country. I do not know what the altitude is, but probably around 2,000 metre. The air is decidedly cooler than at lower levels. There it is hot, while here it is cool enough for us to wear jackets. I would hate to be here in winter, though some years later I would do just that. The farm is interesting, in that it is not on the same plot of land as the house. Instead, there are several fields belonging to the family scattered over a wide area, up to 30 minutes' walk away. There are corn fields growing right up to the house, but these belong to other people.

33.   Life on a Farm – 18th – 22nd July 2010

As can be seen from the previous Jottings, this farm is well off the beaten track, and takes some effort just to get here. Then why are we here? This is Erica's farm, and she invited me to meet her parents. Indeed I have been anxious to do this for some time. Erica is one of my students, having taught her for the past two years. Last year she came to Australia, in order to have her teeth fixed. The result was just brilliant, and I am eternally grateful to the dentists. In their generosity they did their work for free, because Erica's family is not rich – at least not in terms of material possession, but they are rich in other ways – in love. Now I would see just how they lived.

The main house is built of brick for the outside walls, with wood for the rest of the house. The roof is tiled, while the floor is a concrete slab. It has five rooms. The largest room, in the centre of the house, is used for storing farm goods, and also for doing some farm work. To the left are two smaller rooms, one of which is a bedroom; here F1 and Cindy would share the bed. The right hand side mirrors the left, having two small rooms. The back room is where I slept, on my own; I was really being well looked after. The front room is the family room, around which their lives revolve. A TV is here, but it does not work. There is also a bed in which the mother slept with her two daughters – and by the way, these are not large beds. Now where did Dad sleep? He slept at the local school, not because there was no room in the inn, but because he is the caretaker; it is about 10 minutes' walk away.

There is a stove in this family room, consisting of a central cylinder into which coal is fed, and from which comes a flue, though it is blocked. Around the stove is a flat area which serves as the dining room table. Just inside the door is a depression for breaking up the coal; just be careful you do not step into it when you open the door. There is no fridge. They do have electricity, though not all the time. Lucky for us, it was on for the duration of our stay.

At the entrance to the property, there is a rectangular brick building, measuring about 3 X 4 metres and about 4 metres in height. This is for curing tobacco. I had noticed a number of these structures in the district, and some tobacco growing in the fields. There is not much, however, and our host family has not grown tobacco for some ten years. This is not in any way meant as a protest against the tobacco industry. It is just that tobacco growing is a highly labour intensive industry, thus making it not economically viable. Young leaves, for instance, must be pulled off from the lower parts of each plant, in order to make the top leaves larger. This requires a lot of work.

As you approach the house, there is a barn on the left, looking most attractive with bright green moss growing on the roof. This has an earthen floor, with wooden walls and a thatched roof. There is one door, on the right which opens into the cattle pen, occupied by their cow and its calf. From this room, a door leads off to the sty where they keep their pig.

At the left hand end of the barn is the toilet. This consists of a low stone wall, from which wooden rafters lean onto the side of the barn. Sorry, there is no Western toilet. I do not have one in Tongren either. There is a pit, which is actually rather shallow, 30cm at most, and measuring about 1 metre X 1.5 metres. What I found intriguing is that the pit is covered with logs, but with very little space between them. Your aim had better be good! Or you lift a log out of the way.

There are further rooms added onto the right hand side of the house. Here various farm implements are stored, plus the roost for their five hens and the stable for their mare and its newborn foal; they have a piglet as well. The water supply comes from a spring, which has been tapped, so that is handy. The tap is located at the front of the house, to the left, and this water is potable, unlike the water you get from town supply. It is cold, of course. Any hot water must be heated on the stove. There are no shower, so you grab a bucket and wash in that. It serves its purpose.

On Monday, most of us felt like doing absolutely nothing. Doing our laundry was about all we managed, as this must be done regularly when one is on the road, especially in a drizzly, cool climate like this, as the clothes take a long while to dry. We just wanted to relax and wind down – and sleep, which we did for long periods of time. There is a psychological reason for this, as well as the physical, so it is not just explained by the fact that our bodies needed to recuperate. We needed time to adjust to the conditions. It is called culture shock. F1 and I also enjoyed a Western breakfast, as we take cereal and coffee with us whenever we travel. On one morning we did join the family at their breakfast, consisting of wild mushrooms with garlic and *lajiao* (spicy red pepper), fried in oil and water; very nice.

It was late afternoon before we ventured out onto the muddy tracks. We wandered up to the local primary school for some exercise and views of the district. There are hills everywhere, and crops. It is really quite beautiful. Another reason for getting out was so that we could use our mobile phones, as there is no signal at the house.

The evening meal was truly delicious, especially the potato chips. Potato is one of the crops they grow here. Erica's sister did most of the work. Indeed, I had noticed that she seems to be doing most of the serving in this household, so that when she asked me to give her an English name, I had no hesitation. She is Martha. She likes it. I seem to be giving out a few English names on this trip.

While still being very hospitable, the parents continued to do their farm work, from early morning till late at night. At this time of the year, they are mostly weeding, in order to give their cops the best chance to grow, and harvesting their potato crop. At times it would be quite late before Dad got home. They really do work hard, their lives being etched into their faces. I offered to help out with the farm work, but this was not to be countenanced – so to speak. They do have two sons, but these are away working. The older has no intention of ever returning to farming, but the younger one probably will. It is remarkable that in this family it is the daughters – who are also the two youngest – who are pursuing an education, both of whom hope to get into university, and in fact both of them achieved this aim. This is not generally the case in China, where precedence is given to the sons.

On another afternoon we walked a little further along the road, meeting some small boys with a horse and its foal. There is a doctor here as well, with his clinic doubling as the local general store. This was a new experience for me. The doctor is an old man, cigarette hanging out the corner of his mouth, with a long ash threatening to fall at any moment. Yet he proved to be surprisingly competent and with a good supply of medicines.

This is enough for now. Tune in next time for more information about farm life.

34.   *Animal Farm – 18th – 22nd July 2010*

You cannot have a farm without animals, right? – so it would be unconscionable not to give them special mention.

First up is the cow, which now has a calf. She is not a milking cow. These days Chinese are drinking more milk, but it has not been part of their traditional diet. Consequently, their bodies are far more lactose intolerant than is the case for the average Westerner. Nor is the cow being fattened up for its meat. No, it is a work animal, being used to pull the plough in the fields and perform other such heavy work. I do not think I have come across this before, as usually the buffalo is used. Chinese are not as prone to name their animals as we are, but what the heck; let's call her Daisy, and while we are at it we may as well name the calf as well. I'll go for Buttercup.

The horse is used for carrying loads, and has a specially made cradle which hangs over her back. When we left, our bags were strapped to this. I noticed that there are many other horses in this district which have foaled in recent days. I asked Erica if she had a name for her horse, and surprisingly she said, "Yes". "Oh, what do you call her?" "*Ma*". Good grief! So I said; "And I suppose the foal is called *"Xiao Ma"*? "That's right." Great imagination, as *"ma"* means "horse", while *"xiao"* means "little". Incidentally, my Chinese surname is *"Ma"*, so I guess I am a horse. That's OK, as they are truly noble animals.

This brings us to the chooks. They are full grown, so they are not chickens. There are five of these, one black and four brown. In keeping with our naming policy, I would suggest Sadie for the black one, as she is the queen in cleaning up, being aggressive to the others if they have what she wants. For the brown ones, I would suggest Clarabelle and Annabelle (maybe they are sisters), Florence, and last, but not least, Henrietta. Now these chooks just love the house. Leave the door open and turn your back for one minute and they are in. Many times a day you would find one or other member of the family shooing them out, always gently. It says a great deal about this family that annoyance was never displayed, nor any violence. Each time the hens were shooed out with some humour. On our final day here, we were told that we would eat one of the chooks for dinner that night. Well, you should have heard the consternation on the part of the guests. "Oh no, you can't kill one of the chooks! Not Henrietta, no!" The weeping and wailing reached such a pitch that our hosts had a change of mind, and maybe a change of heart as well. I am sure the chooks too breathed a collective sigh of relief.

Keeping to the bird group, there are ducks in the vicinity, though not on this farm. There is a spring nearby which forms a small stream, running down a gully beside a path. It is quite pretty. It is here that they congregate, splashing around in the water and emitting quacks as we pass. They keep a wary eye on us, possibly afraid that the menu for tonight's dinner might switch from chook to duck.

Goats are also tended in this area, but again, not on this farm. When we were walking out we came across a small flock under the care of a boy.

On the evening of our first day, there was something of a stir when a snake was discovered just outside the front door. I was impressed by Dad, who did not kill it, but gently shepherded it back into the corn field. I guess you come to appreciate Nature and all God's creatures when you are living on a farm.

Last but not least we come to the pig. They buy a piglet each year and fatten it up for Spring Festival. They do have a piglet, which lives with the chooks. The pig is already quite big. It is a great garbage disposal unit; there are no scraps of food lying around here. As well, they feed it a special plant, grown on nearby hillsides, which they mulch in a machine. I woke one night around 3.30 am, to find the mother already at work, feeding plants into this machine. These farmers work hard, but it seems for so little, at least in terms of monetary reward. Now what about a name for our pig? This is easy; I would call him Napoleon. It is indeed true that in this country, all animals are created equal, but some are more equal than others. The disparity between the ruling elite and poor people like this family is staggering. The rich-poor index is 0.47, well above the 0.40 level where social unrest reaches alarming proportions. If this gap does not narrow soon, there could be an explosion.

Some of the neighbours are not Han, but belong to a minority group. Remember that this whole area was taken over by the Han, either through migration or military invasion. This is how China's territory has always been enlarged. Nor is there any sign of these tactics diminishing. Generations ago, Erica's family, who are Han, migrated here from another province. Some years ago, their horse was stolen. The father called in the law, and the culprit, who belongs to this minority group, was sent to gaol. One wonders what the motivation may have been.

Language was always a problem. There are many things I would have liked to have discussed, especially with the father, but unfortunately my Chinese is not up to scratch, and one cannot have the girls translating all the time.

Our final evening meal was going to be special – even if chicken was off the menu. Instead we had pork, together with tofu, cabbage and potatoes, cooked hot pot style. The sauce was made from soy sauce, together with vinegar, garlic and ginger. It was very nice. After the meal, we sang songs. Even the parents joined in, under considerable pressure. Then we exchanged gifts. It was a really good night, celebrated in great spirit. This family might be poor in the material sense, but they are rich in love and simple goodness. It was a privilege to have been able to share their family life, if only for a few days, days – I feel sure – that I will always treasure.

35.   Bijie to Guiyang – 22nd – 23rd July 2010

On Thursday we woke just after 6.00 am. Martha (naturally) prepared breakfast for us in the form of *jiaozi* (dumplings), the outside consisting of a kind of sticky rice, with millet in the middle. It was sweet. Mum and Dad loaded up the horse with our baggage, after first wrapping them in clear plastic sheets, as rain was threatening. Even so, by the time we arrived at our destination, my bag was quite muddy.

We left at 8.40 am, and a most pleasant walk it was. The track may have been muddy and full of potholes, but this mountainous farming scenery is beautiful. As well, we shared a great spirit of happiness. God is good. We took turns in leading the horse, who did not seem to mind who had the reins – even me. She just trotted along, though indeed with a mind of her own, as she chose the path, not me. The foal went wherever its dam went.

At 10.00 am we arrived at the nearest village, Huang Lian, on the main road – if you can call it that. Erica and Cindy went off to book our tickets on the bus, while the locals, most hospitably, provided us with stools to sit on while we waited, not that we had long to wait, as the bus turned up at 10.15 am. Off we went, with me again sitting right up front. At one point we met a horse and cart coming in the opposite direction, but there was insufficient room for us to pass, so the poor guy had to somehow turn his horse around and retreat to a wider section.

Why did we not reverse? Because we were bigger, and that is how it works, with important ramifications for the international scene. Make no mistake, China will prove to be a big international bully. At another village it was our turn to stop and squeeze over to the right as far as we could as three large trucks were coming through. They made it with barely millimetres to spare. In this case, the trucks were bigger than our bus. As we drove through the countryside, I noticed that the crops were mainly corn and tobacco, with some beans, melons and potatoes. Some fields had alternating strips of corn and potatoes. I do not know why they do this, but possibly this method gives some rest for the soil.

By 11.45 am we were back in Bijie city. At the bus station – yes, the really terrible one – we tried to get a taxi, but the price was double the usual. This is often the case at bus and railway stations. All we had to do was to walk about 200 m down the road, where we were able to pick up a taxi at the normal rate. From here we went to the other, newer, respectable bus station. We wanted to get to a place called Chi Shui, but were told that there is no bus there from Bijie – even though there is a connecting road. Why this should be so, I have no idea. It is one of the mysteries of life in China. We were told that we would have to return to the provincial capital, Guiyang. I really had no desire to do this, so we sat in the bus depot for some time thinking over our options, while having lunch. Eventually, we decided to return to Guiyang.

At 2.20 pm, we were on our way again. Along the route we saw an accident, which is not at all unusual; in fact just the opposite. In Australia we are surprised if we actually see an accident; here I am surprised if I do not. In this incident, a tanker had gone off the road and was lying on its side. When will these drivers learn? Our driver was doing some crazy things, like trying to overtake on blind corners. To take our minds off his driving, we had the scenery which is magnificent, with some deep gorges and a beautiful lake. The major crop hereabouts is again corn.

By 6.00 pm we were back in Guiyang. You might recall that this new bus station is a long way out of town, so we took a taxi. At this point, one of our number was not feeling very well, having eaten something which disagreed with her, so it became a race to see if we would arrive at a hotel before she threw up. We made it. Just. We booked into "7 Days" a chain of some 400 economy class hotels scattered throughout the country. I have stayed with them so many times, that I have become a member, which entitles me to a discount. So how lucky am I? – staying in this hotel with three beautiful young ladies! It took us a while to find a suitable restaurant, as this district is commercial, mainly selling clothing, but eventually we found one up a side street. By 9.30 pm we were back at our hotel. It is time for bed. Erica in particular was very tired.

Next morning, Cindy was up early, as she was anxious to return to Tongren. After breakfast, we headed off to the nearest bus stop, so that we could get to the railway station. I have done this before, so I know where to catch the bus – or I thought I did. Since my last visit, the city fathers have put in a one way street, and yes, the traffic was going the wrong way. It took us a while to find the correct bus stop, which happens to be on the next parallel street. At the railway station, we bade goodbye to Cindy and Erica, and also booked our own tickets for Xian. At 442 Yuan it is expensive, but we do have a soft sleeper.

We spent the day relaxing in Guiyang. There was one rather surprising incident. We were in our hotel room, when there was a knock on the window – yes, the window, not the door. We are four floors up, and someone is knocking on the window! Am I imagining things? No I wasn't. Outside the window was a young man suspended from the roof. He was painting the walls, and wanted us to remove items of clothing which were drying on the window sill. That has never happened to me before. Life is full of surprises.

Aussie 1 has had a lot of trouble, among other things, in getting his visa to go to India. Originally he was supposed to come with us from day 1, but without a passport you cannot travel anywhere in this country, where the authorities want to know exactly where you are at any moment. I had to supply an itinerary before I left Tongren. I checked my e-mails to find we had some good news; Aussie 1 would be joining us in Guiyang, with one of his students, Grace, coming with him. At 7.00 pm, F1 and I left our hotel again for the railway station – yes, this time we knew where to catch the bus. Here we met Grace, who was on her own, as Aussie 1 has been delayed further, and will not be coming till tomorrow. We gave her the ticket I had bought for myself, while she gave me the ticket she had bought for Aussie 1. To complicate matters even further, another man had paid for the tickets, so that F1 and I forked out the 900 Yuan owing to him. Got it? I said goodbye to F1 and Grace, and headed back to my hotel. Again, bus routes have changed, and I found myself going in the wrong direction, so I got out and walked the remaining 2 km. For the next day I would be on my own. One needs to be flexible in China; you never know what will happen next.

On Saturday morning I had a wonderfully relaxing time in my hotel room. Check out is a 12.00 noon. I had lunch and spent three hours in the hotel lobby, checking e-mails, when the one and only computer was free, and reading. At 3.20 pm, Echo arrived. She is a good friend and has been for some time. We wandered across the road where we found a good coffee shop, called Createa. For the next 1 ½ hours we sat and chatted, until she had to go and teach. She works very hard. We left together, she going to teach, me going back to the hotel to pick up my luggage. By now I knew well how to get to the railway, where I arrived just before 6.30 pm. I waited in Dicos till Aussie 1 arrived, which he did at 6.50 pm. For the past two weeks he has been cooling his heels in Tongren, waiting on the bureaucrats. Dicos, by the way, is a Taiwanese copy of McDonald's.

Here we had our meal. I noticed a rather petty young lady near us, who was sitting on her own and seemed to be in two minds. I told her that if she wanted to get her meal, I would watch her luggage. She was delighted, and that is what she did. Subsequently she told us she was waiting for two of her friends to arrive, which they eventually did. We became quite pally, taking the obligatory photographs to commemorate this fortuitous encounter. Her name is Belinda. The time came to bid our fond farewells, when all hell broke loose.

Before you board a train in China, you must first put your luggage through an X-ray machine and have your body scanned as well, as is now the usual practice at airports. Here the process is an ordeal because of the sheer number of people who are pushing and shoving nearly the whole time. Everybody is trying to get ahead by pushing in front. There is not much sense of an orderly queue. It is difficult to pick up one's luggage after it has gone through the scanner, as it is such a melee. In just such a chaotic bun rush, a man walked off with Aussie 1's plastic bag, containing his food, which he had only just then purchased at the supermarket next door, where he was ably assisted by Belinda and her friends. Now it was gone. Aussie 1 alerted the authorities, who saw the man on CCTV pick up the bag, but there was no hope of catching him in this huge crowd. He was gone. The security men were apologetic, escorting us onto the train and even offering us a free meal, which we declined since we had only just eaten. Oh the joys of travelling, especially in this overcrowded country.

We sat up for a while. There is a family sharing our compartment together with the one next door. There was the mother, who was feeding her baby, the father and the grandmother. I slept well. I actually awoke at around 6.00 am, but it was so pleasant just lying there, completely relaxed, as the train chugged along. We arrived at Chongqing, a major Chinese city and its wartime capital, around 8.00 am for a 20 minute stopover. I thought this would be it, but we stopped for another 15 minutes at Shapingba, one of the districts, where I stayed for a while some years ago, and where I would live for three years later on. A curious incident then ensued. A woman boarded the train and entered our carriage. An argument took place between her and the man who had slept the night in the bunk opposite mine. It transpired that she had the correct ticket; he did not. Did he get a free night's sleep? Who knows? Much of what goes on in this country is mystery.

We noticed that the towns along our route tended to be drab, dirty and polluted. At one station, there was a fast train on the next platform, so we got out to have a look. China is building these at a rate of knots. Soon China will lead the world having a rail network crisscrossing the country, with trains travelling in excess of 300 kph. I might add that China is also building trains for Australia, but with great difficulty, due to the unrealistic expectations of, in particular, the NSW government. But that is another story.

There is a mountain range separating Chongqing from the plain on which Xian is situated. This involved the train going through many tunnels, and crossing over many bridges, including many river crossings. We started counting. Believe it or not, we crossed one particular river, the Han Jiang, something like 50 times! I reckon I have crossed this river more often than I have crossed the Murray. For a large part of our route, we were paralleled by a six lane expressway, well, more or less. Amazingly, at times, such is the rugged nature of this country that this expressway had actually been built over the river itself. I have never seen this before, where'the roadway is actually following the course of the river. This truly is an amazing country.

We ate our evening meal in the dining car, which is not something I do very much as it is quite expensive. We waited an hour for service. This is because they cook first the food which is taken through the train. This is cheaper too, though it is more comfortable to sit at a table, and talk.

We were due to arrive in Xian at 9.18 pm, but for some reason, we sat outside the city – waiting – for two hours, while two goods trains and three other passenger trains went passed us. I do not know why. It was 11.30 pm. By the time we pulled in, some 27 hours after we left Guiyang. There was a long queue at the taxi rank, so that it was quite late by the time we got to our hotel – another in the "7 Days" chain. I finally got to bed about 1.00 am.

37. Xian – Old City Walls – 26th July 2009

I suppose that for most people these days, the name of Xian is immediately associated with the terracotta warriors, so for us, too, it is the first place we wanted to visit. On Monday morning we walked to the railway station. It is only about a kilometre, but we probably walked further as we were not sure of how to get there. Buses also leave from here to take people to the warriors, but the queue was long and the morning had almost gone. We decided to explore the old city wall.

This wall stands in the centre of the city and is in truly excellent condition. It was built during the Ming dynasty (AD 1368 – 1644), with considerable maintenance in AD 1995, but is based on an older wall dating from the Tang dynasty (AD 618 – 907). It is some 12 m high and about the same in width, so there is plenty of room on the top, enough for a six lane road. A Ramp takes you to the top, after you have paid the 40 Yuan admission price. The northern and southern sections measure 4,440 metres, while the eastern and western sections are a little shorter at 3,100 metres, thus giving a circumference of over 15 km. Now you could walk this, but it would take most of the day. Instead, we opted to hire bikes. This should save the feet a bit.

For another 40 Yuan we could hire a tandem bike. We hired two; Aussie 1 and Grace on one, while F1 and yours truly took the other. At least one of these needs some maintenance; riding it is hard work. You have 100 minutes to complete the circuit; if you do not make it, a stiff extra charge applies. We were to see other bikes racing against the clock to get back on time, and at the end of our ride, we were doing the same. We did make it in, with about 30 seconds to spare, but this and a later experience of the operators showed them to be hard hearted people, interested only in making money. A pity, as they left a sour taste in what was otherwise a wonderful experience. I filled out a questionnaire indicating our displeasure at these people. I wonder if they will take any notice.

From time to time we would stop to take in the views and learn more about the wall. Towers are built at 120 metre intervals, as an arrow could be fired 60 metres. Thus bowmen in these towers could cover the intervening spaces. Each corner is dominated by a larger square tower, except one corner where the tower is round – so work that out. There are displays of some ancient weapons and even some copies of the terracotta warriors. Indeed, we would see such copies in many locations.

Back at our hotel we had a well-earned rest, and I did some laundry. That evening we took a taxi to the Bell Tower. This is a very beautiful building in what is virtually the centre of the city. Its original purpose was to warn the citizenry of any impending attack. The gong still sounds, but for a very different reason. Entry into the tower is 25 Yuan, then for a further 10 Yuan, you may strike the gong, so that now its sounds indicate not an attack upon the city, but an attack upon the walleto1 – more money going into the city coffers. We did not go up the tower, and nor did we sound the gong. One corner of this square is occupied by a large shopping mall. I was taken by the contrasting styles of architecture, the old and the new. Close to the opposite corner is a nice restaurant, specializing in *jiaozi* or dumplings. Here we had our evening meal, which was eminently palatable. They also specialize in draft beer, which was even more palatable.

From here we took another taxi to the Big Wild Goose Pagoda, some 3 km outside the city walls. Here there is a series of enclosed pavements, set with regularly spaced nozzles. Music is played, mostly Western classical with some Chinese, while jets of water spurt up, synchronized to each piece. In the background the pagoda is lit up and we had the added bonus of a full moon. It was magical. In spite of signs warning people not to jump into the fountains, kids were doing just that. In my book they were not adding to the entertainment, but detracting from it, but maybe I am a spoilsport. The repertoire included pieces from Tchaikovsky, Rossini and Radetsky amongst others.

After the performance, crowds of people were wanting to get home, so the taxis were taking advantage of this bonanza to overcharge, as were the auto drivers. Nevertheless we were able to bargain with one of the latter drivers. Grace has been invaluable today in translating and getting us around. These autos, called *la la che*, can carry four people at a squeeze. They have open sides and you travel close to the ground. The ride is quite an experience. We are small and have no protection, but we weave in and out of the traffic, we go against red lights, we even go against the traffic, we have great big busses bearing down on top of us. We made it back safely to our hotel, so our guardian angels were really working overtime.

So we come to the end of a very interesting and memorable day. While there were some negatives it was overwhelmingly a great day. God is good.

38.   *Around Xian – 27ᵗʰ July 2010*

On Tuesday, we visited the Shaanxi History Museum. Xian is situated in Shaanxi Province, not to be confused with Shanxi Province. This museum is not far from the Big Wild Goose pagoda, where we were last night. It is certainly popular, with crowds of people queuing to get in, including some Westerners. It is odd, but I am not used to seeing many other Westerners around. Maybe I like being unique. A marquee had been erected in front of the ticket office, but even then the line had snaked into the hot sun. We crept forward, and then suddenly were whisked through on the grounds that the four of us constituted a group. Of course we are.

The building is large, in the style of the Tang dynasty, and in my humble opinion, really beautiful. The Tang marked a high point in Chinese civilization. The size of the collection is huge – some 400,000 pieces – and they are arranged chronologically, which makes eminent sense to me. The oldest periods of history are on the ground floor, so that as you work your way up you come closer to modern times. You can hire an audio guide for 60 Yuan, but we opted not to, as the exhibits have English as well as Chinese captions.

Exhibits seem to start from the Late Shang dynasty, 13ᵗʰ to 11ᵗʰ century BC, with the development of bronze ware, including some very large tripod cooking basins. Implements of war were sadly prominent. Chariots appeared during the Western Zhou dynasty, 11ᵗʰ to 8ᵗʰ century BC. I find it fascinating that chariots were also being used in the West, although a little earlier. From around 990 BC, they became an important part of Israel's economy under King Solomon, acting as the middleman between Egypt to the south and the Hittites to the north. By the time of his death, he had amassed about 10,000 of them, enough to slow down the Assyrian advance for a couple of centuries. But let's get back to China, where unsavoury aspects of society were also on display, such as the keeping of slaves, and severe punishments, like foot amputations, that were meted out to those considered to be unsociable types.

We took a breather in the "coffee shop", which boasts one table and a lot of art work, though not much that caught the eye. They were expensive, of course, as was the coffee at 20 Yuan. I had a small café latte, but I doubt if it had seen many coffee grains. Nevertheless it was most pleasant sitting there, sipping, and enjoying the company and the air conditioning, while ruminating on the exhibits.

A couple of the terracotta warriors from the Qin dynasty (221 – 207 BC) are also on display. From the Eastern Han dynasty (AD 25 – 220) I was taken with a glazed earthenware piece depicting a toilet directly over a pigsty. I am sure the pigs appreciated it.

Upstairs we looked at pieces from the Tang dynasty (AD 618 – 907). Their porcelain and celadon ware is exceptional. I even saw a personal spittoon. Goodness. Whatever happened in the intervening period? Nowadays, people spit anywhere. They had pieces exhibiting "foreigners on horseback". I have never seen this in any Western museum, where the caption would be "Thracian horsemen", or such like. But here in China the world is divided into two groups, and if you are not Chinese then you are "foreigner". There is a good diorama of the Silk Road, with the three routes outlined in coloured lights. I never knew there were three routes. Actually, there was a fourth, if you include the sea route. During the Tang dynasty, ships sailed to South East Asia and to Africa. There is even a theory that they may have made it all the way to Australia. If this is ever proved, we may find China claiming Australia as another province of their empire, although come to think of it, the necessity for proof has never bothered China before in its insatiable demand for more territory.

From the museum we took a taxi to the Muslim Quarter, which is a tourist area, with narrow alleyways lined with souvenir shops. There is traffic on the wider streets, where I was intrigued to find that bikes are parked literally in the middle of the road. Extraordinary. Here there is no footpath, and with the massive increase in the number of privately owned cars, parking is becoming more and more of a problem. In Tongren, they are taking over the footpaths, so that now I often walk on the roads.

There are lots of different foods to sample: very nice. We had our evening meal here in a restaurant, specialising in a kind of beef soup. First you broke into small pieces pita style bread, which you dropped into the soup of beef and noodles. I would have preferred more vegetables, while Aussie 1 pointed out that it needed more salt. Still it was okay and the serving was large. There is also a mosque here, which I did not enter, as the price of admission is steep, but I was surprised at the architecture. It is the only mosque I know of which is not entirely Arab, as it has adopted Chinese characteristics. The Muslims themselves are not Han people, but Hui, and probably came here via the Silk Road, which began (and ended) at Xian. I cannot imagine the Han giving up their culture to become Muslim.

From here we went to the large modern shopping mall near the Bell Tower, as Grace wanted to do some shopping. The ladies might like to tune out here, as I have some advice for the gentlemen who may be reading this. When a lady wants to go shopping, it is best to make yourself scarce. Find some comfortable spot and settle down to read a book, or whatever. What we did was buy ice-cream – rum and raisin for me – simply delicious, even if it did cost 8 Yuan. Aussie 1 was also looking for an umbrella, as he had lost his favourite one, which had served him well for many a year. Here you could get one for 226 Yuan! Or you could go outside and buy one for 10 Yuan. Take your pick. They both keep the rain out.

It was time to return to our hotel, by taxi again, and for me to do some laundry. I also watched some TV, including a late night English movie, which is something of a luxury for me, since I cannot do this in Tongren. It has been a great day.

39.   Terracotta Warriors – 28th July 2010

The next morning, Wednesday, we were up early. After breakfast we took a taxi to the train station in order to catch bus 306 out to see the warriors. We wanted to start reasonably early to beat some of the expected crowds. The bus trip takes about an hour.

At the warriors' site, one must walk a considerable distance – about 200 metres from the bus parking area to the ticket office, plus a further 500 metres to the entrance gate. The vendors lining the route have to be seen to be believed, all out for the tourist dollar. The price of admission is currently 90 Yuan, but I imagine that will continue to rise. Security is tight; one must present one's ticket no fewer than three times. Probably by now everyone knows the story of how this army was accidentally discovered in 1974 by farmers digging a well. Not long after the first of these warriors were unearthed, some were sent on a world tour. My brother and I were fortunate to see them in Melbourne's Art Gallery. Now, more than 30 years later, I was able to view them in situ. One can but admire the Chinese entrepreneurial genius. Western institutions provided free and invaluable advertising, from which China has been reaping the benefits ever since.

The museum which is open to the public measures 16,300 square metres, but this is only part of a much wider area of some 120,750 square metres (about 350 metres X 350 metres), most of which is the mausoleum of emperor Quin Shi Huang situated 1.5 km away. When this is excavated it should really be something. To date, only geophysical work has been done. Qin Shi Huang became king of Qin state at the age of 13 in 246 BC, and immediately began work on his tomb. He also began his conquests of the other three states, thus combining them into the Chinese (Qin) Empire by 221 BC.

This is so important in understanding China. The empire was formed by military might, so that taking by force is ingrained as being acceptable. Whatever territory China wants it thereby has a right to conquer.

Three pits have been opened to the public, the largest of which measures some 210 metres by 60 metres. As you enter, you see below these warriors in serried ranks: archers in front, the main body behind them and chariots at the rear. The trunks were mass-produced in several patterns, so that mixing and matching has provided great variety. The faces, however, were individually made, thus making each warrior unique. It seems probable to me that the artisans used real human faces as their models, in much the same way that European painters did. To the rear of the pit, researches wearing blue shirts were hard at work. The warriors, some 6,000 of them, are in corridors, separated from their comrades by low walls.

The second pit is smaller, with an additional 1,000 warriors and 90 chariots. There are also glass cases containing some of the warriors for close-up inspection, plus information boards, particularly on weaponry. Pit 3 is the smallest, measuring about 30 metres X 25 metres, and contains only 68 warriors and one chariot. These figures are, however, larger than the others, as befits their rank as officers. Generals are more than 2 metres tall. This third pit is therefore called the command centre.

Pits 2 and 3 were discovered in 1976. Elsewhere bronze chariots were unearthed in 1978. More may still be buried. The tomb of Qin Si Huang is reputed to be a wonder to behold, containing, amongst other things, rivers made of mercury. The emperor was told that this metal ensures longevity, so he imbibed some. The result was not quite what he expected, as it caused his death.

This is but a swift overview of what we saw, but for me of far more importance is its meaning. Did Qin Shi Huang believe that this army could protect him in the afterlife? Does the magnificent scale of the project reflect a massive ego? or a massive insecurity complex? or both? Does it suggest that life is all about armies and power? What are the ramifications for today? We can certainly admire the technical advances of Qin society. I must confess, however, that I do have a worry. It can be construed that this man, this tyrant, is still a role model for China today, and indeed one can argue that this has always been the case. Chinese history has been one of continued expansion, as the state sends out its armies to conquer whatever territory is contiguous. Once this has been added to the empire then more conquests are made. This process is still continuing today and is likely to do so for some time to come. For the glory of China, it is OK to ride roughshod over the territories and rights of other countries. That is my worry.

After viewing the exhibits we had lunch in a Subway – no, not an underground passage, but a fast food chain which makes sandwiches. It just happens to have a silly name. The sandwich and juice were nice, and on this hot day we also appreciated the air conditioning. Outside Grace decided to do some shopping, which she loves. She got a very good price for some mobile phone covers, so we also got in on the act, much to the annoyance of the vendors. It appears that there is one price for the Chinese, but a higher price for everyone else. We also bought the most delicious peaches, before heading back to Xian.

At the railway station we parted company, as F1 and I were looking for books. We caught a taxi to the Han Tang Shu Cheng, or Book City, where I was delighted with their excellent selection of English books. I bought two. We caught a bus back to our hotel.

In the evening we went to a pizza place for our meal. It was just so-so, being too doughy and not cooked enough. Their blueberry cheesecake, on the other hand, was very tasty. Enough for one day.

40.   *Puppets and Pottery – 29th – 30 July 2010*

Thursday was a much quieter day, partly spent checking travel options. In the afternoon we went looking for shadow puppets, which we found eventually, thanks to Grace. These puppets are about 30 cm high and are made from parchment, which in turn is made from cattle or donkey hide, and sometimes from other animals. It is soaked in water and rubbed clean, so that it is translucent, then cut into desired shapes and painted. Limbs are attached separately so that they can be moved by means of long sticks. The operator manipulates the puppets from beneath a screen with a light behind, so that they are seen to dance on the screen. One person operates the puppets, while another plays the music, if you can call it that, as it includes those discordant drums used in Peking Opera. They perform whenever anyone turns up, which means they put on a performance for us four. It is somewhat expensive at 20 Yuan, considering that the performance lasts only 10 minutes, but it was worth it to experience this fascinating expression of local culture. It is a family tradition, going back some 400 years. Today the old man, who played the drums, is turning it over to his son, who manipulated the puppets. Thus the torch passes to yet another generation. The story they played for us comes from a Chinese classic, "Journey to the West".

The beginnings of puppets in China is lost in the mists of time, but one tradition states that they began here in Xian, during the reign of emperor Wudi (156 – 87 BC). He was upset when his favourite concubine, Li, died. A man called Shao Weng made a paper cut out of her, placing it on some cloth. The emperor was delighted. The art became particularly popular during the Tang and Song dynasties. Today there are only two successful troupes left in all of China, one in Beijing, the other in Tangshan. I guess TV draws a bigger audience these days. I wonder what the future will bring. Somehow I think it will survive. We have been privileged to have witnessed such an ancient cultural art form.

Today also happens to be Grace's birthday, so we did several things to celebrate the occasion, including having a street artist draw her portrait, a rather lengthy process, taking well over an hour, as the artist was most painstaking in his work.

Aussie 1 just happens to be interested in pottery – amongst other things – and has considerable experience in this field. We heard that there is a pottery town called, Chen Lu, so we decided to pay it a visit. Consequently, on Friday morning we returned to the bus depot near the railway station. While looking for the right bus, we had an unfortunate experience; a thief stole Aussie 1's camera, actually taking it out of its case, which was slung over his shoulder. This was a nasty experience. When travelling, one must be so careful of one's belongings, ever watchful. The incidence of thieving in this country is very high. Of course he lost not only his camera, but also all his precious photos.

We boarded a bus for Tongshuan, some 2 hours away. This is loess country, wind-blown yellow soil, which sits atop the bedrock, as can be seen from road cuttings. It is this soil which gives the Yellow River its name, gives Beijing its dust storms, and, incidentally, provides much of the fertility for northern China.

The bus to Chen Lu, we were told, did not leave from the bus station but from somewhere else. We took a taxi to "somewhere else", only to find, after a long drive, that there must be two places called "somewhere else" and that clearly we were at the wrong one. Back we went. We did not find the correct bus, so instead took another taxi, the driver agreeing to drive us the entire 20 km for 40 Yuan.

Off we went, heading for the hills – literally. Recent rains have wrought havoc with these narrow, local roads, as there have been plenty of landslips, with sections of roadway gone. One had to drive carefully, or end up at the bottom of the valley. By the time we arrived at our destination, it was lunch time, so we found a suitable place to sample the local wares. This consisted of egg and tomato – a popular dish in China – two meats, and bean sprouts which are the local specialty. We also ordered rice. Now you would think that should be safe enough in Asia, but our hostess told us that rice does not go with the food we had ordered. "Oh, what a pity, but we'll have some rice anyway". Guess what? *"Mei you mifan."* They have no rice; the poor lady was trying to save face, and that is typically Asian. The girls also ordered a pineapple beer, which tasted nice.

This place also had a pottery factory, with many pieces at various stages of completion. One lady was carving patterns into the wet clay of a large pot. Throughout the course of the afternoon, we would visit other places, including a couple of kilns. Aussie 1 was in his element, discussing technical data with the operators. Most of the pieces were mass produced, with very little of the handicraft variety. Not much was for sale, either, and what there was was very pricey. Aussie 1 was interested in a teapot, but at 1,000 Yuan *tai gui le* – it was far too expensive. But we had fun wandering around, even though the day was quite hot. Many of the houses, we noticed, had pottery pieces built into their walls.

We had actually been following a guide book, not Lonely Planet, and it had stated; "Chen Lu eats pottery." Really? "Elegant cups lie by the side of the road." We saw none, only some shards. "The local people wear Lei Fang hats." Not that we saw. Lei Fang is supposed to be a communist hero. He was really a product of communist propaganda and more of a self-serving fraud, who happened to have died young in an accident; at least I assume it was an accident. "Exquisite bowls cost as little as 10 Yuan." We found nothing remotely as cheap as this. "Artisans may hail you in the street." There again they may not; we found it difficult to raise anyone. Maybe we went to the wrong town. Nevertheless, this town has been producing ceramics since the Tang dynasty, with pretty much the whole town being involved in one way or another. Not many towns could boast this record.

At around 4.00 pm, we caught a minibus back to Tongshuang. This town does not appear to have much to recommend it. No doubt the locals, for whom this is home, would disagree. It is quite long and thin, as it follows the course of the river, as do so many towns built in the valleys of this mountainous country.

By 7.30 pm we were back in Xian. It was a slow trip, due to heavy traffic. As we entered the city, I estimated around 100 cranes operating on building sites – and that is only on this side of the city. And this is only one city. This is being repeated all over China. We are currently witnessing the biggest building boom in the history of humankind. Just amazing.

For tonight's meal, we thought we would try the hostel fare. I had a huge sandwich for 20 Yuan – very good value. We returned to our hotel via another of those *la la che*, the four seater, open vehicles which zip around with utter disregard for the rest of the traffic. At one point, however, our driver stopped after he was passed by a police car. We wonder if he has a licence. It was all great fun for us. I was giving cheery waves to the driver of a great big bus which was breathing down our throats. He finally lightened up and gave me a smile and a wave when he eventually overtook us.

So how do you sum up today? While there were some good aspects, it was not our best. Maybe tomorrow will be better.

41.   Xian to Chengdu, Sichuan Province – 31ˢᵗ July – 3ʳᵈ August 2010

Saturday was a quiet day, wandering around Xian. We even spent an hour sitting in McDonald's drinking coffee, while enjoying the air conditioning. In the evening we had a final meal with Aussie 1 and Grace, going to the *jiaozi* restaurant near the Bell Tower, where one can drink wonderful draft beer at 12 Yuan a schooner. At 8.00 pm they left for Beijing.

On Sunday morning, after a sleep in, F1 and I took the 600 bus to South Gate, where we changed to the 609 in order to return to the Big Wild Goose Pagoda. With just two of us, buses are cheaper than taxis. We wanted to explore the landscaped gardens here, which are indeed worth a visit. I like the sculpture of musicians and another of a boys' choir. We brought lunch with us, so ate after we had found a seat in the shade; there are not many of them. A sign read; "Take good care of the green grass and treat the grass well", which says a lot about how

Chinese express themselves. We would simply say; "Keep off the grass". Later we sat in a KFC, munching on chicken, reading and again taking advantage of the air conditioning.

We returned to the hostel, where we picked up our rail tickets for Chengdu. The hostel charges a service fee, of 30 Yuan, but in my book this is well worth it, as you do not have to go to the train station, and stand in line, with all its pushing and shoving, for some time. By now it was starting to rain, and we had not brought umbrellas. Oh well, a little rain never hurt anyone. We went to an internet café, and presented our passports – which you have to do here. I settled down to work for 1 ½ hours, correcting the English of one of our teachers, who wishes to study in Australia. And I thought I was on holidays.

Later, after our evening meal, we went to a great ice-cream place called "Dairy Queen", where I treated myself to a delicious "chocolate blizzard" – interesting name. The Bell Tower after the rain and in the twilight was looking particularly beautiful. Then it was back to our hotel.

On Monday we woke to a very hazy day. The pollution in this city is high. Even when the sun shines, you hardly need a hat. I would not want to live here. At 11.30 am we checked out of our 7 Days hotel and caught the No. 9 bus to the railway station. In the waiting lounge we met two lovely English ladies from Bristol, here on a three week holiday, leaving their boyfriends behind. We got on well. We would be in the same carriage, but in different compartments. The train has actually come from Shanghai, so it travels a long way. On board I had some trouble in the dining car when the staff refused to sell me some beer. I have no idea why. Eventually they did. It cost 6 Yuan per 500 ml bottle.

I slept well, in spite of the guy in the next bunk snoring. I find these soft sleepers to be so comfortable. It beats sitting up all night. By 7.00 am we had arrived in Chengdu. From the train station we got a taxi to Dragon Town Youth Hostel. Later they refunded the 14 Yuan taxi fare; great. We had a walk of around 300 m down a lovely street, traffic free. This whole section of Chengdu has been restored to original architectural styles, so has now become a tourist attraction. We would see tourists arrive by the bus load in the late afternoon, to wander around admiring the architecture, buying souvenirs and eating at one of the many restaurants.

After checking in, we went exploring, finding the large "People's Park" nearby. After doing a circuit we headed off to the city, looking particularly for Tian Fu bookstore. We got lost, which is not surprising, but found it eventually on a corner opposite Tian Fu Park, which is the major park in the centre of the city. It looks quite beautiful, decorated with dark green and gold pillars. One end is dominated by a statue of Mao; one wonders how much longer he will remain. The bookstore has an excellent selection of the classics. From here we walked back to our hostel, rested for a while, before going out again for meal. We found an inexpensive place, but here in Chengdu one must watch the *lajiao*, as their food is renowned for its spiciness. It was a bit light on greens and meat, but otherwise eminently palatable.

Today we have done lots of walking, covering quite a few kilometres. This is not the end, however, of this day, as the evening would bring something very special as you will see from the next section.

42. Chengdu Opera – 3rd August 2010

Our hostel was selling tickets for a performance of Chengdu Opera. I had heard of this and thought this was an opportunity not to be missed. We fairly leapt at the chance. I wonder if you have heard of it.

At 7.20 pm six of us were taken by minibus to Fu Rong Guo Cui, a concert hall. We were given seats in the front row, though on the far left hand side; excellent. Now I was expecting a Western style opera – well, more or less – really a play put to music, where the actors sing their lines rather than recite. But it was not like that at all. Rather it was a series of ten disparate acts, so more like a concert.

The opening was something of a surprise. Two young ladies wearing *qipaus* came on stage carrying between them a long painting. This would be auctioned to the highest bidder. I have never experienced this in the Sydney Opera House. Did you want one? Sorry, too late, as I sat firmly on my hands, not daring even to scratch my ear, for fear that my pocket might end up being lighter by several thousand Yuan. This was repeated for a second, then a third painting, before the concert proper got under way. The presenter was another young woman, who gave most of her spiel in Chinese, but with some English; the latter, while not good, was intelligible.

We began with an orchestral piece, the instruments being mainly drums and trumpets. The sound is similar to Peking Opera, with – at least to my Western ears – harsh, strident, discordant sounds. This was followed by a dance of a king, queen and courtiers, dressed sumptuously, the clothes being brightly coloured, with wide flowing sleeves. This was followed by a fight between three kings, one of whom lost his mask in the stoush. Then it was back to an orchestral act, with the main instrument being an erhu. This, as you would probably know, is a two stringed violin like instrument, played with a bow down the base of the strings, close to a sounding box. The notes are mostly high pitched, but can be remarkably variable. It was good and most enjoyable. Another dance act followed, with young ladies sporting a long plume on the top of their heads. Waving these around formed a major part of their act.

Next we had something different. A man appeared with a termagant for a wife. She goaded him into extraordinary feats of balancing a lamp on the top of his head. This included crawling under a very low trestle. One could see the burn marks on the centre of the trestle, testimony to many previous performances. To end the performance he showed an amazing ability to blow out the flame while it was still sitting on the top of his head. You try it. If you wish to emulate any part of this act, just make sure you take out fire insurance first. The same applies to a later act where fire breathing performers were shooting flames a metre in front of them. No way I'm going to attempt that.

The succeeding act was a puppet show, but not the shadow type we had seen in Xian. This puppet is about a metre tall and was held aloft by the puppeteer, who was controlling the arms by means of two sticks. No big deal, I hear you say. Maybe, but this puppet displayed amazing dexterity, being able to pluck a flower from a bunch and place it delicately on the head of its woman controller. The next item was more reminiscent of our shadow puppets. This was a hand shadow display. In this act, a man, showing unbelievable dexterity – well, yes, he did use his left hand too – was able to get his hands and arms to represent an extraordinary array of animals and other shapes. A light behind him threw the shadows of his hands onto a screen. Isn't it surprising what you can do with shadows?

The final act was the Pièce de résistance, and if I had not seen this with my own eyes I would not have believed it. It is for this that Chengdu Opera is noted, and indeed I have not even heard of this being performed anywhere else in the world. There is a number of performers, each elaborately dressed and wearing masks. They prance around the stage, till, "hey presto", they are wearing a different mask. Hang on, I am sure this guy was wearing a green mask; now it is purple. How did that happen? He did not duck off into the change rooms. Nobody covered his face. It simply appeared. As if from nowhere. Do you know how it is done? As a matter of fact, I think I do.

But I'm not telling. You work it out. I did say "I think", because maintaining secrecy is part of the mystique of this performance.

There is a second part to this act, where the actors change clothes too. I kid you not. In this case, the actor is covered, but only for the briefest moment. A fan is drawn quickly across the body, and – again, "hey presto" (you have to get the magic words right) – she is now wearing a blue outfit, where a millisecond ago she was wearing red. How do they do it? Again I have a theory ... Boy, am I nasty.

After the show I offered my services to the company to improve their English, which really did leave something to be desired. Sadly, my offer was not taken up. Maybe I should have struck a bargain; "I will correct your English, if you tell me how you do it."

It certainly was a great show, well worth the 150 Yuan admission. It was 9.40 pm by the time we got back to the hostel. Then it was bed for me. It has been quite a day.

43. *Qinling Range – 5th – 8th August 2010*

The following day, Wednesday, was a rest day. I really do not like rushing around all the time. There are times when it is necessary to relax, take stock, think and pray. In fact I believe in doing this every day. We did find another book store, called the South West Book Store, and found it to be surprisingly good. Here I bought "The Collected Works of Oscar Wilde" for 85 Yuan. It is rather heavy to be carrying it around, but I do like his witty style, even though he likes the bon mot more than its content. He likes to turn phrases on their heads, even if it does not mean much. I think he is more interested in the clever turn of phrase than in deep truths. To a lesser extent, I think Gerard Manly Hopkins is similar.

There is a story of Wilde attending a party when one of the ladies present made some witty remark. "I wish I had said that" was Wilde's comment, to which the lady reposted, "You will". Years ago I acted in one of Wilde's plays: The Importance of Being Earnest". I was Cecily! – we were rather short on actresses.

On Thursday, we left a couple of bags in storage at the hostel, while we headed off early, bound for Jiu Zhai Guo, which means Nine Village Valley, situated in the north of the province (Sichuan), near the border with Gansu Province, and about 300 km by road from Chengdu. The bus left at 8.10 am; now for the ride. Hang onto your hats.

Initially, the countryside is flat, but it is not too long before we get into the mountains. Soon we came to a hold up. So we waited for about 20 minutes before we got underway again. At 12.15 pm there was another hold up, this time caused by a landslide. There has been a lot of rain recently, causing flooding and loss of life in this province. It was an hour before traffic started coming from the other direction, and another 20 minutes before our turn came, not that this "driver" cares much for courtesy to other drivers, as he pushes in whenever he can. This includes haring past the line of stalled traffic on the wrong side of the road, pushing in when vehicles are coming against him. He overtakes at reckless speed around blind corners, the vehicle swaying dangerously as he endeavours to round tight curves. The road is terrible, and I am sure was never meant to cater for this volume of traffic. No I am quite sure he did not get his licence from a Corn Flakes packet; more like a packet of instant noodles.

At 2.45 pm we had yet another unscheduled stop, this time to fix a tyre. Is anybody surprised? These stops do give us a chance to get to know our travelling companions, amongst whom is a Jewish couple from Haifa. He is studying to become a rabbi, so was wearing his yarmulke. At 3.55 pm there was another stop for petrol. Later still there was yet another stop, again to fox problems with the same tyre. Finally we had a meal stop, which for me consisted of boiled corn on the cob and instant noodles, enough to keep me alive, if this driver does not kill us all.

Certainly the scenery is extraordinary; I just did not want to join it. We have steep sided mountains, with interlocking spurs, rivers running through valleys. We were actually climbing over a mountain range, then down the other side. Eventually, after even the Chinese passengers were complaining, I asked the driver to slow down. Wonder of wonders, he did! It really would not take much to go over the edge as we first climbed then descended these steep sides, the road containing many an s-bend. The temperature dropped, too, as we climbed. On the plain it was 34 degrees, after the rain had cleared, that is.

We arrived at Jiu Zhai Guo at 8.30 pm, having been on the road for more than twelve hours, to cover 300 km. Let us now go forward some days for our return journey on the following Sunday. We left the hostel early in order to arrive at the bus station in plenty of time. There was a number of buses there, but none going to Chengdu, so we waited. After some time, the same rattle trap bus and driver that we had arrived in turned up, and yes, it was the one going to take us to Chengdu. Oh no! What are the chances of that happening? I might add that the air conditioning on this bus does not work, but neither does the TV, so that is good.

We left on time, 8.10 am, the same time we had left Chengdu on the previous Thursday. Again, our progress was hindered by rock falls onto the road, not that these slowed our driver down too much. We came across another bus bogged in a mudslide, with a bull dozer attempting to clear a passage. We sidled our way past. At other places there were road works, effectively blocking off half the road, thus allowing traffic to flow in one direction only, when it did move that is. When we came to a line of stopped vehicles, our driver was up to his usual tricks, haring down the wrong side of the road, then forcing his way back into line when traffic approached. I do not know what the other drivers thought of him, but I think they are a little more patient and long suffering than their Australian counterparts. At another place, a utility had broken down in the middle of the road, thus cutting the traffic to one vehicle at a time, the biggest, of course, going first. We came across yet another accident – naturally. A large truck had its front end all smashed in, so it had obviously hit something, and hit it hard.

Coincidentally, we had another Jewish couple with us on this return journey. The woman, sitting down the back, was petrified, vowing that never more would she travel by bus in China. From now on she would take the train. I don't know: where is the spirit of adventure? Now this bus actually has two drivers, who take it in turns, so I told the lady that she was lucky, because the current driver was the better of the two. Now that was hardly comforting! – but it was true. The second driver, who is completely mad, did not take over till we were out of the mountains and down on the plain. This mountain range, incidentally, is called the Qinling Range.

Once more I could marvel at his country. In the early morning in particular, it looked spectacular, with low clouds shrouding the hills below us, and range after range extending into the distance.

Again the temperature varied as the day wore on. In the early morning in Jiu Zhai Guo it was a cool 23 degrees, and it remained cool as we climbed over the range, but as we descended so the temperature rose. On the plain we were baking at 40 degrees. The driver actually left his front door open to try to bring some breeze into the bus. Remember that the air conditioning was not working.

On this return journey, we were back in Chengdu – in spite of the stoppages – by 5.40 pm. Thus we took only 9 ½ hours, compared with 12 hours for the outward journey, but we had no tyre problems coming back, and the wheels stayed on. God – or Yahweh – is good.

Now I have a comment to make. Some people see travel as a waste of time, a meaningless hiatus between two points, a necessary evil until one arrives at one's destination where one can start living again, doing the really important things. I do not share that view. For me, one moment is just as important as any other. Each is to be savoured; a gift from God. Indeed the whole of life is a journey. Enjoy yours.

44. *Jiu Zhai Gou – 6th August 2010*

Jiu Zhai Gou is a valley, or more properly three valleys, two joining together to form a Y shape.. We are up by 7.00 am, and get the guest house to prepare sandwiches for us, for our lunch. We are told it was only 10 minutes' walk to the park entrance, but in fact it takes us 20 minutes. Maybe they run. Entrance costs a whopping 320 Yuan, though a kind lady tells me I could enter for 250 Yuan as a senior citizen. And to think I thought I looked only 59! Lucky I have my passport with me.

Once inside, you could hop on and off buses which spend the entire day running around the park. Our first stop is 10 km from the entrance, at a Tibetan village, looking absolutely beautiful in this clear mountain air. At 2,280 metres we are at the same altitude as the summit of Mt. Kosciusko, Australia's highest mainland mountain. We are so lucky to get this day, with bright sunshine and azure sky, sprinkled with some puffy white clouds. There are prayer flags here, barely moving with only a zephyr to ruffle them. There are also prayer drums for those who want to turn them. In the nearby river the power of the water is used to turn them.

A flight of steps leads down to the river, where the river is cascading not over barren rock, which one might expect, but between mounds of vegetation, supporting not only small plants, but even trees. This river is the upper reaches of the Jialing, one of the tributaries of the Yangtze, which it joins at Changqing. We cross to the other side via a boardwalk, which has been laid down throughout the entire park. It is quite cool on the eastern side where the sun has not yet risen, but already it is getting quite hot in the sun. We spend the rest of the morning walking upstream. Every so often we come upon a lake; there are some 118 of them in his park. They are beautiful, with clear turquoise waters, in various shades of blue – green. In places we stop to watch the fish swimming lazily below us. I love the reflections of the mountain sides opposite.

After walking for some time, we recross the river to the road and catch the next bus to the tourist centre, arriving at 11.30 am. This point marks the junction of three valleys, 14 km from the park entrance and at the foot of Mt. Wonusano, to the east of which is the Zechawa Valley, while to the west is the Rize Valley. Here we stop for lunch, eating the sandwiches we have brought from the guest house. The food here, as one would expect, is expensive. There is a food court, where one can rest in the shade, but not being able to find a seat, we sat on some steps – not that there are insufficient seats. Heavens no. There are plenty of seats; just too many people! Zillions. You do know what country we are in.

After lunch we found, after some difficulty, the bus to take us up to the top of Rize Valley. We always have a little difficulty getting around when we are not part of any tour group, as our linguistic abilities are somewhat limited. The top of this valley is called Virgin Forest, some 32 km from the park entrance, and 3,060 metres above sea level. There are great views from up here, and an 1100 metre walk through the forest, which consists of tall straight trees, but not much undergrowth. Here plenty of people, including F1, were dressing up in Tibetan costume and having their photos taken – for a fee, of course.

Back on the bus we climbed, for a short trip back to Arrow Bamboo Lake, where we got off. This lake is shaped like an arrow while great stands of bamboo cover the mountainside. It was now 2.30 pm. We walked to a small but beautiful waterfall, which I liked so much that we stayed here for quite some time, just soaking up the atmosphere of this wonderful, peaceful spot. Many tourists came and went, stopping just long enough for the obligatory photograph, while we sat and reflected on God's wonderful world.

From here we walked another 1500 metres to Panda Lake, where more people were dressing in Tibetan costumes. The exit from this lake consists of a 78 metre high waterfall; the first drop is some 50 metres. The descent to the bottom is via flights of steep stairs. We continued walking on past the falls, to find – surprise, surprise – that the crowds are thinning out. There are sections where we were almost on our own, and that is a rarity.

The next lake we came to is the prettiest of the lot. It is called Five Coloured Lake, and yes, you may be able to distinguish shades of turquoise; blue-green, green-blue, green, blue. It is hard to describe in words the beauty of this lake in particular and of Jiuzhaigou in general. It is impossible to express the ineffable. This is one of the most beautiful places that I have seen anywhere in the world. If God can make this, then what must God be like?

From here we caught a bus back to the Tibetan village, where we spent an hour wandering around, raising the hopes of the various vendors. There is a museum here, which we did not have time to explore. It has a tower, sporting the swastika; this has been a symbol for thousands of years before the Nazis used it, not only by Tibetans, but by other peoples as well. I have seen it in Bali, Indonesia. At 6.30 pm we hopped on a bus again to leave this idyllic valley, as gates close at 7.00 pm.

Having eulogized this place to the skies, now let me make some negative comments;

1. At 320 Yuan, it is far too expensive. The government is simply greedy, pushing the price as high as the market will bear. Considering the huge numbers of people coming, it must be raking in close to 1,000,000 Yuan a day.
2. I refuse to believe that all of this money is necessary for park upkeep. Maybe the high price is an attempt to limit numbers.
3. The park is too extensive to explore adequately in one day. The admission ticket should be for two days.
4. There used to be nine Tibetan villages in these valleys. The Tibetans, however, have been driven out. I wonder how many are actually involved in the running of the park. I did notice that the workers are Tibetan, but how much of the loot the government is raking in are they getting?
5. It would be great if there could be areas where one can simply get away, but there isn't. Camping is forbidden, and no-one can stay overnight. There is a great system used at the Grand Canyon, where 90 people at a time are allowed to camp overnight. My night at Bright Angel Campsite at the bottom of the canyon is one of the most memorable of my life. Perhaps a similar system could be introduced here.

This valley is lined with peaks, so the sun kept appearing and disappearing as we travelled; we had a number of sunsets. Work that out. We had our evening meal at a restaurant we came across on the walk back to our guest house.

What a great day this has been; a very special day in a very special place.

We remained in Jiuzhaigou all Saturday. It was a great time to rest, going for walks, exploring the neighbourhood and generally enjoying this wonderful place. The architecture, too, is beautiful, including that of our guest house. On Sunday, as I have already related, we returned to Chengdu.

On Monday, we visited Jinli Street, an old area of Chengdu which has been done up for the tourist trade. Maybe so, but I love these old towns with their distinctive architecture, narrow lanes, water ways, and in particular, the wooden lattice structures. This place has certainly attracted many tourists, including some from other countries, although we did spend some time with a charming young Chinese lady who attached herself to us. These people can be so friendly. That night, back at our hostel, we did something unusual; we watched a video on their CD player. We chose "Prince of Persia". Apart from being unbelievable, it was very enjoyable. A few other guests also dropped by to watch.

On Tuesday, we decided to visit another old town, called Luo Dai. At Xianmen bus station we paid 5.5 Yuan for our ticket; not much for a one hour trip. This bus, however, is somewhat old and lacking in suspension. After we got off the bus, it took us some time to find out just where the old town is located. It is not far away, but you have to know where it is.

The main street is paved, with a water channel running down one side. This feature is common to many of these old towns and I find it charmingly attractive. Most of the buildings are made of wood, though the old "guildhalls" as they are called are made of stone. Vendors in shops on both sides of this street are selling souvenirs and food, but there are some variants. One woman was kneading rice flour prior to making rice cakes. One young man was glass blowing, making exquisite figurines of dragons and the like. He drew an appreciative crowd, to which he paid not the slightest attention, so absorbed was he in his art. There were some sideshows, such as dodgem cars, though often these turn out to be rather crashem cars, especially with teenage boys at the wheel.

We stopped for lunch at a square with an attractive stone tower surrounded by a small moat to one side. This is called the Word Store Tower, its purpose being rather curious. This ancient town is not Han, but was built and occupied by a minority people called the Hakka.

Possibly the best known member of this group is Deng Xiao Ping, one of the major authors of China's modernisation after Mao had died, though he blotted his copybook somewhat with the Tiananmen Square massacre. Now the Hakka appreciated the value of the written word, and hence of the paper on which it was written. It was forbidden to throw scrap paper out, or even to tread on it. All such papers were carefully husbanded, until, when a sufficient pile was collected, they were incinerated in this tower, which is therefore a glorified chimney.

Several stores were hiring period costumes for people to dress in and have their photos taken for 20 Yuan. One store featured a husband and wife combination. Mostly they just sat, waiting for customers. It amazes me how many store owners seem to spend most of their day doing absolutely nothing; they just sit and wait. The wife was targeting young women. When one walked past her lair, she would spring up and try to persuade her to dress up. Often she succeeded. The shop next door was the scene for a different performance, when one young man tried to persuade his reluctant girlfriend to dress up; he took her by the arm and physically dragged her into the shop, though I suspect that her protests were only half hearted.

One of the common sites in this country is children going to the toilet – anywhere. Mothers simply hold them and off they go on the footpath. On one occasion I did see one mother actually put newspaper on the footpath first – but only that once. Here at this tower a woman took the child to the rubbish bin, where the job was done, so that is progress.

After lunch we continued our perambulations, eventually finding a park where we could sit for a while on this hot day. This is not a large place, essentially consisting of one major street and a few side streets, so one can take one's time and enjoy.

Late afternoon we returned to Chengdu. We decided to have a Western meal for a change, so went to Houcaller, one of a chain of restaurants specialising in steaks. I had an "Australian style", whatever that means. Certainly the steak was great – very tender – but it was served with pasta. Heavens – whatever happened to the mashed potatoes and peas? Back at our hostel we watched another movie before turning in. I am trying to get in my annual quota.

The following day was a lazy one. I love this life; one day gallivanting around, and the next taking it easy. We did visit Carrefour, a French supermarket store, where I bought supplies I cannot obtain in little Tongren. This included a new pair of sandals, as my current pair has seen many a day and walked many a mile. It means I have to lug all this stuff back in the train, but what the heck. I did a lot of reading today as well.

We are now coming to the end of this marvellous holiday. There will be one more episode. I bet you can hardly wait.

46. Fenghuang, Hunan Province – 12th – 14th and 24th August 2010

This has been a fantastic holiday, not only rejuvenating the spirit, and resting the body, but also enlightening the mind. But it was time to head home. On Thursday we set the alarm for the unconscionable hour of 4.30 am. Out on the main street we caught a taxi immediately and sped off for the 25 minute trip to the airport. At this early hour there was very little traffic, allowing our driver to put his foot down. I remarked that he must be the second fastest driver in Chengdu. "No, hang on, he has just become the fastest as the other guy has just reached the Pearly Gates. " I said this in jest, but on my return trip from the airport I saw a smashed taxi, which had been involved in an accident.

We spent an hour at the airport, time to have breakfast. F1 espied a KFC, where we had a rice congee and coffee, for about 20 Yuan. At the other end of the terminal there is a posh looking restaurant where the coffee alone costs 58 Yuan. You have to be kidding! F1 headed back to Fuzhou. We had had a marvellous time, together with Aussie 1, Grace, Tracey, Cindy and the others.

Now on my own, I returned to Dragon Town hostel and relaxed in my room until check out time of 12.00 noon. In the arvo I spent some of the time in the hostel and some wandering around the neighbourhood. This Dragon Town is really nice with its old style buildings, paved streets and no traffic. One street has been set up as kind of museum to the city's ancient walls, featuring plaques outlining the history, with some maps. They also have a selection of bricks from every major period going back 3,000 years. Gosh, if we dig up an old brick from the Rocks in Sydney, dating back to the early 19th century, everybody gets excited.

My evening meal was at the hostel where they put on a free hot pot for everyone. I tell you, these hostels are really nice, as well as great value. It was also good to mix with other people from many different countries. One has to be very careful with Sichuan hotpot, however; too spicy for me. Not far from our hostel is a wet market, where we saw more chillies than you can poke a stick at. One young man did have a stick in his hand, as he pounded the chillies into a paste. Before I left I swapped two books I had finished reading for one from their library. I chose an anthology of Chinese short stories, which I am looking forward to reading.

Outside I carried my bag down this now familiar ancient style street, listening to the cicadas chirping merrily in the trees. Once more I caught a taxi, this time to the railway station, where I had a little wait in an extremely crowded waiting room; in other words, situation normal. I did find a seat, but at one point got up to stretch my legs, only to find that a man had dived into my seat. Did he not notice all my gear? Of course he did, but so what? In annoyance, I snatched my bags and marched off. Unfortunately my glasses were sitting on top of my bag. Oh no. Too late, I realised that I had lost them. Hence my first task back in Tongren was to get a new pair, which I did, with some help from Erica, who is my student, but much more than that.

Again, unfortunately, I was not able to secure a sleeper, so this meant sitting up all night. Needless to say, I did not get much sleep. This is the first time I had travelled this route, so for most of the time I had no idea where I was. Not to worry as we actually arrived in Tongren on time at 9.35 am, to find Erica (my "daughter") and her good friend Cindy, waiting for me. I tell you, these girls are fantastic. It has been an absolute pleasure teaching these people. They even helped me carry my bags, made heavy by my shopping in Chengdu. We spent some time together, including lunch.

In the afternoon I did necessary shopping. The most important item, of course, was to buy a new pair of glasses. They cost me only 160 Yuan (or about $25). I have been to this particular shop a number of times now, so they know me, and give me a good deal. The weather is hot. Thank goodness for my air conditioning.

We still have two weeks to go before the new semester begins, giving me adequate time to do some preparation, relax and write up some 16 Jottings on my travels, comprising some 18,000 words. But there was one further trip to come. Not all that far from Tongren, in Hunan province, there is yet another ancient town, called Fenghuang, which I had not been to, even though I had planned to go there many a time; something else had always cropped up. Kim in particular, a local girl, had invited me a number of times. Kim and Erica, incidentally, are the two girls I brought to Australia last year.

So on Tuesday, 24th August, Kim, Erica and I set out. Our start was delayed a little because of rain, but at 10.30 we caught the bus from one of Tongren's bus stations, this one being close to the railway. We had a large, modern, comfortable, air conditioned, diesel bus. As we approached the town, I noticed an old wall, but this is not part of the town. The Chinese just loved building walls. We arrived just before 12.00 noon, but still had a 20 minute walk to get to the old town. By now the sun was out and the day was becoming hot.

The wall is about 6 m high, crenelated at the top. The streets are narrow, so no cars, and once again are lined with shops aimed at the tourist trade, selling souvenirs, jewellery, clothing and food. As we walked I munched on a sandwich, till a beggar approached asking for money. Instead I gave her the half of my sandwich which I had not yet touched. She took it, which surprised me, but imagine her surprise when she started to eat it. My guess is she would have taken one bite then have thrown it into the garbage bin. Why? It contained lettuce – which the Chinese never eat raw – cheese – which is not part of their diet – and, as the Pièce de résistance, vegemite! As Aussie tucker it was top notch, but this is Fenghuang. She would never have tasted anything remotely like it. Later, as we strolled around, I found a man selling macadamia nuts, much to my surprise. How did this Australian nut get here? I have no idea. Is it now grown on Hainan Island, which is tropical? I know Hawaii now grows these Australian nuts, so maybe.

After strolling for some time, along a street parallel to the river, we went to the river itself. The scene is quite beautiful. Perhaps my photos can capture this better than my words. Some of these old wooden houses are propped up on stakes driven into the river bed. There are also a couple of pubs sporting Western names, so I can only conclude that people come here from overseas, though on this particular day, I was it. I love these old wooden houses. I love the wooden bridges too, especially the covered ones. There are also some stone structures, possibly dating from the Tang dynasty (AD 618 – 907).

Once again, people were dressing up in period costumes for a fee and having their photos taken. I did not do this, but I did buy some gifts to give to people back home, especially something for my brother. It was late afternoon before we decided to head back home. This involved catching a local bus to the bus station as it is quite some distance away. The station is well built, as it is on the side of a hill, with the buses coming in from the top, while we entered from below. There are no problems with local traffic.

Back in Tongren we shared our evening meal. What a great day, and what a marvellous finish to the holidays. God is good. I hope you enjoyed them half as much as I did. Now it is back to work.

April Excursions 2011

47.　Zai Ying, Guizhou Province – 1st – 3rd April 2011

Although Chinese are migrating to the cities in massive numbers, it is still largely an agrarian society. This is in marked contrast with Australia, where most of the population live in cities. While I enjoy visiting cities, I really like getting into the countryside as well. Last summer I had an opportunity to spend some time on a farm, a time I will always treasure. I would have liked to have done some farm work, but this was strictly *verboten*. I probably could not have done much anyway; these people work so hard, and for so little return. This is such an inequitable situation, which I would love to see redressed, not just in China, but throughout the world. It is the middleman who seems to make most of the profit, rather than the primary producer.

The farm belongs to Erica's family. Recently, her best friend, Cindy, had invited me to her home, an invitation I leapt at. So on a recent Friday afternoon, Erica and I headed off by train to Cindy's village called Zai Ying. It is not far, taking only an hour or so in the train. We had seats, so that was good, though the train – as usual – was crowded. In all my time in China, I do not think I have ever been on a train which was not crowded, and not only with people either. They carry huge amounts of luggage. I would like to see a baggage car, rather than have oversized bags taking up most of the space between seats. After all, buses have a storage section underneath, so why not trains?

The train stop was not much more than a siding, rather than a station. Its location is curious. The terrain hereabouts is quite mountainous, creating enormous engineering challenges for railway construction. Train lines have been kept quite level by boring tunnels through hills and viaducts across valleys, entailing massive amounts work. This siding is located in a valley, but rather than the usual viaduct on legs, they have constructed a levee across the valley, at a height of some 10 m, with a tunnel in the middle for road traffic to pass from one side to the other. This siding is perched on top of this levee. This is unusual, but has the advantage of providing good views up and down the valley.

The first thing one notices, after having detrained, is the rubbish, piled up on the side of the levee, cascading down the slope. A river runs through this valley, the banks and bed of which are also littered with rubbish. The village itself has a large cement works, spewing out grey smoke, with the noise of its operations, combined with the roar of its trucks, persisting into the late hours of the night. So much for the notion of getting back to nature in the pristine countryside, where the air is pure, the water is clean and the loudest sounds are the twittering of birds. Environmental awareness has yet to penetrate into the marrow of the people in this country.

We were met at the siding by one of Cindy's uncles, the headman of her village. He has a car, so that made life easier, as it is a 20 minute drive to her house. The roads are narrow and rather muddy, except in two places. The first is in front of the cement factory, where we were on a smooth four-laned road for about 400 metres. The second was the opposite, as we proceeded, not only to cross, but also to travel along the stony bed of the all but dry river. What a contrast.

Later I would meet sundry other local dignitaries, most of whom are Cindy's relatives. As we wandered around I kept hearing; "This is my aunty." "That is my cousin." This is my uncle." "That is my cousin." Goodness! How many relatives does she have? It turns out that she has heaps, as her paternal grandparents had five children, while her maternal grandparents had eleven! So she has 14 aunts and uncles, not to mention all the cousins. China has a One Child Policy now, but Mao Zedong had encouraged parents to have as many children as possible.

At the house, I met Cindy's mother and grandmother. The father and son are currently away. There is also a cousin living in the house; anybody surprised? Apparently, he is more of a younger brother to Cindy. Chinese families do tend to be more closely knit than are ours in the West. It was good to meet them, and be welcomed by this family – a real honour.

Over the next two days we would wander over this village of maybe 200 people. It is more extensive than at first appears, with narrow laneways between houses providing interesting nooks and crannies. One feature was a series of holes in the ground, lined at the top with bricks and several metres deep. I had no idea what the purpose of these could be, until Cindy enlightened me. They are storage areas for sweet potatoes, which are a major crop in these parts. Indeed, we had seen rows of these laid out on a plot of land prior to being covered over; the next season's crop. I suppose these holes are a lot cheaper than refrigerators, though accessing them might be a little more difficult, as there are no ladders, and no sides either, as the holes have been scooped out. I guess these farmers are exceptionally agile.

Haystacks are a feature of farms the world over, as a means of providing fodder for animals over the cold winter months. In Europe, I guess the house-like shape has been immortalised by Monet, but in China there is a different shape. They drive large stakes into the ground, or simply use the trunks of trees. One advantage of the latter method is that it also serves to keep the trees warm. Around these the hay is stacked or wrapped. Here too, the hay is composed mainly of rice stubble, rather than wheat. One such tree had leaves piled up around it. Cindy told me that this was for the pigs.

Next to the river a basketball court has been newly built and of this the village leaders are very proud. It was here that we took posed photographs of and with these leaders. Next to the court is the swimming pool. Now before you have images of a 50 metre pool, with clear sparkling chlorinated water, divided into six lanes, let me disabuse you. This pool is divided into two sections, one for the men and one for the ladies, with each being no more than a room of about 10 square metres. The depth is about 30 cm. It is more for cooling down over the hot summer months than for Olympic training. It is fed by a channel of water, which then enters the river. This channel is parallel to the river and is also used for washing the laundry. There is a rectangular section set aside for just this purpose.

On Saturday afternoon we walked into town, some 3 km away. I was taken by a magnificent stone pedestrian bridge across this now dry river. It looked a little incongruous. Apparently it was built to enable school children access to their school, which is not far away. In the town, we visited a middle school, which Cindy had attended. While there I noticed that one teacher was actually teaching a class – and it is Saturday afternoon! Why aren't the students down at the local oval playing Aussie Rules? The teacher came out to invite me to teach his class. Well, yeh, OK, why not? So in I went and out he went; last seen heading into the sunset. Goodness. I taught an impromptu class for about 40 minutes, on the topic of "How to learn English".

Back in the town we spoke with more relatives, while on the road fireworks were lit, with deafening explosions and clouds of smoke. In this country, fireworks are let off in all temptations, dangers and afflictions it seems. Meanwhile, a large meal had been prepared for family and friends, at which some 200 people sat down. The tables were served by a platoon of waiters with military precision. And it was very nice, as indeed was the food that Cindy's mother prepared for us at their house.

On Sunday the time came to say goodbye. It had been a memorable two days, days which I for one really enjoyed. Thank you, Cindy, for your kind invitation. As we left I gave them some small Australian souvenirs. The uncle again drove us to the railway siding, and soon we were back in Tongren.

48. Guanzhou – Getting There – 15th April 2011

No, silly, not Guangzhou; it is Guanzhou. Goodness, there is no more relationship between these two words, than there is between, say Timbuktu and Sydney – or so it seems. The well-known Guangzhou is, of course, a major city in Guangdong Province, which used to be known to ignorant Englishmen, who just could not get Chinese pronunciation correct, as Canton. For the record, the first syllable is third tone, while the second is first tone. This Guanzhou, however, in Guizhou Province, has two first tones. Furthermore, the characters are different. So you see, obviously these two words are nothing like each other. Certainly the places are very different.

There is a man called Matthew (no, not the tax collector), who comes from a small town about 200 km away, and who is a graduate of our fair university here, though in his day it was known as Tongren Teachers' College. The more intelligent amongst my readers may be able to guess its name. Just make sure you get the tones right. He invited me to teach some of his students, and I agreed. So on Friday I caught the 11.40 am train to Xiu Shan, where I duly arrived at about 1.15 pm. I had brought my lunch with me, intending to eat it on the train, but during the journey Matthew sent me a text message saying that we would eat in Xiu Shan, or just outside the town. Ok, then I will keep my sandwich for another time. I can see how this town got its name, as it is dominated by a mountain, *Shan* meaning "mountain". At this point, the municipality of Chongqing runs north south and is located just on the other side of this mountain. Matthew was at the train station to greet me, together with a car, a driver and another teacher, who happened to be in Xiu Shan, and wanted a lift back to Guanzhou.

Off we went, first getting lost in Xiu Shan, eventually heading out of the town with the driver looking for a suitable place to stop and eat. It was 2.30 pm before he found what he was looking for, a small family-owned restaurant. The lady of the house proceeded to cook for us, while the rest of the family played cards. We ate goat, which was very nice, even though they kept calling it lamb. Maybe the Chinese word – *yangrou* – is the same. We drank rice wine, which can be rather rough, but this was not; smooth and eminently potable. It does pack a punch, though, so one small glass is enough.

We were back on the road by 3.30 pm, driving through some amazing country. Steadily we climbed. One can only admire the engineers who planned this road, as in few places was it particularly steep and yet we gained a lot of altitude, as we headed up into this highly mountainous region. And the people still farmed. The smallest piece of flat land is a rice paddy or a vegetable plot, while the hillsides are terraced when not too steep. Any larger area of reasonably flat ground is a village. In this country, people are everywhere. As we climbed we entered the clouds, where we would remain for the two days that I spent here. There was no sun, just cloud and mist, with plenty of mud as well. With all this clear mountain air, one would think my lungs would be having a field day, but far from it. In fact I ended up with a headache. Unfortunately both the men in the front seat are chain smokers, so that for five hours I was breathing their smoke: most unpleasant. At one point we stopped. Why? I wondered. "We piss now!" OK, I guess that is clear enough. Oh the advantages of being male!

It was after 7.00 pm by the time we arrived at Guanzhou. I dropped my backpack at the hotel I would be staying in, and we headed off for our evening meal. This time it would be a beef hotpot, washed down with beer. I met Catherine, also a graduate from Tongren Teachers' College, in fact a classmate of Matthew's and now a colleague. I also met her young daughter, Denise, and another teacher.

After the meal, we walked to the local Middle School; only about 400 metres up the street, of what is essentially a one street town, as there are few side streets. The students were still in their classrooms studying. How many Australian teenagers would be studying in their classrooms at 9.00 pm on a Friday night? Some students are boarders, as this is primarily a farming community. The school has some 4,000 students, which is very large by Australian standards. Have I said anything about the population in this country? Their campus features a football oval and basketball courts. There are some busts adorning the grounds – no, not of Mao nor of any of his cronies – but of Sir Isaac Newton, Marie Curie and Thomas Edison. Wow! Why these? I assume that Science is held in high esteem here. I entered two classrooms and spoke with the students. I am the first non-Chinese who has ever been here. I had a great welcome.

By 9.30 pm I was back at my two-star hotel, ready to settle down for the night. I got the staff to bring me some boiling water in a thermos flask for my coffee in the morning, as I am of the belief that it is not possible to begin the day without coffee. I had brought my own. Unfortunately I did not get them to turn on the hot water, so I had a cold shower. It has a Chinese toilet, incidentally, so one must be careful not to slip while showering, as you are straddling the hole. There was no soap, towel etc., but luckily I had brought my own supplies. There was toilet paper, sitting on top of the toilet, directly under the shower, so naturally the roll was soaking wet. Well, they nearly got it right.

One curious aspect was that I was not asked for my passport; that's right, I said NOT. Goodness, whatever will happen if Beijing ever finds out? This will do for one day. Wait till you hear about tomorrow.

49. *Guanzhou Teaching – 16ᵗʰ April 2011*

My bed was warm and comfortable. I had told my host that I did not want breakfast; but I did want my coffee. I was supposed to meet Matthew at 7.30 am, but the hotel was all locked up, so I just waited for some 15 minutes until someone opened up.

Our first stop was up a very muddy lane to a building which is still under construction, so it has absolutely nothing in it by way of furnishings or fittings. On the third floor is a room which Matthew is using as a classroom for his extra-curricular teaching. This room does have eight small desks and a large blackboard. I talked to the dozen children who were already here. Remember that this is 8.00 am on a Saturday.

Our next stop was to the largest primary school in Guanzhou, where Matthew is teaching. There are three altogether. The smallest has some 400 pupils; I repeat the smallest has this number. In Australia this would not be considered small. The next has about 1,000 pupils, while the one I visited has in excess of 2,000 pupils. For the next two hours I taught two classes. The second was quite small, but we had about 100 pupils in the first. I spoke about how to learn English. Next we sang "London bridge is falling down" with appropriate actions, and finally I showed them some pictures of Australia. At the back of the classroom a banner had been stretched, reading – and I quote: "Welcome American expert Macnnany to CT Childen's English", though to be fair, a little "r" ad been added later to the "children's". I can only assume that they are expecting someone else. As for being an expert, there is a definition for this, to wit, "one who knows more and more about less and less".

Having taught for a couple of hours, it was decided at 10.30 am that we would have an early lunch. Goodness; we seem to spend half our time eating. I will not be starving here. By 11.30 am we were on the street waiting for a hired minibus to turn up, which it finally did around 12.00 noon. Sixteen pupils, plus teachers, parents and a couple of tots would head off for the afternoon.

This mountain scenery is spectacular. It must look even more magnificent when the sun is shining. The rock is limestone, blue-grey in colour. The earth, however, is brown. These two often form alternating strips where rocks have been pulled aside so that plots can be prepared for planting. It is still too early for planting rice – maybe in another couple of weeks – so the plots either have bare brown earth, or water with the stubble from the previous season poking through. Other plots are green from various vegetables, or yellow and green from canola. I never cease to be impressed by the terracing. In this limestone country, many rocks have been shifted aside to clear the ground for the paddies. As we drove along, I saw one farmer struggling behind his water buffalo, turning the soil over, preparatory to planting. Later I saw one of these wooden ploughs, which looked to be homemade.

After about an hour, we came to the Wu Jiang. This is a major river, which I have seen before. You may remember that I went to Sinan on several occasions also to teach English to primary and secondary school students. Sinan is about 150 km upstream on this same river. The river eventually joins the Chang Jiang (Yangtze) at Fuling, just below Chongqing. Interestingly, we are also about 60 km downstream from Shiqian, where the early German MSC used to be, and this is how they got there; they took a boat to Shanghai, then another boat upstream to Chongqing, then up the Wu Jiang.

At this point a tributary joins the Wu Jiang. This is the Ma Yang He. *Jiang*, in case you have forgotten, means "river", while *he* means "stream". This is a gorge, so the road has been carved out of a very steep hillside. We drove only a few kilometres up this gorge, before stopping at a bridge. Here we alighted, and walked through a gate onto a path. What is curious here is that there is a water channel next to it. I assume it is taking water for human use.

The river at the start was a fair way below us, and we walked up a slight gradient. Nevertheless, the river gradually came up to meet us. After about a kilometre, we came to a weir, the source of the water in the channel. It is a really beautiful spot. Three of the boys went further up a track which did not look too safe to me, so I pointed this out to Matthew. When the boys returned they got a roasting. Needless to say, many photos were taken, especially by the official photographer we had, lugging his large video camera, a la TV mode.

Many packets of snacks were brought along, but as each packet or wrapping was finished, the children simply dropped them anywhere; on the path, in the river, in the channel. Not one of the teachers or parents rebuked them. I made sure I was the last to leave, and pointed out to Matthew what the children had done. I then proceeded to pick up whatever rubbish I could as we walked back. Matthew also assisted, though I am quite sure that he would have done nothing if I had not made an issue of it. I asked him if he would like me to say something to the children. So I did. I like the slogan, which we use in Australia, and probably elsewhere; "Take nothing but photographs; leave nothing but footprints". What effect did my harangue have? Only a little time later I saw these same children again dropping their rubbish on the ground. So I guess my impact was little or none.

Back at the gate, there is a limestone cave, so here we relaxed for a while. Next followed a one-to-one conversation with each pupil, only asking very simple questions, most of which were not understood anyway. The whole was recorded for posterity by our cameraman. There were a couple of older students, in middle school, and these were much better at English. This really completed the more formal part of our programme, at least as far as teaching English was concerned. At the gate, we had some group photos taken, and then it was time to head back.

In the bus I found myself sitting next to a boy of about 12. We communicated as best we could. At one point, admiring the scenery, I turned to him and remarked that China is such a beautiful country. To this he replied that Australia is a beautiful country. What a diplomat. Later he would show considerable leadership skills in taking his own photos of the group, and organizing everyone according to his own very definite ideas. This young man is going places.

There was still one further stop to make, as you will read in the next episode.

As we drove back towards Guanzhou, I found myself estimating the time we would arrive. Given the unpredictable nature of living in China, my estimate was bound to be wrong. It was. At one point on this winding mountain road, there is a dirt track which turns sharply back to the left. This we took. It was so sharp that even our small bus took two attempts to make the turn. Where are we going? In fact we did not go very far at all, before coming to a parking area. Here we got out and walked up some stairs. I was told we would see a hidden valley. I was not disappointed.

We came upon a lookout, with the Wu Jiang way below us and distant ranges disappearing into the mist. Not far away there is a cleft in the rock, leaving a tall limestone pillar pointing to the sky. No doubt it is caused by chemical erosion along a joint plane. There is a pavilion here, from where the view is even better. You climb up a flight of steps to the second level, then up a ladder to the third. It is well worth the climb. Many photos were taken. Across the river one could see terracing. Goodness, is someone farming here? It is a very steep drop to the river and no discernible means of access, so I have no idea how the people get there, but it underlines the fact that people and farming are everywhere.

As we got out of the bus, there was a slight drizzle, so one of the girls kindly gave me her umbrella, which I shared with Matthew, while she shared with one of her friends. Earlier, another girl had taken it upon herself to make sure I was adequately fed with the snacks they had brought. They were so kind and thoughtful.

We walked back to the car park, then along a little distance to a house and it was here that we would have our evening meal. The specialty is tofu, and I watched the owner making a large quantity in a vat. Certainly my fellow diners seem to relish the dish. I complimented the chef and she beamed. Maybe I have caught something of Aussie 1's penchant for laying it on thick – with a trowel. It does not seem to harm our diplomatic relations; quite the contrary.

By 7.30 pm we were back in Guanzhou, but the day's activities were not yet ended. Matthew's mother is currently sick in hospital. He asked me if I would like to visit her. Of course I would. I would be delighted. It is a private hospital, also in the main street. The cost is 300 Yuan a day, which is quite expensive. From what I saw, the facilities are somewhat basic. It does not even have heating, and in the winter it must get perishingly cold up at this altitude. After some time with her, I asked Matthew if he would like me to pray for her. No problems; so I donned my Prince of Wales hat and launched, even finishing with a blessing. By next day she was much better; so never underestimate the power of prayer.

Back at the hotel I tried to ensure that for this night I would get a hot shower and also some boiling water for coffee tomorrow morning. Yes, the man would be up in five minutes to fix the hot water. Great; I would not have long to wait. I waited. At least I got the thermos flask, though only half full; that is all I need anyway. At about 9.30 pm there was a knock on my door. A boy was there wanting to improve his English. Goodness. So we chatted for a while, though I really wanted to get to bed. After some time, I had to tell him how tired I was or he might still be there. He told me that his English name is "think"! I kid you not, and including the small "t". Still no hot water; I went downstairs and asked when it was coming on. The man immediately went to a switch and turned it on – presto – just like that. Why in the blazes could they not have done that earlier? – And last night too? No, I will not be handing out any service awards to this particular establishment.

Now for a good night's sleep. Oh yeah? At 1.00 am some bright spark decided to let off fireworks. Why? Lack of thoughtfulness for others is, unfortunately, an aspect of this society. After some time I managed to drift back to sleep. At 3.00 am the bright lights outside went on, while somebody stomped up the stairs outside my window. Couldn't they have tiptoed up, using a torch? Nah, too much to ask. At 6.00 am my alarm went off. I was to meet Matthew at 7.00 am, but he rang at 6.50 am, already downstairs and waiting. So down I went. At least the roller door had been unlocked; I only had to slide it up.

The next hour was for me simply magic. I hopped on the back of Matthew's bike, trying to rest my backpack at the same time, except that it kept slipping off. He asked me if I would like to wear a helmet. Well, yes, I would. This was OK except that the strap was loose. Eventually, after trial and error, I got the hang of it by using one hand to hold my backpack, with the thumb simultaneously tightening the chinstrap. As we were riding out of Guanzhou the local duck man came walking towards us with perhaps 50 closely packed ducks waddling in front of him. It was quite a sight.

The road here is excellent, obviously newly laid. They first build a low retaining wall at the edges of the road and top this with cement. The tarred road is then made flush with the top, giving the whole a very neat finish. Down the centre of the road is a single yellow line. The absence of potholes on this new road made for a most pleasant ride.

At this early morning hour, the mist was still hovering in the valleys, wispy filaments adding beauty to the darker land beneath, the white contrasting with the brown soil and green and yellow vegetation. In Sydney the clouds are above you – in the sky. But here the clouds are also beneath you and around you. It was magical. Matthew's phone kept ringing, but rather than being a distraction, it actually added to the atmosphere, as it has a lovely musical ring, and he had it turned down so low that one could hardly hear it.

Just after 8.00 am we arrived in Yanhe. My bus back to Tongren would not leave for another hour, so I walked up and down to stretch my legs. I did not want to sit down as I would be spending some hours more cramped in the bus. This was just as well, as there is nowhere to sit anyway. The bus station does have a cement floor, but outside was just mud. At about 9.10 am, we left. There was a girl sitting next to me but our communication was minimal. I did discover, however, that she disliked cigarette smoke as much as I do, so when people started to smoke, she asked them to stop. Some ignored her. For my lunch, incidentally, I ate the sandwich I had prepared for Friday lunch, and yes, it was still eminently edible.

The driver absolutely insisted on loud music throughout the entire trip; no let me correct that; noise. I do not think I could dignify what I heard by calling it music. What is wrong with silence? Do these people have such deep rooted insecurities that they cannot abide a moment's silence? This noise was often drowned out by an even louder and more raucous noise, as the driver drove on his horn. As you may gather, the trip was not the most pleasant. Be that as it may, I arrived back in Tongren safe and sound (?) at about 2.30 pm.

I have been asked – quite a few times, I might add – how much I was paid for this weekend. The answer is – not a lot. I experienced magical scenery. I met wonderful people. I had an opportunity to spread some goodwill. I hope I helped people learn more of the world's international language. If I was a tourist, I would be paying for everything. As it was, all I paid was 17 Yuan for my train ticket to Xiu Shan. True, I was not paid much money, but this is unimportant. I think I was more than adequately compensated. Besides, I do not need the money. Do You?

PHOTOGRAPHS

Kaili Stadium (chap. 1)

Catholic Cathedral, Guiyang (chap. 3)

Central Square, Kunming (chap. 8)

Dian Chi Lake, Kunming (chap. 9)

Dali University (chap. 11)

Catholic Church, Dali (chap. 11

Yu Long Xue Shan (chap. 13)

On Ba Ma Xue Shan (chap 14)

Tiger Leaping Gorge – the rock (chap 15)

Side canyon into Tiger Leaping Gorge (chap. 16)

Goats on Tiger Leaping Gorge (chap. 16)

A Dali weaver (chap. 18)

Provincial museum, Henan – Michael & Mary (chap. 26)

Iron pagoda, Kaifeng (chap. 27)

Longmen Grottoes (chap. 28)

Pagoda Forest, Shaolin Temple (chap. 29)

Cultural Centre, Zhengzhou (chap. 30)

A lady got left behind (chap. 31)

A beautiful lake, Bijie (chap. 32)

F1 at the barn (chap. 33)

Erica and her horses (chap. 35)

Bijie countryside (chap. 34)

Old city wall, Xian (chap. 37)

Drum Tower, Xian (chap. 38)

Terracotta warriors, Xian (chap. 39)

Shadow puppets, Xian (chap. 40)

Bell Tower, Xian (chap. 41)

Chengdu Opera (chap. 42)

Qinling Range (chap. 43)

Shu Zheng Lake, Jiuzhaigou, Sichuan (chap. 44)

Luodai Ancient Town (chap. 45)

Fenghuang (chap 46)

Guanzhou countryside (chap 48)

Ma Yang He (chap. 49)

Wu Jiang Gorge (chap. 50)

Sinan (chap. 51)

Hong Kong (chap. 52)

Lamma Island, Hong Kong (chap. 53)

Meitan (chap 54)

In the classroom (chap. 55)

Sea of tea (chap. 56)

Amazing balance (chap. 57)

99 bends (chap. 58)

Over the Abyss (chap. 59)

101 Building, Taipei, Taiwan (chap. 60)

Very Pretty (chap. 61)

Footpath? (chap. 62)

Shuili Valley (chap. 63)

Sunrise from Cistercian Monastery (chap. 64)

Sun Moon Lake (chap. 65)

Sunrise, Alishan (chap. 67)

Banyan tree covering house (chap. 68)

Sunset, Kenting beach (chap. 69)

Hot springs, Lyudao (chap. 70)

Taroko Gorge (chap 71)

Defensive wall, Diao Yu Cheng (chap. 76)

Damaged house (chap. 77)

Wang Xing's village (chap. 78)

Lieshimu – martyrs' tombs – Bijie city (chap. 79)

Eastern side of the valley (chap. 80)

Village in the valley (chap. 81)

Room for one more? (chap 82)

The new washing machine (chap. 83)

Back of C house (chap. 84)

Tending the cattle (chap. 85)

Muddy roads (chap. 86)

Family room (chap. 87)

Terraced hillsides (chap. 88)

Farmhouse in the mist (chap. 89)

Chengdu Old Town (chap. 91)

Li Bing's water divider (chap. 92)

Bride and friends (chap. 93)

a good place to swim (chap. 94)

Hagia Sophia (chap 97)

Reflections (chap. 97)

Plant sculptures, Taiyang Dao (chap. 98)

Zuangong Hotel, Yaabuli (chap. 99)

In the mall (chap. 100)

Yamur River and Russia in background (chap. 101)

Russian Restaurant Zhong Yang Da Jie, Harbin (chap. 102)

Main street, Yanji (chap. 103)

Crowds queuing at Chang Bai Shan (chap. 104)

Heaven Lake, Chang Bai Shan (chap. 104)

Hot springs, Chang Bai Shan (chap. 105)

End of the Great Wall, Tiger Mountain, Dandong (chap. 106)

Xinhai Beach, Dalian (chap. 107)

German built church, Qingdao (chap. 108)

Beach 6, Qingdao (chap. 109)

St. Michael's Catholic Cathedral, Qingdao (chap. 110)

Summer Work, July 2011

51.   Third Visit to Sinan – 8th – 10th July 2011

On two previous occasions I have gone to Sinan, a country town in Guizhou Province, to teach English. After finishing classes in Tongren I headed off for a third visit on Friday, July 8th. It was close to 7.00 pm by the time I arrived, after a five hour bus trip. Dick was waiting anxiously for me. We walked about 400 metres to a riverside restaurant where his fiancée, Amy, was waiting, together with three student helpers, Jenny and Susan from Zunyi and Lucy from Tongren. They are all at Sinan Teachers' College. Jenny's folk are greengrocers, as was my father, while Susan's folk are rice farmers; Lucy's family has a small restaurant.

Now we had been to this restaurant on a previous occasion, when we had eaten duck. For this meal, however, we chose chicken. Now the chooks were outside in a cage, so first you select your chook. The chosen one is taken out, weighed and then ... well, you know what. The lucky chook became entangled in the rope of the scales, and was getting a little stressed as the man was trying to extricate it, none too delicately I might add. I said a prayer for the chook, to thank it and God for what we were about to receive. Dick noticed, so I explained. No food is forbidden to us, but we have the responsibility to treat each animal with due reverence, and thank God for Sheir gifts.

After the meal, it was surprisingly difficult to get a taxi in this small town, as taxi after taxi did not want to take us to my hotel. We eventually shared a taxi with another teacher – who also paid. The next morning we started teaching a lot later than anticipated, due to the scarcity of pupils. Apparently, my superstar status has not yet reached this far, in spite of a banner stretched outside the school, announcing my immanent arrival. Can you believe it? You can? OK, but did you have to say this quite so vigorously? I went for a walk along the river bank while waiting. The steps leading to the top of the levee bank reek of urine, with faeces also lying around. Not good.

I taught three classes from 9.30 to 11.30 am. Then we broke for lunch, including beer, which I do not usually drink in the middle of the day. We retired for a siesta, though I do not usually sleep in the middle of the day either; nor did I this time.

At 4.00 pm, we walked into the town where we met the girls loaded with parcels. These we carried down to the river, which we walked along for about a kilometre, stopping on top of a covered aqueduct. It is a pretty spot, between the fast flowing Wu River looking clean and fresh, and the limestone hillside, the grey-white rock interlaced with black organic deposits. Vegetables were washed in the river, pork, seaweed, sausages, green vegetables and mushrooms were threaded onto skewers, while Dick got the fire going. They have a portable barbecue which folds out, with a detachable grate on top. It is easy for storage and for carrying. The fuel was charcoal, with sticks, paper and paraffin as the starter. The food was skewered then roasted on the grill, basted with sauce, made from soy, chillies, chopped vegies and oil. Later, steamed bread was toasted on the embers – very nice, as was the whole meal.

It was truly delightful, eating in this lovely spot, as the sun set and fishermen powered their crafts up and down the river. Not all these fishermen, however, are good, as many use dynamite and poison to catch their fish, thus polluting the river and killing many other kinds of life. Not good.

By 8.00 pm, just as it was getting dark we were back in town. I would not want to be on that track in the dark, as it would be somewhat perilous. Back at the hotel, I found that the zealous cleaning staff had thrown out my toothpaste, my toothbrush and my comb which I had been using for thirty years – the comb, that is, not the toothpaste or toothbrush! I am glad we clarified that. What a pity.

On Sunday I headed back to Tongren, so I really did not do much work, and had a wonderful time doing it. I wanted to get back, as I was going to be heading off again on Tuesday. This you will hear about in the next episode.

52.   To Hong Kong – 12th – 13th July 2011

My visa was due to expire on July 20th; hence, it became necessary to renew it. No problems: all you have to do is wander down to the nearest police station, right? Wrong-very wrong. You return to wherever you got it before, with the government thinking this would be back to one's country of origin. It just so happened, however, that I got mine in Hong Kong, so this would be a huge saving, both in time and money, though I would of necessity have to remain in HK for some time, as without your passport you cannot travel. First stop would be to Shenzhen.

On Tuesday 12th I boarded a train for this city. I could not get a sleeper, so had perforce to settle for sitting up. It was just so crowded. Naturally, when I finally squirmed my way through to my seat, it was already occupied, but the occupant graciously vacated it for me. There were ten seats in my compartment, but there were sixteen people. Children were sitting on small plastic stack seats, while some adults stood. Even so, train crew would still be constantly pushing their trolleys back and forth. Why they do it so much I do not know. The man beside me was smoking, so I asked him not to. This was no problem for him, as he simply got up to smoke at the end of the carriage. It is illegal there too, but nobody is going to enforce this. As from May 1st this year, smoking in public places became illegal, but in effect there will be no change, as it will not be enforced. It is more important to be seen to be doing the right thing. That is China.

At the first opportunity, some two hours into our journey, I asked a passing guard if I could upgrade to a sleeper. He said he would find out, so off he went, to return a little later with a welcome affirmative answer. Not only did he lead me through the train, but he even carried my bag. What I noticed, much to my surprise, was that many of the carriages were virtually empty, yet they told me there were no vacancies. Admittedly, many more people got on as we travelled further. I was asked to wait in the dining car for some time, as the guards would be having their lunch till 1.30 pm. I did not mind this one little bit, as I had a table to myself to write on, and I had some blessed space. Here I paid the extra 170 Yuan. I landed in a compartment with three other people, with a shirtless man stretched out on what was to be my bed. He got up when I arrived, but I noticed that the bedding was wet with his sweat. Oh the joys of travel.

My evening meal consisted of instant noodles, which had been given to me before I boarded the train and which turned out to be very spicy indeed – thanks Erica – so I washed it down with a 350 ml can of warm, flat beer, which cost me 5 Yuan. That night I slept surprisingly well. Thank God I could stretch out on a bunk and not have to sit up all night. On the opposite bunk there were two people sleeping together; a boy of about 7 and presumably his elder teenage brother. They looked beautiful. I am reading a William Faulkner novel, "Light in August". He really likes joining words together e.g. "womansinksmell", though I have no idea what this gains. The next morning, for some reason, there was no hot water on the train, so I drank my coffee cold. Don't expect five star restaurants on trains.

In Shenzhen I was to be met at the station, but no-one was there; he turned up eventually, but I waited close to two hours. It was good to meet some friends in this city; and some people whom I have not met before. I was taken to two apartments. The first has two rooms, the larger about 10 square metres, with the other one only about a metre across, with toilet/shower down one end and the kitchen at the other. One person lives here. The second apartment has two major rooms, each about ten square metres. The first has a bed and a double bunk; two people sleep here. The second room has a double bed where a husband and wife sleep, plus their baby. She is expecting another baby soon. The other rooms are the shower/toilet and kitchen.

Thus you have five people crammed into such a tiny space. Needless to say, there is no room for an elaborate wardrobe. Meanwhile the sister of these two brothers, Erica no less, is renting an apartment in Tongren, sharing it with her friend – the size? – a miserly 4 square metres, with one bed and a small desk; there is no wardrobe for clothes, and no water. The washroom is elsewhere in the building.

I slept in a much roomier hotel room. I was under the impression that the border with Hong Kong was only 700 metres away; no, the bus to the border is only 700 metres away, then you get on the bus for a journey across town of more than an hour. I arrived at the border at 10.30 am, to find crowds of people wanting to cross. It would take two hours to do so. The sheer number of people in this country has made travel uncomfortable.

I could not find where to buy a bus ticket for Kowloon so opted for Mong Kok instead, as it is very close to where I wanted to go. When I got off the bus, I hailed a taxi, but even though we did not have far to go, he did not know where, so we did a tour. It cost 60 HK$. It was raining too: this is the monsoon season. Finally I made it to the AITECE office, where I would be staying. AITECE is an organisation under whose umbrella teachers are recruited for China. It was not late in the day, but I just had enough time to get to the visa office in the city, but you will just have to wait till the next episode to find out what happened then.

53.   Is 8 a Lucky Number? – 7th – 14th July 2011

The Beijing Olympics began at 8.00 pm on the 8th day of the 8th month of the year 2008. The Chinese believe that 4 *(si)* is an unlucky number because of similarities with the word for death *(si)*, while 8 *(ba)* is considered to be lucky since it sounds like the word for luck *(fa)*, though all this is complicated by the different pronunciations and words in different dialects, not to mention the different tones.

After completing the requisite forms, I had just enough time to get to the visa office in Hong Kong to lodge my application before closing time at 5.00 pm; I took my No. – 401 – and waited. They were up to No. 386. 387 came up, then 389 etc., right up to 400. Good. I am next. 402, 403, 404 came up. Goodness, what happened to 401? I went up to the counter to ask that very question, only to be told in no uncertain terms to go back to the end of the line and get another number. The lady at this particular counter was not happy. She was working at window No. 8.

Well I really did not have much choice, so got another number and waited. There were eight windows operating, so I was praying that I would not get No. 8. The probability was on my side; I have 7 chances out of 8. I got window 8. Oh dear. She looked at me, looked at my papers, and said; "Your application is rejected. You do not have the university registration number and you do not have a health certificate." I have a feeling she was going to reject my application no matter what I had. Never before had we needed the university number, and the health check had always been done afterwards. But what can you do? I hate bureaucracy.

I just had to rack up to a hospital in HK and get the health check done. All was well here. And we had to contact the university, asking them to fax their number, which they did. The weekend intervened, so on Monday I returned to the fray, now armed with the required documents. I picked up a number and waited. Again, there were 8 windows operating. I was praying I would not get window 8 yet again. After all, the chances of getting 8 twice in a row are 1 in 64, slim odds indeed. I got window number 8! The lady took my papers, went through them and said; "You must photocopy your health check." Goodness; what next? "Where do I do that?" "Over there." Eventually I did find the photocopier and photocopied the original. Once more I put all my documents together and gave them to the lady at counter 8. "Come back on Thursday."

On Thursday I returned, paid the cashier the required 150 HK$. I picked up my new visa, and then went back to my favourite lady in HK, at window 8. I wanted a copy of my health certificate so that I could take this to Chongqing. No luck. She told me that she only takes the copy, not the original. So now I have neither the original nor a copy. I know: I should have made two copies. So now, I just may have to undergo yet another health check in Chongqing. Since I have been in China, I have had more health checks than for the whole of the rest of my life, even though I am perfectly healthy. In fact I have never missed a single class through illness.

I had a whole week in Hong Kong. On Sunday I walked to a nearby church, St. Theresa's, for Mass. It is about a 20 minute walk. Back at the AITECE office, I prepared a cut lunch and set off for one of the other islands, Lamma Dao. I boarded the 113 bus from across the road, getting off at the Aberdeen fish markets on HK Island. In amongst hundreds of fishing vessels there is actually a ferry. I took this, using my octopus card to pay, to Lamma Island, getting off at Mo Tat Wan, where I had lunch.

I wanted to walk across the island, but this only takes an hour and a half, so I took my time, exploring as I went. I stopped at a small beach near Tung-O for a swim. It has been wet and cloudy every day, but this was the only day when we had no rain and in fact had a little bit of sunshine. The swim was lovely. I brought my togs but no towel; in this heat, you are a lather of perspiration anyway, so that a towel is somewhat superfluous.

From here I took a side track to walk to the top of the island for a commanding view over the island and across the sea to Hong Kong Island. And – oh bliss, oh joy – it was not crowded. You could actually walk for some distance and not see anybody. What a change from China, where there are always hordes of people at any public site. Most of the people I did come across were westerners, and I chatted with most of them, who were mainly on holidays; one Canadian man was working in HK.

By 4.00 pm I had reached Sok Kwu Wan, a little earlier than I had hoped, so I wandered around for a while, before sitting down, taking in the scenery and resting. At 5.00 I chose the Mandarin restaurant, one of a string fronting the shore, for a seafood dinner. They had a set menu, curiously consisting of one abalone, three prawns, four baby octopuses, some rice and vegies. They offered a cup of tea for free, which I said I would gladly swap for a beer. They agreed. The whole cost 100 HK$, which I think is eminently reasonable.

After the meal, I caught a ferry back to HK harbour, which took about 40 minutes. We were motoring along, but it was so pleasant watching the HK shoreline glide past, with its tall buildings and interesting architecture. Even though we were travelling quite fast, we were overtaken by a couple of catamarans which made us look as if we were standing still. There were many other boats on Hong Kong harbour, which truly is very busy indeed. It was beautiful watching the setting sun reflect off the water. There is no payment on this ferry until you get off, when you swipe your card on the machine at the exit point.

So all in all I had a really great day, maybe because I saw no number eights all day.

54.   Hong Kong to Meitan, Guizhou Province – 15ᵗʰ July 2011

On Thursday morning I was able to pick up my new visa. It is actually a rather strange document. It is dated 19th July, which is OK, as my old one expired on 20th July. I am allowed one only entry into China – not multiple entries – and this must be before October 19th. Well that is OK too. But the strange bit is that the number of days I am allowed to stay is 000. Work that one out. The next step is for the university to convert this into a residence permit. Have I ever mentioned how much I hate bureaucracy?

I wanted to fly to Guiyang from HK, but it appears I could not do that, though I have done it before. This meant flying from Shenzhen. The flight was due to leave at 7.20 pm, so I left the AITECE office at 2.00 pm, to allow me plenty of time. Remember that it took two hours to cross the border coming into HK. The first part involved getting a taxi to Kowloon Station, from where one can get a bus. The taxi driver had some difficulty. He dropped me off somewhere down in the bowels of the earth, telling me to go through a set of doors. I did and found myself in a concrete stair well. Perforce I had to follow it up and up and up, eventually coming out at street level. Now what? The station entrance was only about 100 metres away – if you knew where to go. After that it was plain sailing.

Back in China I was able to turn on my mobile phone again; it does not work in HK. At the airport in Guiyang, lovely Echo came to meet me. I would stay with her family for the next two nights. It was good to spend time with them, including her husband and 4 year old son. On Friday night we went to a seafood restaurant. The highlight of the night was a live prawn flopping onto the table in front of me. I picked it up and popped it into the boiling water. That night, I awoke in a cold sweat, with an upset stomach, necessitating a quick trip to the bathroom. Could this be "The Revenge of the Prawn"? Guiyang is a long way from the sea, so maybe the food was not all that fresh.

Next morning, I left with Echo, who went off to work while I caught the 222 bus to the bus station, which is situated a long way out of town. It is also huge. The ticket office has a bank of about thirty windows. Goodness, which one do I use? I went to the information desk to ask which window I use to buy a ticket for Meitan. It saves a lot of hassles. "*Hao shi jiu*", or No. 19, the lady said, so no problems. I was told the bus trip was another 6 hours, but it turned out to be less, more like 4 1/2 hours, so that was good. One of my students, Catherine, comes from this town, so she came to the bus station to welcome me, as did David, who would be my host.

Meitan is quite a small place built on the banks of the Mei Jiang. I would be guessing, but it looks to be a town of around 100,000 or so. I was looking at the farms as we travelled, wondering what the produce is, and what fuels the economy. Rice and corn appear to be the principal crops. Later I was to find that many grapes are also grown, as is tea.

There is a hill overlooking the river, which we climbed one afternoon; something like 400 steps lead to the top. They love building steps. On top there is huge teapot, and this is the town's claim to fame; it is the world's largest teapot; it looks to be about 40 metres high. This whole hill is quite a nice park, but you need to buy a ticket to enter. I went up one afternoon with David and three absolutely delightful 12 year olds – two girls and one boy – who are in my grade 6 class. Our ticket also entitled us to a boat ride, so a park attendant took us up and down the river in a small boat. I loved it. These moments are so special.

Meitan also has a pleasant open square, some attractive bridges and even a swimming spot. Quite a few people were in the water on the hot afternoon that we went there, but nobody was swimming, as so few people can. The water looked inviting, but I was not told (no surprise here) where we were going, so I had not brought my swimmers.

There is also a Catholic church here ... or was. It was taken over by Mao. There is a plaque outside dedicated to the "Ninth Chinese Red Corps". Was there any compensation? Did the Communists build another church? What happened to the Catholics? All these questions never occurred to my genial host, who happens to be a member of the CP, as is his father, and as was his grandfather before him. You can say nothing wrong about the CP. I might add that his attitude underwent a slight metamorphosis over the next couple of years.

My hotel is quite comfortable, and at 100 Yuan a night, it is quite affordable. My room has two beds, one hard and one soft, so take your pick. I chose the hard. It has air conditioning, which is a godsend in this hot weather and a computer. The latter, however, appears to have a virus. Whenever I open it, I get a string of "ps". It is hard to stop; as fast as I delete, I get more pppppppppppppppppppppppp...Great. Then, when I start typing, there are no "ps" at all! To complicate matters, the only way I can write is in an e-mail, which I can then send to myself. Later, back in Tongren on my own computer, I would make all the necessary corrections, like adding all the "ps".

Altogether I am teaching about 120 students from grade 3 to grade 8, but these are spread over three grades; grade 3, 4, 5 together, grade 6 on their own and grade 7, 8 together. This is not my level, so am struggling a bit. How on earth did I get myself roped into this? I am not a primary school teacher. Next episode I will give you an idea of what I decided to do with them.

55.　First Week in Meitan – 18th – 22nd July 2011

My class plan has been fairly simple. In each class I attempt five things; 1) pronunciation; 2) tell a story; 3) vocabulary; 4) say something about Australia, especially through pictures; 5) a song. Games are used on and off. The songs include; "Old MacDonald", "London Bridge", "Peace is flowing like a river", "Song of Joy", "It's a Small World" and "I'm a little teapot". I thought the latter particularly appropriate given the big teapot (the biggest teapot in the world) sitting on top of a hill overlooking the town. Nobody has ever referred to it simply as "The Big Teapot"; it has always been called "The Big Teapot, the Biggest in the World". So I guess this is rather important to them. We have a similar tendency in Australia, with "The Big Sheep" at Goulbourn NSW, "The Big Banana" at Coff's Harbour NSW, "The Big Pineapple" at Caloundra Qld, and "The Big Lobster" at Robe SA. Does anybody know of any others?

My hosts have been too kind, feeding me like I have not eaten before. I am eating too much and exercising too little. I need to address this. Each afternoon I have been going out with one or more of the students.

On Monday, I went with two grade 6 girls, Tina and Belinda, who are bosom pals, and Joe, each of whom is the only child in their respective families. We went by car to a resort, not far out of town.

There is an enclosed pool for swimming and a river close by. The pool seems to have been taken straight out of the river, as it is murky, with no visibility. You have no idea how deep the pool is, though I think it is very shallow. You would not want to dive into it.

It was most pleasant sitting on a second storey verandah, sipping drinks and eating grapes. Around 6.30 pm, we had a meal, as there is a restaurant downstairs, al fresco style, set up in the courtyard. No doubt they could move inside during inclement weather. Though every day here has been hot, it does get cold in winter, and it snows. The altitude, so I found out, is about 800 m, a little lower than I had thought.

At the meal, I was sitting with some of the local big wigs, all CP members and government officials. We drank *bai jiu*, or white wine, this lot made from corn. Be careful, as it could blow your head off. This did not stop the chief big wig from scoffing it down; "*Ganbei*" he would say – "bottoms up" – and down it would go. The best I could do, without collapsing in a fit of coughing, was to sip it, like a liqueur, which it really is. The serious part of the conversation concerned "*guanxi*". You do not get anywhere in this country without contacts. Surprisingly, these men were against it. I agreed with them saying it leads to mediocre leaders. David was praised for his initiative in getting me to come and teach his pupils.

On Tuesday I went with three other students, to climb the Big Teapot Hill (the biggest teapot in the world, don't you know?)

Wednesday was rather odd. We went with a boy to visit his family, but they knew nothing about it. We found Dad with his shirt off working in a yard. We were then ushered into the house of his auntie where we drank water and ate watermelon. And that was that. David asked him if he had any other plans. No he had not. So we wandered off to find a restaurant for dinner.

On Thursday we went with a girl. All of these come from one child families. Her grandfather was a teacher, and is still living in an apartment attached to the local primary school. This school has some 2,000 pupils, so a little larger than most of our Australian counterparts. In fact, I would venture to guess that it is larger than any of our primary schools in Australia. Some of our towns are not this big. We had a meal here, very nice, but a little spicy. The girl is very bright, but as yet lacks social skills, being very abrupt. Close to this school is a large square, rising in concrete tiers up a hill. Next to this is the Catholic church which the CP appears to have purloined, not the first time they have done this.

On Friday afternoon, after classes, Lily (one of the teachers) and I went to yet another home for evening meal. This girl is in grade 7, and with her were her two best friends, also grade 7 girls. She stands out by the fact that she is quite tall and has cut her hair very short – she looks like a boy. I asked her why she did this, and she said that it was only because it was so hot, and short hair is cooler. I had been wondering if there was more to it, and she really wished that she was a boy. She is quite bright, too, with their kitchen wall plastered with about 20 awards she has received for academic excellence.

Her apartment is not far from my hotel, in an older part of town which is undergoing restoration, so that her apartment is quite new, is spacious and features a split level. It was designed by the father, who is an architect, and he told me he was inspired by Western styles. He likes the split level design partly because it makes the bedrooms quieter. The mother is a housewife, and they have a 20 year old son, who was away at the time of our visit. They have a large TV, which can also be used for karaoke. The building backs onto a steep hill, which is being farmed, so there was corn and other vegetables right outside the kitchen window. The meal was really nice, except for the spices. One dish had me in some trouble, almost ready to explode. I hope nobody noticed.

That lands us, at the end of week one. I wonder what will happen next. One never knows.

56.   Of Swims and Tea – 24th – 30th July 2011

Classes for this fortnight go from Monday to Friday, with Saturday and Sunday off. This surprised me a bit, as I had expected to be teaching over the weekend as well. So what would we be doing? David, my host, seems to think that he must organise me 24 hours a day, 7 days a week. I have assured him that I am quite capable of entertaining myself.

On Friday night, after our meal with that student I mentioned in the previous episode, I went for a swim, with Lily and her husband, who is a police officer. The three of us went in his van to a spot about 15 minutes' away, over a new expressway which is being constructed, to a small river. There is a weir here where dozens of people were gathered to swim – well, to splash around anyway. Nor was our species the only one. A family of ducks was in the water, searching the bottom for food. Nearby was a buffalo, with only his head above water. I think he was happy.

We walked along a raised concrete path beside a corn field to a spot maybe 200 metres upstream. Lily does not swim, but her husband does – sort of. He does a kind of dog paddle and a kind of freestyle. I swam downstream for some distance then back again, close to a cliff face where the water is deeper. The rock type here is limestone, so the cliff face has caves in it. Elsewhere in this vicinity the rock is shale. I thoroughly enjoyed myself, as the water was delightful, and warm. I would not want to swim here in winter, however, in the snow.

At this time, Shanghai is hosting swimming championships. The coverage on TV concentrates on the Chinese athletes, which is no surprise. One night I watched the Chinese water polo team compete against Greece – and they lost. It is very unusual for the Chinese media to report on any event where China loses. At this point I would like to add that China is not a sporting nation. Australians love sport for sport's sake. You cannot say the same about this country. You will find outstanding Chinese athletes, including swimmers, but as I see it, people are not competing for the love of the sport. Rather they do so for the love of the Motherland. It is all about making China Great. It is all about winning. Winning, not swimming.

My second swim was in the same river, but further upstream, where the river has been dammed by another weir. Again I enjoyed swimming for some distance up river, the only one doing this. Later I was told that swimming is not allowed so far upstream, as the water is used for drinking Oh dear! But it was so good.

I was to have five swims here altogether at four different spots. I loved it. One place was curious, in that you needed to cross a small creek in order to reach it. A local entrepreneur has attached a raft to a line in order to pull people across, charging 1 Yuan per head. It is only few metres wide; you could wade across. He is making a killing. Further along, another enterprising person has wrapped a bit of canvass around some poles; hey presto, you have a changing room, and another 1 Yuan per head, please. This is the real reason China's economy is booming.

The remaining two swims were in the Mei Jiang, not far from my hotel. Again I was told to swim no more than 200 metres upstream. No problem; as this gave me plenty of room to swim up and down, without interference from other people who were congregated around yet another weir. There is a toilet here which is absolutely revolting, and a changing room, which is expensive. I simply wrapped a towel around myself, a practice I perfected many years ago on Coogee Beach – to change, that is, not to go to the toilet! I am glad we cleared that up.

On Saturday morning, David, another teacher, and I climbed a local mountain overlooking the town. It was an easy 50 minute walk up a gently inclined road, providing a good view, with the whole town spread out below. Unfortunately it was too hazy (polluted) to see clearly. Over the slopes of this mountain are tea plantations, with women working as we watched. They were picking the leaves with one hand, while holding an umbrella with the other, as a protection against the sun. I do not know why they did not wear bigger hats. I noticed yellow fly paper amongst the bushes, set to catch insects which would otherwise eat the leaves. Fine- except that they catch any insect, including those which eat the insects which eat the leaves.

As you may have gathered, this district is noted for its tea. One really worthwhile excursion is to a place not all that far away called "Hai Cha", or "Sea of Tea", which is a rather apt description, as you come to a region of rolling hills, covered in rows of tea bushes. It looks very attractive. Some people were working while we were there, three women tending the bushes, while a man was watering. Another woman, however, had found a hollow to curl up in and sleep. Well it was a hot day. We were able to walk down the rows of tea bushes, though there is not much space; not only is it single file, but you are still brushing the bushes on either side. Later I would be given samples of the local tea.

57.   Meitan Culture – July 2011

While here, I saw some examples of local culture. Opposite my hotel, on the other side of the river, there is a small park. Each evening there was some version of local opera. Typically, a couple of men would dance around each other, while one chanted poetry in a high pitched voice, to the accompaniment of an orchestra. One man plucked a small stringed instrument; another tattooed a drum; a third banged a stick against a cymbal; while a fourth clashed together those discordant cymbals, which so grate against Western ears. Nor am I alone in disliking these sounds, as young people here do not like them either. All the people involved looked to be over 70 years old. It was quite some time before they stopped, the chanter by this time being exhausted, but he never missed a beat. He had committed to memory a truly massive body of material.

Up town, in the main square, I saw a similar performance, with about ten men and women dancing around in a circle while brandishing tessellated sticks, about 50 cm long. One man was particularly energetic in waving his stick around his body: over his head, between his legs, all the while twirling around. Meanwhile a man with a large brush was writing characters on the pavement, not that he wanted to convey some message, but simply to demonstrate his artistic talents, as calligraphy is most definitely an art form. Elsewhere in this square, as indeed in other squares around this city and all over China, people were line dancing. It has become quite a craze, especially amongst the women.

The pièce de résistance of this town's cultural attractions was performed by one of the minority peoples. Seven women and three men, dressed in their traditional costumes, were standing on bamboo poles, balancing themselves with hand held poles. One woman was the leader, blowing a whistle to co-ordinate their performance. Together they manoeuvred themselves into several patterns, every so often taking a breather by sitting down on their poles. Can you imagine just how difficult this is? Bamboo is round. I would have thought it to be virtually impossible to stand on a round pole in water, as it would immediately twist as soon as you stepped on it, unless you distributed your weight at all times precisely dead centre. But they did it. I for one am absolutely amazed. One can only wonder at the number of hours spent practising, and the number of times they took a spill, before perfecting their skills.

I watched their performance with David and some of the students late one day. Afterwards we once again climbed the Big Teapot (The Biggest in the World!). The price of the admission ticket included a boat trip on the river. This was great. On our first visit here, we had taken up this option, boarding a small craft with an outboard motor, under the control of one of the park attendants. We had a choice of fast boat or slow. I opted for the slow; I was in no hurry and really wanted to soak up the experience. It was so pleasant coasting down river, then up river. On this second occasion, however, there was no boat ride. Why not? Well the minority people were still performing on their bamboo poles. Can you imagine the havoc that would be cause by the wash of a passing boat? The water needs to be very calm indeed.

There are a number of signs on this hill. One warns "caution slippery, you slow". Well that is clear enough, even if the English was not written by one of my students (naturally). But you might like to ponder this next message, concerning the Big Teapot:

Mandarin House.

Succeed, women look into the phoenix, all parents of the expectations of the Chinese nation.

Mottled shade, legends have a kind face, hand-held Huijian, riding a lion, the body Meitan golden Buddha came under the Flaming Mountain, No. Manjusri, the wisdom sword cut off his troubles to opposing deterrent Roar Magic resentment, and guide people to the proper use of wisdom, common sense, knowledge for knowledge results, critical thinking, analysis of pathogen, and even know the meaning of life and value, breaking the stupid dark shelter, get rid of the shackles of fame, to life on track, Zhiwu good deeds. Over the years, Meitan children with the hope people have a wisdom and academic success of a desire visit Manjusri habits.

"Heaven pot" days, pot of tea in the gallery to create the same time, to respect the customs of Meitan people over the years, specially brought in from the Emeishan a Manjusri statue. Manjusri in the opening to the day, has gone through half a month rainy Meitan, blue skies, a flash of light in the open, rays shine, lasting tens of minutes to allow the presence of people marvel at, such as the gods come. Since then, the worship of the people are doing.

Any clues? I might add that this is not the only inscription on this hill that defies my understanding. Though the words might be English, the language certainly is not. If you are going to put up a sign in Chinese, then go to the trouble of having someone translate it into Chinglish, why not make the further effort of turning it into good English? Otherwise it is virtually useless. I suspect that as far as Meitan is concerned, there was simply nobody around who could do it.

This district is obviously doing very well financially, especially from their tea. Just outside of Meitan there is a brand new village dedicated to tea. It boasts clean new buildings in a pleasant architectural style. There is a hotel built besides a landscaped area, with paths, shrubs and a waterway. It is all very attractive. With all this background, it not surprising that I was presented with a range of tea related gifts when the time came for me to leave. These included various kinds of tea, drinking vessels and a book on the district. I was also showered with many other gifts from the children. Many of these they had made themselves, from cards to origami cranes. I even got a pair of sandals made from rice husks, the traditional peasants' footwear.

These of course must remain in China, as you cannot bring plant products into Australia. It was very touching.

After two weeks here, it was time to leave. I had not exactly been looking forward to this venture, as I do not consider myself to be a primary school teacher, but as it turned out I enjoyed the experience enormously, though it is just as well I had people to translate for me.

Now I have been asked to return during the winter break, but I do not think I will, as I consider it important to return home each year. If you do not, you can lose touch with your roots. Besides, I really would like to meet some of my cousins whom I have not seen for nearly 50 years, not since my mother and I travelled to Brisbane at the end of 1961.

So it is goodbye to Meitan – perhaps till next time, who knows?

Summer Holidays 2011

58. Tian Men Shan, Hunan Province, Part 1 – 10th – 11th August 2011

Having spent much of this summer teaching, I wanted to go somewhere just for a holiday before going off to my new abode in Chongqing. There was one place I had been wanting to visit for some time, near the city of Zhangjiajie, which used to be called Dayong, in northern Hunan Province, only 6 ½ hours by train from Tongren. Not far from the city are two famous mountain ranges. The more distant has been of recent days made famous as the location for the film Avatar. I wanted to go to another much closer, called Tian Men Shan, or Heavenly Gate Mountain, only 11 km from the city.

Accordingly in early August I set out with two companions, Joanne who is a native of this province and the ever faithful Erica. The train ticket was very cheap at only 29 Yuan, but no seat. I got one anyway, making four of us crowded onto a seat built for three. Just as well this country does not as yet have the same problem with obesity that we have in the West. Poor old Erica had to stand, though eventually she too squeezed onto the end of a seat. Later she was even nursing a child, her maternal instinct coming to the fore. I cannot imagine this happening in the West.

We left Tongren at 10.25 am, arriving at Zhangjiajie at 5.00 pm. It was a simple matter to catch No. 6 bus, which followed a very circuitous route before dropping us off in about 20 minutes at a 7 Days Inn. The tariff was 300 Yuan a night, which is a bit expensive, but there are three of us. There is a travel agent in the hotel so that makes it very convenient. We booked our trip for the following day, before going out for our evening meal. We found a restaurant nearby, where the food was quite nice, though a little oily. At least hereabouts the food is not spicy. After our meal we went for a walk, finding a pleasant park where people were frolicking. I wanted Joanne to dance, as she is a dancer, coming from the Music Dept. Next we found a supermarket where we bought supplies, chiefly lunch, for tomorrow.

The two girls slept in one bed, quite a common practice here, while I had the other. In spite of the noise of the traffic, I slept well. At 8.00 am we left, catching the No. 6 bus to the cable car, which is quite close to the train station. I had been through here before on the train, and had noticed the cable cars, as they actually go over the track, but then did not know where they went. Now I know. There is a massive tourist construction going on between the cable car station and the train station, so that it takes some 15 minutes to walk from one to the other; you have to walk around it.

The tickets are expensive, but I expected this. I paid 258 Yuan for Erica, 231 Yuan for me (senior citizen these days), and 187 Yuan for Joanne (student concession). Unfortunately, Erica could not get a concession since she had been robbed, so lost some money and her ID card. In this country you cannot do anything without ID. She had to go back to her own town, some 10 hours away, just to apply for a new one. It will take three months to come through. Bureaucracy. Expensive or not, this trip would be really something very special.

This cable car ride took 35 minutes to get to the top of the mountain, traversing a distance of some 7.5 km. Sometimes we just skimmed the tops of the trees, while other times we were swinging high above a valley. At one point we rode to the top of a sheer cliff. I found it spectacular and exhilarating. Not everyone, however, was sharing my delight. There were seven of us in our capsule. The terrified woman next to Joanne clung to her hand tightly, while her mother on the other side sat grim faced throughout the ordeal. Both were sick, and Joanne was not feeling so good either. Actually I am not sure how it helps to cling to someone who is just as terrified as you are.

The view from the top is really something. It is much cooler up here, as we have ascended some 1,280 metres, to an altitude of 1,480 metres, and below us clouds were softly enveloping trees on the mountain slopes. The temperature felt like mid-20s, whereas the expected maximum in the city below was 37 degrees. This is quite a difference, though I imagine it must be icily cold up here during the winter. We are actually on a plateau, which you can walk around, though it is not exactly flat. We walked up to the highest peak, where we were above a sea of clouds and as we walked, the sun was sucking the clouds upwards. I found it fascinating watching them stream upwards past us, revealing glimpses of steep cliffs, distant peaks and valleys far below.

Our path was made of paving stones. For some reason, the Chinese do not build paths from natural soils, but must cover them with paving stones and of course, especially in mountain regions, many steps. These paving stones are made of limestone, since this is the local stone. Well, that might make it more convenient, but in this climate I would not bet on their longevity. Already cracks are appearing, and that is all you need. Water seeps in, turns to ice in the winter and expands, thus forcing the cracks further apart. As well, the water combines with CO_2 to form a weak acid (carbonic –H_2CO_3), which in turn erodes the limestone further. The chemical formula goes something like this; $H_2CO_3 + CaCO = CaO + H_2O + 2CO_2$ – i.e. for those interested.

At this point you are probably falling asleep. We had a break by stopping for lunch, so this might be a convenient time to finish this edition. See you after lunch.

59. Tian Men Shan, Part 2 – 11th – 13 August 2011

Our lunch spot is a tourist hub, with souvenir shops, food for sale, tables and chairs. We sat down under the shade of an umbrella and opened up the lunches we had bought yesterday. We had been walking for a couple of hours, so were looking forward to a rest and something to eat. We could see a large pavilion atop a neighbouring hill, with a chair lift taking people up and down. We did not go up. Heavens, if you get sick in an enclosed cable car, what will you be like on an open T-bar? There is a Buddhist temple here too, brand new, and with an area of 1 ha, quite large, though an older, smaller temple has been here for 400 years. They like building these on mountains. It is quite beautiful, as always. Erica was enthralled, as, surprisingly, she had never been to a Buddhist temple before.

Now came the most spectacular part of our walk. Most of the distance, our walkway goes through trees, vegetation on each side. Sometimes it hugs the cliff top, with a railing to ensure you don't go over the edge, but a large section is actually built onto the side of the cliff face. There is nothing between you and a drop of hundreds of metres. In Australia, we commonly carve walkways into cliff faces, but nowhere have I seen anything like this. It truly is astonishing. I would hate to be part of the construction team. In fact they were building a new section while we were there, and I watched one workman perched over the abyss, with no safety harness in sight, as he drilled more holes. Stark raving mad.

One section actually juts out about 4 metres, with people queuing to go out and have their photos taken. Yes, there were crowds of people;

need you ask? Some sections of the walkway are quite narrow, and where trees are growing out from the cliff face, there is room for only one person at a time. I noticed some people did not appear to be enjoying themselves too much, clinging like limpets to the cliff face and refusing to look out over the edge, fear etched into their frozen visages.

In time we completed the circuit, bringing us back to the cable car. We hopped on, but not to return to the city. Wai-ai-ait; there is more. There is a half way station and here we got off. You then get into a 20 seater bus to go back up again. A fleet of these buses spend the day going up and down, ferrying tourists. This section is also included in the cost of the ticket. Now it becomes more worthwhile.

The road up, called Tongtian, or Heavenly Road, is amazing. I have never met anything like it, as it zigzags its way up the mountain. At one point it goes into a tunnel before turning back on itself to go over the tunnel. In all there are supposed to be 99 bends in this road, although I did not count them; too busy admiring the scenery. It is not exactly the Nullarbor Plain, where you can drive for 150 km without a single bend. I was having a ball.

Up the top, you get out, but actually you are not quite at the top yet. But you are close. All you have to do is to walk up the steps, called Tianti, or Heavenly Ladder. Now there are supposed to be 999 of these, but in fact there are only 887. I know, I counted them, or at least Erica and I did in turn. You need to be fit. All the way up we were encountering perspiring, puffing tourists, faces red, pulling themselves up by the railing. At the top of these stairs is a great big hole in the mountain. This used to be a cave, but it collapsed in AD 263, following an earthquake. It is 131 metres high, 57 metres wide and 60 metres deep. It is so big that from time to time aircraft have flown through it. Now that would be a thrill.

We made our way to the top, with Joanne, the youngest of our troupe, having most difficulty. I don't know, but this younger generation ain't like their grandparents. Here we took the obligatory photos. There are professional photographers here, going through the motions. You stand like this, put your hands up like this, then like that, etc. They've done it all before.

At the bottom of these steps, more building is taking place in order to cater for yet more tourists. What is another million or so? There is a service area here, with food and souvenir shops. I have some gifts from here, bought by Erica for friends in Australia. Back on a bus we climbed for the trip down those 99 bends or whatever, to the cable car station. From here it is only 15 minutes back to the city. What a wonderful day. We capped it off by finding a restaurant for our evening meal. It was a good meal, at about 20 Yuan a head.

The next day was far more restful. Joanne did not even surface till 9.30 am. We checked out at noon, leaving our bags at the hotel, while we explored the city. We took a taxi to a new tourist complex, dedicated to the minority peoples hereabouts; the Tujia, Bai, Mao and one other. There were some outside exhibits, but the museum itself was closed, or perhaps not yet open. There is statue of a tiger with a small boy. Apparently legend has it that the boy, who later became the Tujia leader, suckled from the tiger, so that honouring the tiger has always been part of this people's culture. It is a bit like Romulus and Remus, only in their case it was a wolf.

I decided we would walk back to the hotel. Fine, except that muggsy here went the wrong way. No wonder the ladies complained. We stopped for our evening meal at the best restaurant of the three we had used in this city. It was also cool. From here we got a taxi back to our hotel, where we stayed for some time, before getting yet another taxi to an internet café near the railway. We were to stay here for four hours. I slept for some of the time. In the early hours of the morning, we walked to the railway station, around that huge new tourist complex, where we found that our train would be delayed. I lay down across some seats and tried to sleep. There is sign here which reads; "Do not lie". I agree; one should always be truthful.

Finally the train arrived, and finally we left, at 5.40 am, as dawn was breaking, silhouetting Tian Men Shan in the distance. Two of Erica's classmates happened to be in the same carriage, returning to university after the holidays. We got back to Tongren around midday. We had enjoyed a truly, truly wonderful experience. God is good.

These would also be my final days working at Tongren University, as I have been "kicked out": over 60 years old is considered to be "too old". Really. So I am moving to Chongqing, having been accepted by Sichuan International Studies University (SISU). It would prove to be a great move.

Summer Holidays 2012 – Taiwan Series

I know, I know; Taiwan is an independent country, and has been so since 1949. Nevertheless, China claims it as its own, as indeed it claims lots of other territory. Since, however, I visited Taiwan during my time in China, I have decided to include it. Agree or disagree. At the end of this series, I will give an overview, but first I would like to say something about each of the places I visited, beginning with the capital and largest city, Taipei.

60.   Taipei – Four Sites – 6th – 10th July 2012

Getting around the city is not difficult, due to its very efficient MRT (Mass Rapid Transport system), otherwise known as the underground rail network, which in other cities is called Metro, the Tube, or simply the Underground. You can buy tickets for individual trips, or day passes, two day passes etc. Passengers line up at designated doors on the platforms, where train doors open precisely. China has the same system, only there people tend to push onto trains before others have a chance to get off. Taiwanese people are a little more polite.

The first attraction for me was to ascend the tallest building in the city and the second tallest in the world, after the 828 metre high Dubai Tower. This one is considerably lower, however, at a mere 508 metres. It is called Taipei 101, because it has 101 storeys, plus another 5 below ground. It is also a surprisingly large building in terms of area. Some 10,000 people are employed here, a small town in itself. Inside the top of the building is a massive ball of 600 tonnes (about the weight of 130 elephants); it is there to pull the building in the opposite direction when hit by the strong winds of typhoons or earth movements from earthquakes, thus damping most of the movement, and keeping the building stable.

At the top there is an exhibition of coral, not the formations found just below the surface of tropical seas, but the deep sea variety that can be turned into jewellery and art works. There are some beautiful carvings here. From the observation deck one has a view of all Taipei, spread out below in all directions. It is well worth a visit. There is also an exhibition in honour of the Olympics. Naturally this featured Taiwanese athletes, but unlike China, it included other countries as well.

Another must place to visit is the National Palace Museum. To get there, you take the train to Shilin, then 304 bus to Gugin. There are 3,200 national treasures stored here, brought from China in 1949 when the Kuomintang fled China. There are rare books, paintings, carvings, calligraphy, jewellery, gems, pottery, bronzes, imperial archives and other artifacts from every major period of Chinese history, beginning from the Neolithic period. This collection is larger than that in Beijing. There are many works from the Qianlong period (1736 – 95, though his life spanned from 1711 to 1799). I particularly like celadon and *wucai* (= 5 colour porcelain). Different clays from each region of China determined the type of pottery and porcelain. I also admired the intricate carvings in wood, ivory and rhinoceros horn. Some people have amazing skills.

Many tour groups were going through while I was there, their leaders carrying the essential triangular flag. You can even hire guides to give commentaries in English. It was a hot day, around 35 degrees, yet it was cold in this museum, with the air conditioning so high. Why do they do this?

China of course, wants this magnificent collection returned to China, saying it has all been stolen. Maybe Taiwan can use this as a bargaining chip in turn for recognition. I did say "maybe", but in truth, Beijing does not compromise; it wants everything. After the Chinese military invades and conquers Taiwan, I am quite sure that this whole collection will be packed off to Beijing.

Another place I visited was Chiang Kai-shek's official residence. This took some finding, but I got there eventually. I could not enter the house, which was closed off, possibly because it was after 5.00 pm when I got there, but the grounds are extensive and beautifully landscaped. There are rose gardens, orchids, even a row of melaleuca from Australia. There is a small wetland section, complete with boardwalk and descriptions of the various plants and animals to be found there. Indeed I saw squirrels, lizards, insects and birds of various species. There is a lovely pavilion near a set of carvings of various animals. There is no doubt about it, but CKS knew how to live well, though I suspect his wife was mostly responsible. I had previously visited another of their residences in China at Longmen Grottoes, near Luoyang.

To refresh your memory, May-ling was one of the Chong sisters; another, Ai-ling married a wealthy financier in Shanghai, who became not only China's richest man, but also Finance Minister. The third, Cing-ling, married Dr. Sun Yat-sen, the founder of republican China and of the Kuomintang. It is said that one married for power, one for money and one for her country. May-ling only died a few years ago at the age of about 105.

One further memorial needs to be mentioned before I close this edition, viz. the Chiang Kai-shek Memorial Hall. This is more than just a hall, consisting as it does of three buildings and a large entrance gate. The elaborate gate alone measures some 75 metres across and 30 metres high. One of the buildings is the National Theatre, while another is the National Concert Hall.

It was here that I bought a five CD collection of songs from Theresa Tang, otherwise known as Deng Li Jun. I have admired her singing for some years, as she is much admired in China as well as in Taiwan. Tragically she died in mysterious circumstances while on a tour in Thailand; she was still in her 30's. It is rumoured that she was murdered by Chinese government agents, because of her support for Taiwan, but I doubt if this is true. The collection cost me NTD 700, but well worth it. NTD = New Taiwanese Dollar, and at the moment there are some 31 to the Australian dollar, so I paid about $4.50 per CD.

One curious thing I noticed about Taipei, which would be echoed in other cities, is the dearth of fruit and vegetable shops. Where do people do their shopping? Maybe they eat out. Maybe they eat very little fruit. Yet fruit and vegetables form a major part of my diet.

61.   Taipei – The Red Line – 6th – 10th July 2012

As in many cities which has a metro system, lines are colour coded as well as numbered. The red line in Taipei is one I ended up using a fair bit, as it has a number of sites of interest along its route.

The end of the line is Tamshui, marking the mouth of the Tamshui River, where it debouches into the Pacific Ocean. I walked for some distance along the shore of this river. It is lined with many stalls selling snacks of various kinds. On one night I had my evening meal here. The street parallel to the shore has the more usual shops selling clothing etc. Many people walk up and down the esplanade, or ride bikes. One enterprising young man was selling a device to make large soap bubbles; he appeared to be doing well. Tamshui also has a Christian church and museum. I got talking with a young man there, who told me something of the earlier Christian missionaries.

Beitou is actually just off the red line. You get there by special train, which traverses a whole one stop. This is an area of hot springs, of which there are many on this island, sitting as it does on the junction of the Pacific and Asian Plates. The first spring I visited is very hot at some 90 degrees, and even though the day is hot, it is steaming. There is a smell of sulphur, and with a pH of 1.5, this water is highly acidic. It is H_2SO_4 – sulphuric acid – so don't fall in. Nearby is a more salubrious pool at a mere 35 degrees. The site and building were developed by the Japanese during their occupation. It is a quite pleasant spot and I thoroughly enjoyed my soak.

Shilin is another site of interest on the red line. For one thing, it has a Catholic church, so it is here that I went to Mass on Sunday. There is a good feel about this parish. I like the way the prayers of the faithful were read by people from their seats in the body of the church, not from up front. The priest is Indonesian, which surprised me. I learnt a little about the church here in Taiwan, but I intend to say more about this in a later edition. Shilin is also noted for its night market. These, as I was to find out, are very common throughout Taiwan, some being a lot better than others. The one at Shilin is among the better ones. What happens is that a side street, with possibly several other streets leading off this one, is closed off to traffic. Stalls line both sides of the street, selling snacks mostly, with crowds of people wandering along, sampling their wares; not a bad way to have one's evening meal.

Two stops from Shilin on the red line is Yuanshan, and here there is a temple dedicated to the memory of Confucius. I was to discover that there are many such throughout Taiwan. At the train station I asked directions of a young man, who informed me that my Chinese was not good, but not bad either. Thanks mate. Later I met him at the temple; coincidence? No. He had followed me to ensure I found my way. I must say that I found the people here most helpful and hospitable.

It is right to honour Confucius, who has had a huge influence upon Chinese people, wherever they may be found. He stressed order, harmony and obedience, admirable virtues in themselves, but have been interpreted to bolster the legitimacy of totalitarian regimes. It is refreshing to see that Confucian virtues can co-exist with a free and modern society. This transition has yet to happen in China.

The weather is hot – ideal for swimming – but this pastime, popular in my own country, is not popular either in Taiwan or China, since in both countries very few people can swim. Consequently neither country tends to build its cities on the coast. The normal practice is to build inland, especially on a river, even if the coast is not far away; look at Shanghai, Fuzhou, Guangzhou, Shenzhen for instance, and Taipei here in Taiwan.

I was told that the closest beach is at Jinshan, more than one hour away by bus. So there I went. I got off the bus to find that there is not much there; it is just a town. Fine, but where is the beach? I asked. *"Shatan, zai nali?"* Locals gathered around, and I found the beach is no less than 3 km away. Goodness. Even a policeman on a motorcycle rode up to see what the attraction was (me?). He offered to give me a ride to the beach. Wow! So I hopped up behind and he drove me to the beach. Thank you. He took me to the end of the beach and told me to get in at that spot. OK.

The sand is an orange colour and a bit hot to walk on without shoes. The surf, however, is as flat as a tack. The surrounds are not particularly attractive. There were not many people about, even though the day was hot, and not surprisingly, nobody was in swimming; not one person; nobody; nix. They just paddle by the shore. I was the only one who actually went swimming. All was well, till I got stung by a jelly blubber, but it was no big deal. Thank goodness it was not a box jellyfish, such as is found in northern Australia; these can kill you – very painfully.

When it was time to leave, I headed back up the beach, not the side where I came in. I had to go through a gate, where I noticed a man at a booth. Then it hit me: you have to pay to use this beach. In Australia, all beaches are free. I could see the puzzled look on the gate keeper's face, wondering why he did not remember me! Now remember, it was the policeman who had shunted me in the back way!

I walked past a scout troop, both boys and girls, who seemed to be involved in some exercises, not including swimming, and eventually found my way to the bus stop, where I should have got off in the first place. There I met a group of young people. We proceeded to talk about all sorts of subjects for the next hour or so. The subject of our conversation, and the conclusions I drew, will appear in a later edition.

I enjoyed my time here in Taipei. My next stop would be Taichung, a city on the west coast, about 200 km away.

62.   Taichung – 8th – 11th July 2012

62.   Taichung – 8th – 11th July 2012

It seems that every second city in this country begins with "Tai", including the country itself. I gather that it is the same "tai". After several days in Taipei, I caught the fast train to Taichung (or "Taiwan Centre"), not that I was in a hurry, but it was convenient. It certainly is fast, travelling at some 300 kph. It is interesting that this small country has this fast train, while Australia, with such vast distances, does not.

At the Taipei station, I fell in with a group of Americans who were here to sell helicopters to Taiwan. They will need them. The ride was also amazingly smooth. Even with several stops along the way, it took only an hour to cover the 200 km to Taichung. This is the third largest city in Taiwan, after Taipei and Kaohsiung, with a population of about 1 million. I did not visit Koahsiung, but this is a southern city and appears to be the industrial heartland of the country.

I was recommended a hotel, a fair way from the fast train railway station, but closer to the normal railway station, the bus station and other attractions. The shuttle bus was free. Other buses around the city have a curious payment method. You buy a card from any 7-11 store for a minimum of NTD 100, then you add however much money you like, depending upon how far and how often you wish to travel. These cards are not only swiped as you get on the bus, but also when you get off, presumably because you pay different amounts depending on how far you go. But this means that people must get on and off the bus from the front, thus creating a deal of congestion. The back door is still there, but is blocked by seating. Curious. I have not seen this system used anywhere else, not even in Taiwan. Bus routes also tend to be confusing, with one bus actually doubling back to its point of departure. I took a few wrong buses in this city, but that is life.

This city too has its temple to Confucius, a rather magnificent one. The street nearby has a bronze mural depicting scenes from Confucius' life. Nearby there is a large gateway commemorating the "martyrs of the revolution". No, these are not noble communists killed by the evil Kuomintang, such as you find in Chongqing; nor are they noble patriots killed by the evil communists – and there are plenty of these – but are people executed in 1911 by the Qing Dynasty, just prior to its fall. Apparently 72 people were beheaded.

In the evening I went in search of the local night market. Even with the aid of a bus, it still took me well over an hour just to find it. In usual fashion, the street is blocked to traffic, and is lined with shops. There are clothing stores here, as well as those selling snacks. It is not a bad way to have one's evening meal. Many of these snacks are foods cooked over a coal fire, and include squid, tofu and various meats. Once again, this city has few supermarkets, fruit or vegetable shops, but a large number of convenience stores.

Opposite my hotel is an attractive park, Zhongshan Park, complete with a pond, bridges, lawn and walkways. Zhongshan is another name for Dr. Sun Yat-sen, who is greatly honoured here. This is the spot where the original settlement was founded in 1721. The park also has a large statue of a goat, so maybe this is a symbol of the city – I do not know – but Guangzhou has 5 goats as its symbol. I found this park a good place to relax in the evening, when the weather was a little cooler. It has been hot during the day. The hotel, of course, is air conditioned.

One of the attractions, not only in this hotel, but in most of the ones I stayed in, is that breakfast is included in the tariff. Great. This particular hotel boasts both a good Western breakfast and newspapers, including English ones. Each morning, as I enjoyed a hearty breakfast, I read the papers. This both allowed me to catch up with the news, and also to learn a lot about Taiwan, not just the local news, in terms of what was happening, but also the feeling behind the news. Later I will tell you what I learnt.

Beside this park I found a very good bookstore, so was able to buy a book in English to read as I travelled. I bought "North and South" by Catherine Gaskell, for only NTD 80, or just over $2. If one is sitting for hours in a bus or train, it is good to have something to read. I had been reading a book by Jeffrey Archer on George Mallory, an English mountaineer, who may possibly have been the first to climb Everest in 1924. He died in the attempt, but did he die on the way up Everest, or on the way down? His body was not discovered until 1995, at an altitude of 8,500 metres, about 400 metres below the summit. One of his climbing partners was George Finch, an Australian, who was the father of Peter Finch, a well-known Australian actor.

Another surprising fact about Tw's cityscapes is that although the streets are clean, there are very few rubbish bins. You may have to walk quite a few blocks before you find one. Rather than use public bins, it seems every shop owner has sheir own, which they keep hidden, just in case some other dastardly soul is tempted to put rubbish into their bins. Rubbish trucks playing the same tune over and over and over again roam the streets, like lions seeking whom they may devour. The inhabitants rush out of their homes and shops, black rubbish bags in hand. These they throw into the back of the truck. In Australia the council workers do this, though often the rubbish truck lifts each bin hydraulically, emptying its contents into the back, and then setting the bin back down again.

Footpaths in this city and others in Taiwan, are interesting in that it seems pedestrians are the very last people considered. Often, one cannot even walk on the footpaths, because they are filled either with wares spilling out from shops, or with motorcycles. There are far more motorcycles than cars, and yet it seems that little thought has gone into where to park them; so they are simply left on footpaths.

I enjoyed my time in Taichung, though it is probably not the most exciting city I have ever been in. Nor would I list it amongst the "must see before you die" places. It was time for me to head for the hills – literally – to make my annual retreat.

63.   Shuili – 11th – 20th July 2012

At Taichung train station, I met an interesting family. He is an American from Chicago, where I had such a happy time, while his wife is from Singapore. They have a seven year old daughter. I had been reading my book till we fell into conversation, then when it was time for me to catch my train I inadvertently left my book in the waiting room. Oh no! And I was nearly finished. I went back, and found that the American had it; great, though I got the impression that he would have liked to read it himself. I finished it on the train, before leaving it (deliberately) with my friend in Shuili.

I was told to get off at Ershui, which I did, but had not realised that I needed to change trains here. I went to the local tourist office, right at the station, where I met a lovely lady called Melody, whom I suspect may be a Catholic; she is certainly Christian. She could not do enough for me. I bought my ticket for the next leg of the journey with her, and she even came onto the train with me to ensure I sat up the front. This train line is cute. The trains are small, the track is narrow, and you can indeed sit right up the front next to the driver, who has his own little cabin. It is a short line, with only four more stations, terminating at Checheng. I was to get off at Shuili. There I arrived at 4.45 pm, only 1 ½ hours late, to find Joe and Francis waiting for me. We would drive up the mountain to their Cistercian monastery, where I would spend the next week.

Shuili is a small town, maybe 10,000 people at most would be my guess. It is situated right in the centre of the island, in the mountain region which runs down the spine of Taiwan. A little bit of geology might help here. Taiwan is like the nose of the Asian plate which juts out a little into the Pacific Ocean, where it meets head on with the Pacific plate – we are talking plate tectonics here. The latter is crashing into the former and is also sliding north. As a result, Taiwan experiences earthquakes which can be quite damaging. The central mountains are being piled up as a result of this collision. The eastern side of the island is quite a narrow plain, tapering off to a point. This side is where most of the indigenous peoples live. The western side of the island has a large flat plain, where you find not only the bulk of the population, but also most of the agriculture and industry.

Shuili is famous for its pottery. I would visit this one day with Francis, just before I left. He was a gracious host, thank goodness, as I do not think I could have found it on my own. It is called the Snake Kiln, not because it has much to do with snakes, except that their kiln is very long indeed, so maybe it looks a bit like a fat snake. It was built in 1927. This kiln may very well be the largest in the world. Certainly they boast a pot, which certainly is the tallest, standing 5.56 metres high, just beating the previous record held by a pot in Queensland. The surrounds of this pottery are quite attractive.

Checheng, the terminal station on this line, I also visited one day. This used to be the site of a large wood mill. Under Japanese occupation, there was much logging – and I will speak of this again later. This town still thrives on wood, but more as a tourist centre. They also make many wooden artifacts, either for decorative or practical purposes. The air is redolent with the smell of freshly cut wood, which I for one find very attractive indeed. I did not buy anything, for three reasons: 1) I have no room in my bag; 2) I cannot take anything with me back into Australia, and 3) I do not need anything. There were many school children there at the time of my visit, and some of them were in a classroom where they could try their hand at making their own artifacts. What a good idea. From the noise they generated I gathered they were thoroughly enjoying themselves.

Each afternoon at Shuili I would go for a walk to get some exercise. Sometimes I would walk down the mountain to the town – it takes about 45 minutes. Shuili has a 7-11, as have most places throughout Taiwan, so one advantage in coming down the mountain was to enjoy a yoghurt and a beer.

You can climb back up the hill in about the same time if you really push it; in places the gradient is quite steep. In this hot weather the perspiration would be dripping off me, but it is good for your health. On a couple of occasions I got caught in thunderstorms, but these do not last long, so I took shelter under the awning of someone's tin shed. I probably looked a little ridiculous on the second occasion, as the tin roof overhang was too narrow, so I was holding a used plastic food container over my head for about 20 minutes till the rain eased. On one afternoon I walked up to the top of the mountain, where the road ends and you can look out over a valley on the other side.

As one climbs either up or down the mountain, great views of distant mountain ranges unfold, as well as of the valley below. A river flows through, dividing the town of Shuili. On the further side of the town, the valley broadens, and as it does so the river anastomoses, dividing into several streams then rejoining. It looks very pretty. The monastery is located on the northern slope of this particular valley, which is somewhat unusual, in that I would expect most valleys to be running north-south, rather than east-west. The view of the ranges in the distance is inspiring, with several peaks rising to over 3,000 metres. We do not have any mountains in Australia this high.

This is the wonderful setting in which I was to make my annual retreat. Next edition will be a little more reflective.

64.　*Cistercian Monastery – 11th – 20th July 2012*

For a week, this monastery, deep in the central mountains of Taiwan, became my home. It is a wonderful, peaceful place, overlooking the valley. There are three main buildings. The chapel is in the centre, with classroom and library above it. The main building houses the dining room, monks' cells, laundry etc. Further up the hill is the guest house, which can accommodate five people. I loved the view over the mountains, receding into the distance. And I loved seeing the stars at night.

I joined the monks at prayer, including Mass each day, and at meals, which are normally eaten in silence. Each morning I was invited to give the homily, with one of the monks translating as I went. Hopefully they garnered some pearls of spiritual wisdom, if not from me, then from my translator!

I tried to fit in to the community as much as possible, with a minimum disturbance to their usual routine. Indeed I discovered that their willingness to be disturbed exceeded my willingness to disturb. As a result, I was able to spend time with each of them. It is a very small community, with only six members. Two are priests and two are new members. One is my friend, Theo, with whom I taught in Fuzhou. Each day he would give lectures to the two younger ones.

They form an extraordinary group, and this world sorely needs them. We live in a world where great progress is being made in many areas, e.g. scientific development, yet one which lacks a proper underpinning to all our hustle and bustle. Communism has failed; unbridled capitalism has failed; religion has largely failed. Hinduism is too nationalistic; Buddhism is largely irrelevant and is reduced often to mere practices and superstition; Islam is caught up in paranoia, with its endless killings, its sexism and misunderstanding of the Trinity. Christianity has often got sidetracked. The new Trinity is Power, Profit and Pleasure.

Yet Christ alone has the power to transform this world. These men make Christ the centre of their lives, and through their prayerfulness, through their union with Jesus and with each other, through their powerlessness, they are the real powerhouse of the Church. This is so different from what the world understands by power; it is not the force of coercion, it is not the force of armies and has nothing to do with domination of others. Life should be about union with God (prayer), union with each other (love) and union with our world (creation).

Yet these men are also so ordinary, very human. The newest member comes from one of the aboriginal groups. Another comes from Malaysia. Another comes from the U.S. and had spent many years working for the United Nations, especially in the care of refugees. The superior comes from China, where he spent 25 years in prison under the communists and so impressed his captors that after his release the Chinese authorities allowed him to spend some time studying in the U.S., arranging both his passport and visa; they even reduced his age by 10 years! – at least on his passport. He truly is a wonderful man.

If at this stage you are pondering the possibility of your own calling to be a Cistercian monk, in a sudden burst of fervent enthusiasm, let me first point out some aspects of their lifestyle. Their daily horarium goes something like this:

3.30 am rise, then Matins is sung in the chapel, followed by reading and breakfast. I hasten to add that my own fervour does not go so far, so I never joined the monks for Matins; the other hours, yes.

6.00 am Lauds (morning prayer), then Mass.

8.00 am work meeting, then work till 11.00 am.

11.45 am examen, Sext (prayer at the sixth hour), lunch then rest.

2.00 pm None (prayer at the ninth hour), then work till 4.00 pm.

4.30 pm community reading.

5.30 pm Vespers (evening prayer) followed by the evening meal.

7.00 pm meditation

7.30 pm Compline (night prayer).

8.00 pm retire. You would want an early night after that regimen.

So much of the day is spent in prayer and work.

About 10 minutes' walk down the mountain there is shrine dedicated to Our Lady of Fatima. It was built by a monk who was born in Fuzhou and died in Hong Kong at the ripe old age of 110, who also built four others at various other localities where he had been stationed. This one features Stations of the Cross al fresco style. Many local Catholics make this a pilgrimage site.

There is a flat piece of ground here where the monks grow corn, cucumbers, melons and even coffee, but there is a shortage of water. So I offered to find some water for them. First we needed two suitable pieces of fencing wire. With these I marched up and down, covering the entire site. The wires, as you would know, are held loosely in the hands, and in the presence of water they move of their own accord. I have no idea how it works, but it does, at least with me. I think that just possibly the moving water generates an electric current, which in turn induces magnetism. I can find both the location of the water and amount, but have no idea of its depth or other qualities, such as salinity. One other monk also found that it worked for him. We did find water at several locations, but they told me from other information that it is very deep – hundreds of metres. It would cost an arm and a leg to drill for it.

There is so much life here, apart from the prolific vegetation. There are beetles, butterflies and birds with lots of cicadas filling the air with their summer sounds. Incidentally, "cicada" can be pronounced correctly two ways, either "a;" or "ei". I even saw a largish, yellow snake with black markings trying to slither over a wall, which proved to be too high, so I followed him as he went up a path, up a flight of steps then into the undergrowth. He was no threat to me and I was no threat to him.

The monastery has a library with both an English and a Chinese section. I spent some hours here, becoming reacquainted with Thomas Merton, amongst others. It is years since I read him, and was struck by how much our (my?) theology has changed over the years. We just do not express ourselves in the same way; nor is our content quite the same. For example, Merton tells us to practise the virtues in order to get close to God. In my more formative years, the virtues were stressed. Today I would turn it around the other way; be conscious of how close God is, form a personal attachment to God (Jesus) and the virtues will follow. "You are the people of God; he loved you and chose you for his own. So then, you must clothe yourselves in compassion, kindness, humility, gentleness and patience." Col. 3/12. Notice that for Paul, the relationship with God comes first. I found good spirituality in "Truly Human, Truly Divine" by Michael Casey.

Eventually the time came to say goodbye. It has been a time for quiet reflection, for prayer – especially for people (and yes, Sarah, you figured prominently), and for fraternity. Sarah is a friend in the U.S. undergoing treatment for cancer – and she was cured. Maybe the prayers of these monks were a major factor. Hopefully I am a better person as a result of this week. Whether the monks are any better for my presence among them is a moot point.

65.   Sun Moon Lake – 17ᵗʰ – 18ᵗʰ July 2012

Situated almost at the geographical centre of Taiwan lies a beautiful lake, one of a chain trending north- south in the central mountains. This one, Si Yue Tan, is the largest, at around 30 km circumference. The lake derives its name from its shape, being composed of two parts; one part is almost circular (the sun), while the other is crescent shaped (the moon), with an island at the join. *Si Yue* means "sun, moon". Apparently these shapes were even more in evidence before the Japanese built a hydroelectric dam here. The surface of the lake has an altitude of 750 metres.

Conveniently, the lake is not all that far from the Cistercian monastery, being situated in an adjacent valley, so that towards the end of my stay, I took a bus to the lake, and spent one night there. I found an inexpensive hotel opposite the bus terminal and tourist centre, so it is very convenient. As usual, I found the staff at the tourist centre to be most helpful. I liked their computer, of a type I had never seen before. It has two screens, so that the operator sits on her side of the desk, while from the other side you can see what she brings up.

After lunch I caught a bus to the other side of the lake to a cable car. The ticket cost NTD 250 (about $8), but it gives you a great view of the lake. It rises to a height of 1044 m, then down again to another valley, where there is an aboriginal village called Naruwan or Formosan Aboriginal Culture Village. Actually it is rather a showcase for aboriginal culture from various tribes, such as the Parwan. Their houses are expertly made from small pieces of flat stone, mainly shale, fitted together to make a quite sturdy structure, as it needs to be in this earthquake prone region. Roofs are made of thatch.

It reminds me of Celtic architecture. Isn't it interesting, that different peoples, in different parts of the world, with absolutely no contact with each other, yet about the same time, come up with similar ideas? We are truly one. Houses of other tribes were constructed from larger stones piled on top of one another, others from logs, since there is a plentiful supply in the surrounding forests, while others are made from bamboo.

Inside the houses one could read – in English – explanations of various tribal rituals. One of these involved swinging very high up on ropes; I gather this was part of a wedding ritual for a bride. One man was making glass ornaments very skillfully, using a blow torch, though I doubt if this was a part of their traditional culture. In an auditorium, another group performed one of their dances, while dressed in traditional costume. I got talking to some of these people, and was impressed by their attitudes – but more of this later. When you are a small tribe, however, it is inevitable that you will be conquered and swallowed up by a bigger tribe. There is always a bigger fish. Many people were selling snacks, which I sampled. One man even called me over and simply gave me a potato he had just baked; delicious. They are such friendly people.

I spent a couple of hours wandering around this interesting place, before heading back. Then I could not find my ticket. I searched everywhere in my bag, but to no avail. Eventually an attendant pointed to the back of my hand, which had been stamped when I came in. You cannot see anything, but it comes up in ultraviolet light! I must be getting old. It was so peaceful and quiet as I headed back down via the cable car. I was the only one in my car.

By 4.50 pm I was back at the lakeside. It was not yet late, so I decided to walk the 7 km or so back to my hotel around the lake. It was a lovely walk, partly on the roadside, partly on boardwalks. I could watch colours changing on the lake as it got darker. I stopped for about half an hour at a temple, partly to have a rest. This temple boasts the largest lion in Asia. As I was sitting there, minding my own business, I was peremptorily ordered to get out of the road by an officious woman who wanted to take a photo! (Hey, what's wrong with me?) She did not say either "please" or "thank you". I wonder where she was from? What good is it to visit a temple – or a church – if it is just about observances and not change of heart?

This raises one of my main objections to Buddhism, at least judging from its adherents, in that it seems to be so bound up with superstitious observances. I have a suspicion that Siddartha Gautama would turn in his grave, unless, of course, he has been reincarnated! They have so many practices of things you must do if you want "luck", "happiness" or "long life". For example, there is a matchmaker god, with a temple here on this lake – and I quote verbatim, making no apologies for the standard of English in this notice:

"Hold to ask the god of matchmaker for a happy marriage. Hold incense in front of you, face the god, and repeat your name, and address to him (sic), then drop divining blocks on floor. If answer provided by blocks is positive you can take a piece of red thread from god's hand (sic) and place it in a red packet. After praying to the Old Man (sic), you carry the packet with you and place it at the head of your bed as you wait for your perfect match." Goodness. Incidentally the Old Man under the moon is the matchmaker god, whatever that means. When faced with such utter nonsense, it saddens me that we as Christians have so much to offer, yet people are unaware. Maybe we are not living in relationship to God as we should be.

Back at the Centre (as it is called), I was sitting on a bench enjoying a well-earned beer, when I heard a family speaking in English, arguing whether the correct pronunciation is "aluminium" or "aluminum". I said the former, unless you happen to be American, and they are not. We then had an extensive conversation on English and other matters. This family is Taiwanese, currently working in Hong Kong. I learnt something from them, as will appear later. I spent about an hour drinking tea with them.

Next morning I woke up early. Goodness, don't tell me I am getting used to monastic routine. After breakfast I went for a walk around the lake shore, but in the opposite direction from the previous day. There is a Christian church nearby, built and used by Chiang Kai-shek, who was a Christian. He also liked Si Yue Tan, coming here regularly.

Nearby there is a most pleasant garden spot overlooking the lake, and here I stopped to spend some time in quiet. On the other side one can see the mountains rising to a height of over 3,000 metres, higher than anything in continental Australia. A Korean girl came along, on her own, taking photos. I asked if she wanted one of herself, and she did, but she was using an incorrect setting on her camera. I told her about fill-in flash when you have a light background, but your subject is in shadow. Then we talked about many things, including Korea's attitude toward China – but more about this later.

That afternoon I caught a bus back to Shuili, so that by nightfall I was back in the Cistercian monastery. Sun Moon Lake was a most pleasant interlude, and I would recommend it.

66.　Chiayi – 20ᵗʰ 22ⁿᵈ July 2012

The time came to say goodbye to the Cistercian monastery and its wonderful community. Francis drove me down to the station, and I caught a train about 9.10 am, travelling again on this quaint railway line back to Ershui. Here I made a point of catching up once again with Melody, that most helpful Christian lady at the tourist office. At 10.15 am I caught another train to Chiayu, where I booked into a hotel. After lunch I went for a walk to get a feel of the place.

It took some time to find the city museum, after people had given me wrong directions, and I found myself walking up and down the same road. It was well worth the trouble. This museum houses a marvellous exhibition of bronze ware, pottery and ceramics from China, covering a large span of history, beginning from the Zhou dynasty (1100 BC), and moving through the Tang (AD 618 – 907), the Song (AD 907 – 1279), the Ming (AD 1368 – 1644) and especially the Qing (AD 1644 – 1911) dynasties. The bronze ware comes from the Warring States Period (476 – 222 BC). I loved the intricate, delicate filigree patterns.

Most of this collection had come from one of the Qing emperors, Qian Long. He is by far the most prominent of all of the twelve Qing emperors, partly because he reigned for so long (excuse the pun), from 1750 to 1795, actually retiring a few years before his death. He had a passion for ceramics, collecting many from previous reigns, and he also set up his own kilns. What will happen to all of this after China conquers Taiwan? It will probably all be shipped back to China, yet none of it belongs to China, not even to the city of Chiayi. All of it has been legitimately purchased over the years and is privately owned, being on loan (I think permanently) to this museum.

From the museum I walked to Chiayi Park, small but attractive; indeed I found this to be a small but attractive city. The park contains walkways under trees, statues, a skating rink, a baseball park and the de rigueur temple in honour of Confucius. From here I walked back to my hotel, stopping for my evening meal. The man at the counter asked if I was wearing shorts. Well, yes, I am. "Then you get a $5 discount". Goodness, I must wear shorts more often. To wash down my fish hamburger, I bought a 187 ml bottle of Australian wine for only NTD 120, or less than $4. Wow!

There is another museum in this park, a cultural museum. I actually returned here the following afternoon, intending to spend no more than an hour here. Exhibits show something of the history of the place, some architecture and some prominent families. An hour would be more than enough. Unfortunately, just as I was arriving at 2.30 pm, it started to rain, then it got heavier, till a full-blown thunderstorm broke, with the rain fairly belting down. That's OK; though I had neglected to bring my umbrella, thunderstorms generally do not last long. This one did. I sat and waited, chatting with some local people, and learning more. At 5.00 pm, closing time, I was turfed out, so I sprinted to the nearby Confucian temple, where I waited a further hour. Yes, I can still sprint – a little. I did not walk this time, but caught a bus. Life is fun.

The next morning I caught a bus for some distance to the Museum of the Tropic of Cancer, about 3 km away, as this city lies on this imaginary line, some 23 ½ degrees north of the equator. The first monument was set up in 1908 during the Japanese period. A number of exhibits is featured;

1)   Astronomy, with an explanation of many facts;
2)   U.S. and Russian space programmes, including life size models of some spacecraft and satellites, e.g. Sputnik 1. I guess this has passed into dim distant history, yet I clearly remember watching it pass overhead in October 1957.
3)   An interactive display of general science;
4)   An explanation of the earth's tilt, and the effect this has, though it did not mention the desert belt around the globe on either side of both tropics (Cancer and Capricorn);
5)   Piped music. Big deal, I hear you say, yet one of the tracks featured Dame Kiri Tekanua singing the Maori Farewell, a truly wonderful piece of music. What a pleasant surprise.
6)   An extensive exhibition outside, including a globe of the world, yet failing to add New Zealand, ironically. Dame Kiri is a Kiwi.
7)   They showed a children's 3D animated film about a dinosaur whose planet was invaded by aliens, highlighting the lengths she

went to in order to protect her as yet unhatched egg. It was an unusual and unexpected extolling of a mother's love.

I also found the local Catholic church, so spent some time here, chatting with a sister and learning more about the church in Taiwan.

Chiayi streets tend to be narrow, on a grid pattern and not without interest. On the one hand they are clogged, especially the footpaths, as is the case everywhere it seems in this country, but on the other hand they are colourful, with signs hanging everywhere, also adding, of course, to the sense of clutter. I spent two nights here in this fair town. Breakfast was complimentary in my hotel, as was a condom! Goodness, only one?? At breakfast one morning I saw a girl wearing a T-shirt with the word "LOVE" across the front, while another girl had "What is love?" across the front of hers. Indeed. It was time to leave.

67. Alishan – 22nd – 23rd July 2012

At 9.10 am I headed off on a 20 seater bus for a 70 km journey to Alishan, ascending from a mere 30 metres above sea level to some 2,170 metres. There were good mountain views along the way. As you may know, the temperature drops roughly one degree per 130 metres altitude, so that the visitor's centre in the mountains is a good 15 degrees cooler than on the plain. I am glad I bought my tracksuit top, as I needed it, though this was the only place I wore it throughout this whole holiday. The mountain was named after a tribal leader who lived in the mid-18th century, whose name was Abali, and who apparently knew the area extremely well, providing for his tribe all that they needed. Abali Mountain became Ali Shan.

We arrived at the visitor centre at 11.30 am, where I was warmly welcomed by two lovely girls, who could not be more helpful. They were university students, working here voluntarily over the summer; they get training, board and meals but no pay. They could not do enough for me, making sure I had adequate accommodation, walking with me to the hotel, worried that it might be too expensive (at NTD 600 per night, or about $20!). They carefully perused the local map with me, noting local sites, routes and suggested walks. The accommodation was hostel style, but as it turned out I was the only one in my dormitory.

At 1.30 pm I took a small quaint train and was surprised to find how short the distance was to the next station. I spent the rest of the afternoon walking through a forest. Again I was surprised at the smallness of the area. The Japanese began felling cypresses and cedars from 1912 on, so most of the trees are not that old, being regrowth from after World War II. To take out the logs they built a railway, which is how I wished to come up here from Chiayi, but unfortunately this old railroad is no longer serviceable.

Some older trees still remain, some over 2,000 years old. One tree is called the "Three Generations Tree", because after it was felled, a sprout grew from its trunk and later another sprout from this growth. Nature is so resilient. Another tree is 2,300 years old, has a 12.3 metre circumference and is 45 metres high: remarkable. Predictably, there is a temple up here, but not so predictably there are groups of Falun Gong, with placards stating that they are good. This group of course is banned in China. The devotees just stood there for much of the day.

As early as 3.30 pm I was walking into the visitors' centre when I met the two girls leaving, going to their quarters, so we stopped and chatted for some time. I have been most impressed with the young people of this country. Truly, they are doing something right, and are not just obsessed with power, money or whatever. There is something wholesome about them.

I found a restaurant for a good evening meal, then had an early night, not that I got to sleep early, as the people next door were singing and talking till late. It is good to hear them being so happy. Maybe I should have joined them.

Next morning I had set my alarm for 3.45 am, but need not have done so, as my worthy companions in the next dormitory woke me up. They certainly did not get much sleep last night. Why so early? The thing to do here is to get up early to watch the sun rise from the peak. You have to be kidding! The whole time I have been in these mountains it has been cloudy and threatening rain, so there is no hope of seeing any sun, either rising or setting or any time in between. But there is more to it.

Hundreds of people walked up to the railway station. I had bought my ticket the night before, costing me only NTD 50, rather than the usual NTD 80, in deference to my grey hairs. Wonderful, especially since I am not a Taiwanese citizen. There is a viewing platform at the terminal railway station, commanding a view of the valley below, or it would if you could see, but there were just so many people there, that I opted to walk a further ten minutes to another viewing platform on a nearby ridge, Mt. Ogasawara: much better. The altitude here is 2,488 metres, which is higher than Kosciusko, Australia's highest continental mountain. Just before 5.30 am a reddish glow did in fact appear in the east, followed by a gradual lightening of the sky, while we stood in the mist, some people using umbrellas, for all the good they would have done, since the moisture was all pervasive rather than falling from above. It was also pleasantly cool, so that I really needed my tracksuit. Nevertheless it was magical, standing there, watching clouds in the valley below, everything so quiet and still, very peaceful. There is something about mountains which soothes the human spirit.

Mountains are special places for many different peoples. For the Chinese, *qi*, or life spirit, is concentrated in mountains as it is considered to be light, so rises. This *qi* can give one vitality and can be curative. I am sure that the effort to climb may also have some effect. As well, mist or cloud is considered as the feminine principle, while rain is considered as the masculine – yin and yang. The two together is symbolic of intercourse, and hence life giving.

For those of us in the Judaeo-Christian tradition, mountains are places where God is most present – between Heaven and Earth – and so are places where theophanies occur. Moses received the Ten Commandments on Mt. Sinai, Elijah met God there as well "in a still small voice". The Transfiguration took place on a mountain, and so the list goes on. For me, in particular, they have always been very special places; and yes, God is there.

Instead of taking the train, I decided to walk back to the centre, as many other people did as well, walking partly on the road, partly through new growth forests. By 7.00 am I was back at the hostel, ready for breakfast.

By 9.10 am I boarded a bus back to Chiayi, after a truly wonderful interlude. The bus had allocated seats, which surprised me and I found myself sitting next to a Korean girl, who is studying Chinese in Taipei. Two of her classmates were also on the bus, a young man from Thailand, and his girlfriend from Slovenia; they were obviously very keen on each other.

Back at Chiayi, I immediately caught a bus for Tainan – yet another "Tai".

68.   Tainan – 24th July 2012

As usual here in Taiwan, breakfast was provided as part of the tariff. This particular breakfast, however, was a little unusual, at least for me. There was weak cold tea with hot corn soup, a platter of vegetables plus fruit, and to finish a doorstop slice of toast with sausages. Where is my cereal and coffee? But there was quite a lot – enough to keep me going throughout the day.

The morning was spent looking for the Catholic church, which I found eventually after much asking of directions. I found myself at a Protestant centre, where a lovely Christian lady took me in hand, actually driving me in her car to the Catholic centre, which did not look anything like what I had expected. I wanted to sit down with people in the know and talk about the Church in Taiwan, not just from idle curiosity, but because I had a serious purpose in mind. Discussions were most fruitful. But I need not go into them here. Suffice to say that Taiwanese believe in many gods, thinking that the Christian God is just one more, and not the favourite, it seems, since Shey has the reputation for being slow to grant requests! Goodness, is that God's purpose? There are also few local clergy, with many coming from overseas.

I walked a lot. The footpaths here have the usual blockages with motorcycles, which I have mentioned before, but as well shops often spill out onto them, leaving even less room for pedestrians. To add to the obstacle course, gutters are high, so that you are up and down as well as veering in and out. So you walk on the road.

In the afternoon, I caught the 88 bus to Anping, the port area. As usual with both Tw and Chinese cities, they are sited at some distance from the coast. This, however, is where the Europeans settled, so there is a lot of history here. A plaque identifies five periods in Taiwanese history;

1)   Aboriginal, with separate tribes scattered throughout the island and seemingly happy to keep it that way.
2)   European settlement from the late 15th century, first the Portuguese, then later the Spanish and Dutch. It was the Portuguese who called the island Formosa (beautiful). The Japanese were also attempting to annex the island.
3)   Chinese. In 1644 the Ming Dynasty fell to the Manchus, but an army held out in Xiamen, Fujian Province under the command of

Zheng Cheng-gong, otherwise known as Koxinga. In trying to escape the Manchus, he attacked and defeated the Dutch in 1661. In 1683 the Manchus (Qing) took the island. A major revolt against Chinese rule took place in 1783. During Chinese rule, Tainan was the capital of the island.

4)   Japanese. In 1895, after Japan defeated China, by the Treaty of Shimonoseki, China ceded Taiwan to Japan, giving up for all time any claim whatsoever to the island.

5)   The republic. After Japan's defeat in WW II and the defeat of the Kuomintang, Chiang Kai-shek and his remaining forces fled to Taiwan and set up a government which remains to this day.

There is still part of a wall remaining from a Dutch fort, called Fort Providentia, built in 1653, and a Dutch well in much better condition in what is now known as Chihkan Tower. The site was a school for a time, but is now a museum. A plaque praises the contribution made by England and France to Taiwan's development, bringing knowledge, techniques and culture. I have never seen any such acknowledgment in China.

A much larger Dutch fort, Zeelandia, was closed when I was there. Around the port area there used to be warehouses belonging to major trading companies, though not much remains now. There is, however, one interesting site. A British built warehouse of Tait & Co. became the centre of the salt industry during the Japanese period, then was abandoned and left derelict for some 60 years, during which time it was almost completely enveloped by a banyan tree. Extraordinary. Today they call it the tree house.

The morning had been fine- sunny and hot, but as I emerged from the tree house it started to rain, so I headed for the nearest restaurant for a late lunch, and sat there from around 2.00 pm to 3.30 pm, while a thunderstorm raged. I got chatting with a Taiwanese couple who are university students.

After the rain cleared, I walked around for a while, before catching the No. 2 bus back to town. It is not a large city; with a population of around 800,000 it is the fourth largest. Even though I had just the one day in Tainan, I learned a lot. I did a lot of walking, so had an early night. I would head off for the south on the morrow.

69.   Kenting – 25th – 27th July 2012

After breakfast, I left my hotel in Tainan at 9.30 am to catch a train to Kaohsiung, only 40 minutes away. Distances are not great in this country. This city is the second largest in Taiwan, with something over a million people. It is the industrial and trade centre, with a lot of manufacturing (with its resultant pollution) and a large port. There did not appear to be much to attract me to remain here, so immediately upon arrival I bought a bus ticket to Kenting down in the south. I bought an English language newspaper to read on the bus, and attempted the crossword, but unfortunately found it to be American and not international. I really do not know the names of American personalities or small towns etc., not to mention American expressions.

Kenting National Park is the first one established in Taiwan, in January 1982. I am surprised at such a late date, more than a century after the world's first, being The Royal in Sydney, dating from 1879. I think Yellowstone in the U.S. was second, in 1883. It is situated on the Hengchun Peninsular, which forms the tail of the island, tapering off to a point.

At Kenting I booked into a hotel called A Gong Resort, then walked around town to get a feel for the place. It is not much more than a single street lined with shops, restaurants and hotels, with some stores. There is no internet cafe, no fruit or vegetable shops and no supermarket. It must also be the dirtiest place in all of Taiwan, which I have found to be very clean. There is rubbish lying around in many places. What a pity. Yet this strip really comes to life at night time, when that Taiwanese specialty, the night market, begins. This street then becomes lined with portable stalls, most of which lie unused during the day. They sell foods of many different kinds. Some stalls even have a portable oven where they bake pizzas while you wait.

After an hour's rest in my hotel room, I set of for the most southerly tip of Taiwan, to Eluanbi lighthouse, some 9 km down the road. It was a good walk. I could have got on an organised bus tour, but a brochure I picked up indicated that this would cost virtually an arm and a leg; I preferred to use my arms and legs for walking.

I got there just after 5.00 pm and spent quite some time wandering around the pathways there, which meander for about 3 km, before finding a seat at a lookout. One could gaze out at the Taiwan Straits on one side, the Pacific Ocean on the other with the Bashi Channel in between. Quite apart from soaking in the tranquillity of the scene, I appreciated the rest, having walked so far about 12 km today. Another man joined me here, so we chatted for a while. One of the things I really appreciate in Taiwan is that you can visit sites and find not all that many people, unlike China, where every place is swamped with crowds.

There is much coral around here, and also evidence of early human habitation. The probability is that people from the Philippines first came here around 10,000 years ago. The 22 metre high lighthouse is fortified, complete with moat (no water in it), glace, and castellated walls with slit holes to fire through. I do not know why. Certainly the lighthouse is valuable, probably having prevented hundreds of shipwrecks since it was built in the 1880s.

By now it was getting dark, so I asked if there was a local bus – not a tour bus – heading back into town. Yes, there is -great. Together with some 13 other people, I waited at the designated bus stop, but no bus came. Maybe the others joined me because they thought I knew what I was doing! Eventually, after about 50 minutes, an empty tour bus drove past, going in the opposite direction. The bus driver saw us, turned around and drove us back to Kenting, and for no charge. I have found Taiwanese people to be so obliging. It was just as well, because it started to rain heavily. If I had have walked I would have got soaked. As it was I was safely ensconced in a restaurant enjoying my spaghetti carbonara and Taiwan beer while the rain pelted down outside. I was not going to use the night market in this weather. Then it was back to the hotel for rest, shower and do laundry.

The next day dawned bright, sunny and hot; just the day for a swim. In the morning, however, I wanted to explore the hinterland. I would have liked to have climbed a nearby mountain, but there is no track and I was told it has been sealed off as being unsafe. The landscape is lush green and is in fact dairy country, with brahmans being the preferred breed, the cattle being accompanied by egrets, which flew off as I approached.

After lunch, I headed along the coast to a beach, but alas, no swimming. Recently a typhoon had approached the southern tip of Taiwan, bringing with it rough and dirty seas. The water was of a brown colour, whereas I believe normally it is more like a clear teal. There is a rather plush hotel here, with small children pools, but nothing in which one can have a decent swim. For a while I sat under the shade of Australian casuarina trees, gazing out to sea; most pleasant.

Next morning I walked about 400 metres up the road to the bus stop, out in the open. It was so hot that I sat in the shade instead for more than half an hour. Just after 10.00 am we arrived in Fangliao, where I immediately bought a train ticket for Taitung on the eastern side of the island. Unfortunately there were no seats, so I managed to squeeze myself into a small space behind the last seat of the carriage. I was there about 30 minutes, reading, when a woman who was passing, saw me, spoke to the conductor, then led me through several carriages to the first class carriage, where there were plenty of seats, enabling me to complete this leg of the journey much more comfortably. Wonderful. People can be so nice. The first shall be last and the last first.

It took only about half an hour for the actual crossing of the island from west coast to east coast, going through a number of mountain tunnels. The countryside is again lush green. I finished my book as we travelled, about the Salem witch trials of 1692- just horrid. How could people do this? Yet as I write this, news has come through of the Muslim Taliban beheading 17 people simply for dancing. This is really evil, the evil of ignorance, superstition, petty spitefulness, jealousy and especially the attempt to control others.

We had arrived at Taitung.

70.   Taitung and Lyudao – 27th – 28th July 2012

Taitung is not where I would build a city, coastal, yet at a distance from the sea, while the railway station is set at a considerable distance from the town and even further from the sea. Curious. I caught a bus into town, looking for a suitable hotel. But first, I needed to buy a hat. I lost mine somewhere between Kenting and Taitung and I do not want to spend long in the hot sun without some protection. Luckily I soon found what I wanted. There is a visitor centre close to the hotel, so that was good. That was my next port of call to plan my stay here.

I wanted to go to the National Museum of Prehistory, but once again, it is situated at an inconvenient distance of around 8 km. I took a taxi. Entrance for me was free, either because of (a) my good looks or (b) over 65 years old. Has to be the former! According to this museum, the first humans arrived in Taiwan about 15,000 years ago, considerably earlier than I had been led to believe in Kenting. It is not clear where the people came from – from China or the Philippines or maybe both. During previous ice ages, of course, the shallow seas to the west and south of Taiwan would have been even shallower, perhaps dry. Interestingly, there does not appear to have been much advance in civilization once the waters rose and the people were cut off. There is a parallel here with China, which fossilized once it cut itself off from the outside world after 1421.Something similar happened to the aboriginal people of Tasmania, who actually went backwards after Bass Strait was flooded, forgetting how to fish and how to light fire. There is a lesson here; we need each other. I spent a very pleasant two hours here until closing time, when I got thrown out, so to speak, but the museum was kind enough to order a taxi for me, which took a considerable time to arrive.

For the next couple of hours I wandered around the town and discovered – much to my delight – fruit shops. Wonderful! It is weeks since I have had an orange, for instance. Time to relax back at the Eastern Hotel, as the next day would be special.

Close by the visitors' centre there is a bus depot, from where I caught a bus to the port of Fugang, some distance up the coast. I fell in with a group of young people, which is just as well, because you needed to know where you were going. At the port I paid NTD 960 for a return ticket on a boat to Lyudao, or Green Island. It was a most pleasant 50 minute trip across.

I had expected to find a visitors' centre at the wharf of Nanliao Harbour on the island, but no dice, though a sign pointed up the road. It began to rain, so I sought some shelter for a while, so that it took me a further hour to walk the 2 km to the visitors' centre. Once again, everything is most inconveniently located. Here I got a map, since what I really wanted to do was to go to Jahbrih hot springs. I found that they were located at the other end of the island, meaning I needed to retrace my steps 2 km back to the wharf, and it was a further 6 km from there. What do people do? They hire a bike or motor scooter, but to do this you need ID (passport) and unfortunately I had left mine back in Taitung.

Back to the wharf I went, through the town of Nanliao and out onto the coast road, which is 19 km in length, encircling this small island. I had gone only another couple of km when I was hailed by a man on a bike. He stopped to ask how I was –so very kind. Well, I was fine, except that I have some hiking to do. "Hop on" says he. "I can't do that; you already have three." "We'll fit." And we did. Andrew drove, with his wife, Yi Lun, behind him and son Byron in front, while I perched behind. This saved me a good deal of both time and energy. It turns out that Andrew comes from Hungary, while his wife is Taiwanese.

For the next two hours we soaked in these hot springs, called Jahbrih, obviously not a Chinese word. There are many other languages in this country. They are right next to the sea itself, in a series of circular pools. There is also a natural rock pool into which the sea washes. The water temperature is not too hot, warm mainly, but the pools do vary. There is just a hint of sulphur. The rain, too, had cleared though the skies remained cloudy. It was wonderful, the more so in that there were not the crowds of people that you get in China. It was most pleasant talking with this family. I hope all goes well for them. Most people seem to stay on the island for a while, but I needed to get back and the last boat was leaving at 4.30 pm. Why so early?

While Andrew and his family headed up to the headland, which I had investigated before getting into the pools, I started out to walk the 6 km back to the wharf. Along the way I fell in with a charming young Taiwanese lady, Joyce, who was intending to walk around the entire island. It would be dark before she finished. It is a lovely walk, with great coastal scenery, here and there the sea gouging our caves and revealing its true teal colour.

By 5.30 pm I was back in Fugang, with some time to wait for the next bus to Taitung. I spent the time watching fishermen at work. Back in Taitung, I walked a couple of blocks from my hotel to a street which had been cordoned off for a night market, the most sophisticated I had seen in all of Taiwan. Tables and chairs had been set up down the middle of the street, the first time I had seen this. They also had sinks, so one could wash one's hands, with pipes tapping into the mains below the road for the water supply. So here I ate, and the food was superb. I had fish balls, dumplings cooked on a spit, washed down with Taiwanese beer. For dessert I had the most delicious waffle with ice-cream topping.

Truly this day was just great, one of the very best here in Taiwan. On a slightly sour note, I lost my phrase book which I always carry around with me. Possibly I left on the bus, as I had been using it when talking with a group of young people. First I lost my hat and now my phrase book; do these things come in threes? Wait. Tomorrow I would head off to Hualien my last stop on this tour.

71.　*Hualien and Taroko Gorge – 29th – 31st July 2012*

In the morning I walked down to the bus depot to catch a bus to Hualien, the next town to the north up the east coast. I was told there was only one bus and it had left at 6.10 am. Goodness, why so early? I had wanted the bus, rather than the train, because it follows the coast more closely. So at 7.40 am I caught the town bus to the railway station, where I had an hour wait. I read the Taipei Times. At 9.45 am we were just pulling out of the station when there was a huge commotion, and the conductor stopped the train. I think some passengers had got onto the wrong train.

As we travelled I reached into my carry bag for my camera. No camera. Oh no, don't tell me I left it behind! It may be in my back pack. I searched my backpack. No camera. This is terrible; not just the camera, but all my Taiwanese photos gone. First I lost my hat, then my phrase book and now my camera! Am I losing "it" as well? I really wanted that camera. What do you do when you really, **really** want something?

I grew up in a parish dedicated to Our Lady of the Sacred Heart, and all my life she has been the one to go to. This was just such an occasion. I was thinking that possibly I had left it in my hotel room at Taitung, so as soon as we arrived in Hualien, I went to the railway police to report it missing, and to ask if they might ring the hotel. They were most obliging. The hotel sent someone to check my room but no, it was not there. "Ok, thank you very much." There was nothing for it but to find a place to stay in Hualien, which I did, close to the station, bus depot and tourist centre. As soon as I booked in I searched my backpack thoroughly, though actually I did not need to. Why not? – because the camera was sitting near the top, just under my breakfast supplies. Who put it there???

The hotel is called the Chen Tia. The floor levels are curious. I am on the 5th floor, but this is also called the 3rd floor. Where is the 4th? – there isn't any, because 4 is associated with bad luck. *Si,* fourth tone, means "four", while *si,* third tone means "death". In my hotel in Taitung, there was no 4th floor either and no 9th floor as well. People can be so superstitious.

I spent the afternoon walking around town, down to the harbour, which is protected by both walls and large triangular shaped blocks of concrete, designed to break the force of the waves, as this coast is prone to typhoons. Indeed one is coming, chasing me as I move north. A man was fishing, perched precariously on the tip of one of these blocks. All it needed was a bigger wave and the fish would be feeding on him. There is a statue to Mazu here. To refresh your memory, she was the lady from near Fuzhou who drowned about 300 years ago. She is honoured as protector of sailors, which is somewhat ironic. What she really is – and she would know this – is an image of Mary. And we know how powerful she is.

Hualien is a marble town, as tonnes of it are mined in the nearby mountains. Remember that Taiwan used to be under the sea, until lifted up through collision with the Pacific Plate. The limestone in this area, laid down about 200 million years ago, was then subjected to both pressure and heat – regional metamorphism – turning it into marble. The bus stops are marble; there is marble in the footpaths; the town seats are marble. It is beautiful.

Next day was special. I woke at 6.00 am and after breakfast strolled over to the bus depot to buy a ticket at NTD 250 for Taroko Gorge. It is cheaper to buy tickets as you need them but this entitled me to go where I liked and get on and off buses all day. We left at 7.50 am, and I rode the bus all the way up to the top end of the gorge at Tianshang. The road continues over and through the mountains to the west coast, as this road is the Central Cross Island Highway. Here I wandered around for a while before sitting down in a cafe to enjoy a cup of coffee. Two streams join here, making for great scenery. An attractive bridge has marble in the footpath and a marble balustrade.

Time to move. I walked the 2 km back down to Lushui, where there is a camping ground. There is also a geological museum, with all explanations in Chinese only, unfortunately. It includes an exhibition of geological specimens, which was a bit of a surprise. Now it is many years since I studied Geology, and I have forgotten more than I remember, but it seemed to me that quite a few of these specimens have been incorrectly labelled. I pointed this out to the curator, who asked me to identify the samples, which I did, though also pointing out my lack of expertise, suggesting he get a qualified geologist to check them out. From here there is a 2 km walking trail through the bush, built by the Japanese, which is quite delightful, supplying great views of this part of the gorge.

The trail led down to Heliu, which also has a camping ground, and from here I waited for the bus to take me 4 km further down the road to Yanziko, where I got off, since this is where the gorge is at its best. It truly is beautiful, with folds in the marble rock showing where it has been squeezed together, squashed between the Pacific and Asian Plates. Cliffs tower hundreds of metres above, while the gorge itself is so narrow, only a couple of metres at one point, with the river rushing below. It is worth a visit. The roadway is in and out of tunnels and at this section there is even a separate walkway for pedestrians, so it is that much safer. To further emphasise safety, tourists are given safety helmets to don, free of charge. At places railings have suffered some damage from falling rocks, so that wearing helmets is not a bad idea. Remember that this region is prone to both earthquakes and typhoons, and one is coming. A little rain has already reached here, as it moves up the coast.

I walked a further 8 km down this road through this extraordinary gorge, and yet saw only a part of it. It would repay a revisit. This whole area, about 30 by 40 km, is a national park, the second largest in Taiwan, and boasts an array of wildlife as well as fantastic scenery. There are, for instance, some 108 different species of butterflies here. There are many walking trails throughout the park. I walked as far as Changchun, where there is a temple, called Eternal Spring. It is actually built right over a spring – whose waters, I guess, flow all year round, emptying into the Liwu River. The aboriginal people here are called the Taroko, and hence the name of this gorge.

The rain is getting heavier, so I decided that this would be enough for one day. At Changchun I caught the bus back to Hualien. The forecast is for increasing rain over the next few days. That night it rained heavily. Back at the railway station I bought a ticket to return to Taipei. Unfortunately there were no seats and I really wanted a seat, and the next train which had a spare seat did not leave till 4.00 pm. So I waited, spending the day both relaxing and wandering around Hualien, but mostly reading at the railway station, as it was raining most of the day. This is my final full day in Taiwan, as tomorrow I fly back to Hong Kong. If ever you get a chance, visit this gorge.

72. Hualien to Chongqing, China – 31st July – 7th August 2012

On Tuesday, 31ˢᵗ July, I left Hualien just after 4.00 pm. It is a very interesting trip, as one is heading north on a very narrow strip of land between the steeply rising mountains to the west and the Pacific Ocean to the east, the former is part of the Asian Plate, while the latter is part of the Pacific Plate.

We got into Taipei at around 7.00 pm. My first task was to find the bus station from which I could catch the airport shuttle the next day. It took a good hour to locate it, through the drizzling rain, the forerunner of the typhoon which had been chasing me up the coast. Next was to find a nearby hotel and luckily I found a suitable one directly opposite, though at first sight it looked anything but suitable, as it is located on the third floor of a rather unkempt building, the entrance being located up a dingy flight of stairs. But the inside is clean, and the room quite presentable; and it was inexpensive.

I slept well but woke up rather earlier than intended, due to a form of entertainment issuing from the next room, with sounds clearly audible through a wall which must have been paper thin. Let us just say that a young couple was thoroughly enjoying each other. It seemed that they had come to what we might call a conclusion before I went off to breakfast. By the time I returned they were starting again. Isn't it wonderful when people love each other?

It was raining quite heavily, so I remained in my hotel room and watched a movie on TV. Obviously, one cannot underestimate the quality of entertainment in this fair establishment. As soon as there was some abatement in the weather, I checked out and walked across to the bus station, leaving almost immediately at 10.40 am. My companion was a very interesting gentleman from Belgium, called Alfons, who is working on energy solutions and security. What an interesting world it is.

At the airport my flight was delayed, taking off eventually at 3.40 pm, with the weather closing in. At 7.00 pm the airport was closed. My travelling companion on this leg was a young lady – from America, as it transpired – who was writing in Chinese. I told her how much I envied her with my poor Chinese. I also told her that I had lost my phrase book, whereupon she promptly gave me hers, identical to the one I had lost. My companion on this flight has spent three years studying Mandarin in Beijing, so said she now no longer needed such a simple phrase book. Thank you.

We were back in Hong Kong by 5.30 pm and at the AITECE office by 6.30 pm, welcomed by fellow Aussie, Jim. We talked till late. We do share a most important common interest, in that we both barrack for Collingwood. For the uninitiated, this is an Aussie Rules team – the best, I might add – which has made it to the final four this year. We will see how they go, though their finals record is not the best. In the morning I was able to talk with Rita, a hardworking and ever obliging secretary and pick up my computer. After lunch I left to catch the train to Guangzhou. All went smoothly on the 2 hour train journey.

In Guangzhou East railway station one goes through security as this is an entry point into China. From there I found my way by the metro system to Guangzhou railway station, where I proceeded to purchase my ticket for the next leg of my journey, to Guiyang. I found that the next available seat was not till the following day, 2.40 pm; there is no sleeper available, so I will have to sit up all night. Welcome back to China and its crowds of people. I booked into the nearest hotel, right next to the railway station, where in fact I had stayed before. It is a comfortable hotel with a screen which doubles as both a TV and computer – excellent. One minor point was that the plug in the sink was stuck, meaning I had to bail the water out using a glass tumbler.

The next morning, when I went to check out, I was asked to pay an extra 10 Yuan because the tumbler had been cracked. I agreed on the proviso that they reduce my tariff by 10 Yuan, on the grounds that the room was faulty, and that the tumbler would never have been cracked if the plug had not been stuck. Our positions were adamant, until the concierge said he would call the manager. Good; that was exactly what I wanted. As soon as he saw this, he agreed to my terms.

At 1.40 pm I headed to the station to find the correct waiting room; there are ten, probably each of them equally crowded. At 2.45 pm we left. I bought my evening meal on the train, which they bring around – this is convenient – washed down with a Tibetan beer, which, I might add, is very weak, both in alcoholic content and in taste. I got snatches of sleep through the night, and did a bit of reading, finishing "The Help" by Kathryn Stocket. If you have not read it, I would highly recommend it.

We arrived in Guiyang at 10.15 am after a 19 ½ hour journey. Sitting up all night meant I did not get much sleep. I would meet with Echo at 4.00 pm, so I spent those waiting hours in Dicos, a fast food chain emulating McDonald's, where I had breakfast, including a welcome cup of coffee, and lunch. I read a lot, or sat and watched the people. I also bought my train ticket for the final leg of my journey to Chongqing. I caught the 253 bus to the vicinity of Echo's place, and had to wait only a short time for her husband, Rupert. As it turned out, Echo did not finish work till 6.00 pm; she works very hard indeed.

The next day was a day of resting and walking around the district and spending time with these wonderful people. They would like to move to Australia; perhaps they could teach Chinese; both of them speak excellent English

On Monday, 6th August it was time to head back to Chongqing. After lunch with Echo, I got back on the 253 bus for the return trip to the railway, while she went off to work. We had not gone far, when our bus was stopped by the police and the driver fined 100 Yuan for overcrowding. Goodness, overcrowding is part of life here; the police could make a fortune if they fined every overcrowded vehicle.

At the railway I booked into a very nice hotel, right at the station, so conveniently located. At 3.00 pm, I had a reunion with Aussie 1, who is back in China for a couple of months teaching English, before he returns to India. I met up with a former student from Tongren, plus two new people. We had a very good meal, including Peking duck, and even better company, with Echo and Rupert also joining us. It was a memorable night.

Next morning, the hotel provided breakfast, but Chinese style, with dry breads, vegetables, hardboiled egg and soy milk. I still prefer my cereal and coffee. I was in good time for my 8.00 am train. I spent most of the journey finishing "North and South" by Catherine Gaskell, a very good author. I found the story a little long and the plot a little contrived, but she is dealing with a most important topic; the relationship between management and workers. There is hope that co-operation will win out in the end.

I cannot pretend that this was the most enjoyable train trip of my life. It was just too crowded to access my luggage, which I had placed on the overhead rack. Quite a few people were travelling without seats, standing most of the time. The toilet was really dirty. I was with a family, where the father and a younger man were smoking cigarette after cigarette, even though this is illegal, and even though there was a baby in the carriage. When the baby needed to relieve itself, the mother simply held it out so that it peed over the carriage floor. I was not impressed either with the father throwing his rubbish out of the carriage window. Welcome back to China.

As we travelled north the weather became hotter. In Guiyang it had been cool and showery, both because of the monsoon rains coming up from the south, and the city's altitude at over 1,000 metres. But Chongqing is hot. At Chongqing railway station I had my evening meal, then caught a bus back to my apartment, after an absence of more than five weeks. But what wonderful weeks they were. God is good. My next episode will be the final one in this series on Taiwan.

73.   A Point of View 23rd September 2012

At the outset here, I would like to make it patently clear that what follows is a personal view, based not only upon my experiences in Taiwan, but also on my interpretation of historical events. Feel free to disagree. What follows, however, may be considered controversial in some quarters.

Before I went to Taiwan, I was asked what I thought of Taiwan's status. I replied that this was in no way dependent upon me, as I am an outsider. I added that I did not think it concerned Washington or indeed Beijing, but that it was up to the people of Taiwan. If they considered themselves to be just another province of the empire, then fine; I have no problem with that. But if they thought of themselves as a separate, independent country, then that should be respected by all and sundry. What in fact the people of Taiwan did think, I did not know. Now, I think, I do. I did not conduct a plebiscite, but I did talk with many people.

The first thing that struck me was the social atmosphere of the place. They have freedom of the press, freedom of religion, freedom of assembly and freedom of speech. They are a democracy. All of this shows; you only have to pick up a newspaper or hear people talk- so very different from China. The language used is so different. Now China refers to Taiwan as a breakaway province. This is fair enough, but it is clear that it is also an independent nation in its own right, and has been for more than 60 years. Nobody can dispute the fact that it has been governing itself for that length of time; it has not been governed by Beijing; it has not been controlled by the CP. And it has been doing very well without external interference.

What I discovered is revelatory. I did not meet a single Chinese person. This is a surprise, and came up as a result of conversations. I might say something like, "Well, you Chinese..." which seems innocuous enough, but I found myself dealing with an angry reply: "We are not Chinese; we are Taiwanese." Nobody admitted to being Chinese. One man became quite angry: "We hate China. China is a bully." That is a point of view I never found in China. Most Taiwanese people have ancestors who have come from China, but that does not make them Chinese, in much the same way as my ancestors came from Ireland, but that does not make me Irish. I am Australian. National pride in their achievements and patriotism are evident. All over the island you find National Museums, National stadiums, national this and national that – not provincial. In China people always talk about Taiwan and the Mainland, but that is Chinese talk, not Taiwanese, where they talk about China and Taiwan as quite distinct entities.

People told me, much to my surprise, that Taiwanese languages and culture are different from China. Well in many ways they are similar, but the differences are significant. Mandarin is spoken, though in their own way, but so are other languages not found in China. Much culture has derived from China, but much has not, and they have put their own stamp on it.

Re the hatred, I came across some evidence of this while reading a newspaper article about a certain Taiwanese businessman who invested in China, taking his company there. Now you would know that if you are not Chinese then you must usually have a Chinese partner. But isn't he Chinese? Apparently, for the purposes of business, he was not, but was classified as foreign. His Chinese partner then proceeded to get what he wanted from him, viz his company secrets and his money. Once this was achieved he was told to go back home. The victim took his Chinese partner to court – to a Chinese court, so you can imagine how much justice he was likely to get. Surprisingly the court ruled against his partner, but not, I might add, for him. The partner was ordered to pay damages of hundreds of millions of Yuan. So justice was done? Not really, as he did not see any of the money; half went somewhere – I forget where – and the other half was taken by the Communist Party.

It is good to get some historical perspective. You may remember the five periods of history that I mentioned in a previous episode: aboriginal, European, Chinese, Japanese and the present. Interestingly, it is only the Chinese who are jumping up and down saying "Taiwan belongs to us". The Europeans are not doing this and nor are the Japanese, even though they may have some legitimate claims to do so. In 1895, for instance, China ceded – CEDED – Taiwan to Japan – forever. From that moment, China ceased to have legitimate claims.

Even Mao Zedong recognised that Taiwan did not belong to China, though he was pushing for its independence.

Throughout my travels I also met people from other countries, and some of these expressed their opinions, and again this may not be representative of their countries. Both Japanese and Koreans distrust China and do not like it, nor did they like Chinese claims upon their territories. I did not meet any Filipinos nor Vietnamese, but I know that they, too, resent China taking their territories.

So what is going to happen in the future? Will China get Taiwan back? Of course they will, just as China will continue to take other people's territories. Who will stop them? What we need to realise is that throughout China's entire history it has been increasing the size of its territory at the expense of its neighbours. It considers that it has every right to do this, as each territory thus acquired has "been Chinese from ancient times", a mantra which is deemed to be sufficient unto itself, without further explanation. It also has the advantage that if anybody dares to criticize this aggression they shout; "Do not interfere in our internal affairs!" – by whose definition? There are some 54 minority groups, all of whose territories were overrun by the Han. I see no sign of this nationalistic greed abating and the empire will continue to expand into every contiguous territory. Someone told me recently that he had read a book whose central tenet was that China has no further territorial claims. I thoroughly disagree. It is currently in dispute with The Philippines, Vietnam, Malaysia, Indonesia, Japan and Korea, to name a few.

What worries me is that we have a parallel with Hitler's territorial ambitions in Europe. There it became clear that appeasement did not work. This only emboldened Hitler to make a grab at yet more territory. I am afraid that if China is not stopped now, we could be in for serious trouble in the future. If Hitler had been opposed early enough, we may have avoided the Second World War. It is something to think about.

74.   *Xian Nu Shan, Chongqing – 1st October 2012*

A couple of us were invited by the director of the Lancaster Programme, to join her family for two days of the week long National Day holiday. This is ideal as it gives us a chance to get away, but still leaves plenty of time to relax at home. We were picked up by car just after 6.00 am on Monday, so it was an early start and were driven to Great Hall Square where we joined a tour group. This means everything is arranged; all we have to do is to follow our leader's yellow flag. We need not have got up so early, as it was some time before we departed.

It took about two hours to reach Wu Long, which is both a town and the county in which Xian Nu Shan (Fairy Mountain) is located. The first attraction, which they called a meadow, we reached in a kind of train. It looks like a small train, but it runs on tyres; quaint. The meadow is an area of perhaps 1 sq km of rolling grassland, the sort of country you can find up and down Australia's east coast, where it is generally devoted to pasturing either sheep or more often cattle, but not the sort of country you tend to find in China. It is beautiful, especially as now the grass is so green and the day was sunny – very unusual in our climate. In fact I think this is the only sunny day we have had in the past five weeks, and the winter has yet to begin. To make it even better, the higher altitude meant we had little pollution, with the sky actually blue; heavenly. Susan's 7 year old daughter, Coco, wanted a kite, so this was purchased and a pleasant time was spent flying it.

From here we went to a market area, where you can buy all sorts of interesting food items. Meats include pork, chicken and dog, hanging up in whole carcasses. There were many different kinds of seeds and dried products. Some of the mushrooms were quite large, up to 30 cm in diameter. Coco was given a sunflower. Now sunflower seeds are very popular in China, but I have never seen anybody picking them from the sunflower itself. They are nice too.

At the visitor centre, there was a large white board for people to sign, stating that the Senkaku Islands belong to China and not to Japan. Currently the two nations are fighting over them. At this centre, Coco went missing – or so we thought. We found her with the tour guide; she had simply looked for the yellow flag; clever girl.

Back on our tour bus, we headed for the hotel where we would spend the night, but not to check in, or even to drop off our bags, but only to have lunch – a late lunch at that. The afternoon's activity was a walk from the top of a sink hole, down many steps to the bottom, some 280 metres below. This is limestone country. Probably dolomite, a magnesium calcium carbonate, laid down during the Cambrian Era, about 500 million years ago. I do not know when it was raised from the sea floor to form high land, but it would have been much later. Then erosion began; water seeping through joints would have carved out –by chemical action rather than physical – underground caves and streams. In time a large cavern was formed, large enough so that the roof could no longer be supported and it all came crashing down, leaving just three places where the roof is still in place, forming arches, or as they are called here, bridges. They are called *Tianlong Qiao, Qinglong Qiao* and *Heilong Qiao;* Heavenly Dragon Bridge, Cyan Dragon Bridge and Black Dragon Bridge.

The largest is Qinglong, at about 100 metres high. With a thickness of about 170 metres, the top is about 280 metres above the canyon floor. It apparently looks like a dragon when you get rain and falling water. Many things in China look like dragons, where elsewhere people would say it looks like a bride's veil or whatever. Heilong Bridge is about 220 metres high and 107 metres thick, so it has different dimensions. Tianlong Bridge is somewhere between these two, but has more evidence of roof collapse. Heilong is more like a tunnel, as it is quite deep, thus being considerably darker inside; hence the black dragon. There is a dragon etched into the rock as you emerge; it is a favourite photo op. It all makes perfect sense really. There is also a lovely little waterfall falling out of a crevice to join a river flowing out of this canyon, but at the moment it has very little water in it, apparently much less than in days of yore.

At one end of this canyon, or sinkhole if you prefer, there is an old temple. Apparently it was used as the setting for a movie called "Curse of the Golden Flower". I have not seen it so have no idea what is it about, though one can guess. There are a couple of old style coaches as well, which I found very interesting, as one can see how the wealthy got around centuries ago, when the horse provided the major means of transport. They are remarkably similar to Western coaches, though I am sure that each developed independently of the other, providing yet more evidence of the unity of the human race.

We rejoined our bus to return to our hotel for evening meal. This, however, was not the end of the day's activities, as we piled back on our bus for a half hour ride to a concert venue. Traffic was heavy, so there were many delays, but we managed to get there by the skin of our teeth before the starting time of 7.00 pm.

The venue is truly remarkable. You approach up a box canyon where vehicles are parked. You then walk up steps and through a tunnel, about 150 metres in length. The roof is curved with projectors at the apex. These show slides of the boat haulers at work. Before the Three Gorges Dam was constructed, men were employed to haul boats over the rapids. In some places the sides of the rivers (Yangtze amongst others) were so steep, that paths had been dug along the cliff face, so that these men could do their work. I have seen some of these paths as I traversed the Three Gorges before the river level rose. The photos show how very hard this work was, with men straining at their ropes, muscles bulging, wearing only a loin cloth. Some were barefoot; some wore home-made sandals. I have a pair of these and did not find them very comfortable.

This concert is all about these men. As you emerge from the tunnel, you find yourself in another box canyon. Seats are arranged on one side, with a capacity, I was told, of 2,700. The seats themselves are interesting. Each is a fixture, made from cane, and the backrest of each has a lighted panel, with the seat's number and row: what a good idea. These lights can be left on during the performance or turned off.

The display of lights was simply amazing, using both conventional spot lights and lasers. The screens on which these lights were projected included the floor, a building on the right hand side and the canyon wall, not to mention the air itself. Thus an appearance of a flock of doves flying overhead was produced using lights.

There were about half a dozen items, focusing on the life of these boat haulers. Dance was combined with song. One such song told the tale of a woman who grows up in her family, but must leave when still very young to marry a boat hauler. On the day of her wedding she cries at her hard lot, the only time in her life when she is allowed to cry. From now on she must accept her lot and make the best of it. Singers were also located within the audience and on the cliff face opposite. At one point lines of men hauling ropes came up the aisles between the seats. It was all very impressive.

There would be three performances on this night, but this would be the final night. We were very lucky to be here. We were also lucky to get here on time, as those who missed out would have to wait for the third performance; they would have a very late night indeed. We got back to our hotel about 9.30 pm. It has been a long day, and we were all ready for bed.

75.   Furong Dong – 2nd October 2012

I think we all slept well; the beds were comfortable. There were some drawbacks, however. The hotel relies on solar power for its hot water, but its system is inadequate, with the result that we had no hot water for showers, not that it mattered, as they did not provide towels and I had neglected to bring one. No matter, as I can have a hot shower when I get back to my apartment in Chongqing. Watch this space. The toilet is Chinese style squat, not Western.

After 7.30 am breakfast, we all piled back into our bus for a very long drive indeed- all of 100 metres. Then we all got out again. This is an organised tour, and for all of these it is de rigueur to go to shops to purchase various goods. Both the tour guide and the bus driver get their cut of whatever we buy. This particular shop appeared to specialise in goods made from natural products, such as towels made from bamboo and massage oils. The layout is in the form of a maze, in order to maximise customer exposure to goods within a limited space. I noticed that some goods were repeated, just in case you had a change of mind. Some of our travelling companions bought goods, but I did not. There was nothing I needed.

Later this day we would visit yet another establishment, this one a factory making knives, mainly for kitchen use. I really need a sharp kitchen knife, but the ones they were offering were too big for my needs. The knives you buy in supermarkets are not very sharp. This company has an eye on the international market, so we sat down and listened to the spiel and watched the demonstrations. It must have been effective, because quite a few people did buy packets of knives. David even bought an electric razor, which I too would have done if we had been here six months ago when I needed one. Prices were quite inexpensive. As we filed out we were each presented with a fruit knife; now that is welcome. I noticed in their show room that they were selling at 25 Yuan.

There remains just one place to describe on this tour- a limestone cave (*dong*). It is situated about half way up the bank of the local Furong River, about 200 metres above the river. This river is a tributary of the Wu River, which joins the Yangtze just below Chongqing. The bank here is quite steep. This means that the road up is narrow and windy, in fact too narrow and too windy for our large 40 seater bus. I do not know why they do not leave large buses down the bottom and use smaller ones to run up and down the mountain. Our driver, Horatio, has a habit of swinging wide on curves- too wide, in my opinion. Maybe at some time in the past he did not swing wide enough and ended up with his rear wheels in a ditch, so that now he is extra cautious. I know buses do have to swing wide – I used to be a bus driver – but not as wide as he was going.

Why is he called Horatio? I hear you say. It is the name we gave him. Well Horatio likes to blow his horn when going around bends. He likes to blow his horn when passing traffic. He likes to blow his horn if there are pedestrians around. He likes to blow his horn if has not done so within the previous 30 seconds, just to make sure it is working. There are in fact TWO horns on this bus; a softer one and a louder one. Our Horatio definitely has a preference for the latter. So why did we call him Horatio? Some of you may know that there is a certain fictional British naval hero set in the time of the Napoleonic wars called Horatio Hornblower. So now you know.

In due course, after some delays due to the police ensuring that traffic became one way on this narrow mountain road, we arrived at Furong Dong, entering at 11.00 am, together with a million or so other people. It was far too crowded; remember that this is National Day holiday, and China's population is massive.

I have been into many limestone caves in various countries and they are amazing. Stalactites and stalagmites take such a long time to form, at the rate of about 1 mm per year, or one metre per thousand years. The structures they form are beautiful and detailed. This cave, however, may now be too dry to be forming new structures – a fossil cave. It is some 1,860 metres long and between 30 and 50 metres across, with the vertical height being about the same. Surprisingly, it was not discovered until 1993 and opened to the public in 2007. It does have very good examples of mysteries – stalactites going sideways – and the cascading effect you get down columns. There was also good use of lighting, to provide colour, and of course, some use of imagination, with structures bearing such exotic names as "Stone Flower King", "Canine Crystal Flower Bed" and "Coral Pool". The main attraction, however, is "Origin of Life", a stalagmite looking like a phallic symbol. Surprisingly, there was no "Jade Dragon". Dragons are usually everywhere.

We emerged from the cave at 12.10 pm and then waited for quite some time for our travelling companions who had opted not to enter the cave, but had taken a boat trip on the Furong River instead. It was rather late by the time we had lunch. Then it was time to head home, getting back to Chongqing around 6.30 pm. Susan had organised this trip for us, so David and I invited her to have a meal, so we found a buffet style restaurant near Great Hall Square. It appeared to specialise in meat, which was delicious. I saw one man pile his plate with so much bacon, that I assume he was feeding a small army. You cooked the food yourself at your table on a hot plate. It is really a very good idea.

From here we were driven back to SISU, arriving not too late. Now for that hot shower that I missed out on last night! Alas, this was not to be. There was no water in my apartment, not even for a wash. I told you to watch this space. So I had to go to bed as I was. Thankfully, the water was back on again when I awoke next morning, so then I had my shower, though the water was somewhat brown in colour, with lots of sediment coming from the pipes.

It was a wonderful two days. Thank you, S for organising it. For the rest of the holiday, I relaxed at home, wrote up this tour and prepared classes.

76.   Diao Yu Cheng, Chongqing – 29th December 2012

This place is important, not only in the history of China, but also in the history of Europe, much of Asia and possibly of Africa as well. Now that appears to be a rather outrageous claim to make, but it is not without justification.

This town, called Fishing Town in English, is only about 1 ½ hours from our university by car, but I had never heard of it, until one of my students gave a speech about it. It has a long history, being occupied first by the Ba people, the aboriginal inhabitants of this whole region. According to legend, it got its name from two incisions cut into a rock overlooking the Jia Ling River. Ancient peoples thought a giant had stood here to cast his rod into the river to fish. It would be some rod, as the river is some 200 metres below. This does, however, give a clue as to why this town became so important. From a military perspective, it is easily defended. Not only does the Jia Ling River provide a barrier on one side, but two other sides are protected by the Qu River and the

Fu River; thus only one side is open to a land assault. As well the town sits atop a steep bluff.

Its military significance became apparent in the 13th century, when the Mongols were on the advance. Just to refresh your memory, Genghis Khan became supreme ruler of the Mongol tribes, uniting them into a formidable fighting force, before beginning to invade the surrounding territories in AD 1206. Genghis died in 1227, being succeeded by his son Ogedei. He died in 1241, and according to Mongol tradition, all princes had to assemble to choose a new Khan, thus putting a temporary halt to further invasions; by now the Mongol armies had entered Eastern Europe and were ravaging China and many other countries. Ogedei's death halted further invasion in Europe, thus saving Western Europe. Mongke, a grandson of Genghis was eventually elected Khan after considerable infighting, in 1251.

By 1243 the fortifications of Diao Yu Cheng were complete. Subsequently, the Mongols made many attempts to take it, but with no success. Over the next four decades there were at least eight major sieges with around 200 separate attacks. Of these, the siege of 1259 is the most significant. The struggle with the Song Dynasty was prolonged, and in particular this small town had resisted sieges for a long time when many other larger towns had been taken. You may imagine the frustration.

The Mongols decided to continue their attacks through the hot summer months, which was not in accord with their usual practice. As well, the Kahn (Mongke) decided to lead the attacks in person; a big mistake. Mongolia is definitely not a tropical country, and is subject to extremely severe winters. Over the summer of 1259, many soldiers sickened. On 11th August, 1259 Mongke was wounded – possibly with an arrow, but more probably he was hit by shrapnel. It is immaterial, as the net result was that he died on 3rd September. He failed to employ nurses from the Prince of Wales hospital (where I used to work) who had proper qualifications, so that his wounds became infected from tainted water.

Now the year AD 1259 was just a little before the advent of mobile phones, worldwide internet connections and on the spot reporters. Hence it was some time before his body was taken back to the Mongol capital, Karakorum, and even longer for the news to filter out to the far reaches of the empire. In April of 1260 AD, one Mongol army was invading Baghdad, and indeed succeeded in its conquest, almost completely destroying what was then the centre of Islam. They next proceeded to conquer Syria and were now poised to strike into Africa.

This was the state of play when news arrived that all leaders would be required to gather in Karakorum to elect their new Khan.

This they did, the process being both long and rancorous, with civil war actually breaking out till 1264, after which Kublai became victorious. Indeed the empire now split into separate Khanates. Meanwhile, the Mamluks from Egypt defeated the token Mongol army still remaining in the Middle East, thus effectively ending any further Mongol advance. The battle took place in the Jezreel Valley in Galilee in September 1260. This marked the end of any further Mongol advance. The civil war also meant there would be no further advance into Europe.

Hence this small town does have global significance.

When I first heard of Diao Yu Cheng from one of my students, I expressed an interest in visiting it, so she very kindly arranged for two cars to take some of us to see it one Saturday. We left around 8.00 am for the 1 ½ hour drive to the north. The day was cold and overcast, but not actually raining, a typical Chongqing winter's day. It took us some time, driving around the nearest town, stopping to ask directions, before we eventually found our way. You do have to drive out of the modern town, and up the bluff on which the old town was built.

We spent the rest of the morning and early afternoon exploring the site. You can still see the holes in the rock in which wooden poles were affixed for the drawbridge over the main gate. You can also see the marks where mangonels rested. There is also a series of open pits, where the defenders used to mix gunpowder. Large open cisterns for water are now used for carp.

The town finally surrendered in 1279 after a 36 year siege; is that a world record? The reason is that they were running out of food, as they could only grow so much on top of their bluff, yet needed many defenders to man their 8 km circumference wall. In any case, the writing was on the wall for the Song Dynasty by then, with only some pockets of resistance in the south still holding out. The town surrendered on condition that the lives of all the inhabitants would be protected – and they were; the Mongols honoured their promise, which was a little unusual, in that they often slaughtered all who resisted them. It is reported that they massacred as many as 800,000 people at the fall of Baghdad.

After our tour, we drove back to the town for a late lunch at a restaurant which specialises in mutton. Wonderful! – and so rare here in

China, where mutton or lamb is so hard to get, usually only in summer. Then it was time to drive home.

What a great day, and many thanks to the lady who organised the trip. She is a lecturer in Physiology at Chongqing University. In the car, I was sitting next to a three year old girl, who easily picked up some English that I taught her. She would ask me to repeat, and then she would remember. I wish I could do that.

Spring Festival 2013

77. *Songtao, Guizhou Province*

Over the Spring Festival holiday I spent more than three weeks travelling, mainly staying with my former students from Tongren. It was a wonderful three weeks. This was followed by two weeks back in Australia – also wonderful, though in a different way. This is what happened.

I left Chongqing on Friday 25th January, with the train due to leave at 2.20 pm. Now the last time I did this trip, the train did not leave till 5.30, while the passengers were forced to wait, standing up, at the barrier. I was hoping this would not happen again. It did.

Naturally, no information was given as to the reason for the delay. China's fast trains and its metro systems are the equal of any in the world, but the normal train service leaves a lot to be desired. They are dirty, slow, overcrowded and with lots of smokers. It is a six hour journey to Tongren, meaning we did not arrive until 11.30 pm. On the previous occasion, I was to be met by my former students, but at that hour the dormitories were locked, so that nobody was there to meet me. This time, however, those same students have graduated, and yes, they were waiting. They truly are wonderful people.

They had booked accommodation for me at – believe it or not – the Jim Carrey Hotel. I wonder if this American actor knows about it; probably not. It is quite a comfortable hotel. At 9.00 am next morning they returned, including C2, who was most anxious that I visit her home in a town called Songtao, just over an hour away by bus. I agreed.

We left about 10.00 am the next morning on what would prove to be a somewhat disturbing trip. Not far out of town we came across an accident, so very common. On this particular occasion a car and a van had met head on, because one of the vehicles was on the wrong side of the road. This is also very common. It would not be quite accurate to state that there are road rules in this country; let us say that there are loose guidelines to be followed if it is convenient. The result is that in excess of 300 people die on the roads every day.

The next thing to happen is that we found the main road blocked by men holding a banner. They are migrant workers, demanding that the government pay them to go home to their families for the upcoming Spring Festival. I do not think much of their chances. Our bus, in consequence, was diverted onto a bumpy sidetrack. It served, and we arrived at Songtao, a town of about 30,000 people, at 11.40 am. The first thing we did was to have lunch, or at least it was lunch for me, as I had already had breakfast in my hotel room, but for the girls, it was brunch. The town is quite attractive, with a collection of monuments and open spaces. Some ethnic women were wearing their traditional dress.

After lunch we visited C2's home. Why was she so insistent? Their house is somewhat old and a little small, so the family decided to build a larger and better house on their property. In the countryside, you simply build it; no problems. In towns, however, you need a building permit, which should not amount to much. In this case, the government was demanding 20,000 Yuan, which is a sizeable amount. From what I can gather, this is not intended to cover the cost of any paper work, but simply to line the pockets of the Communist Party officials; in a word, corruption. The government is a past master at collecting revenue. Here in Chongqing, for instance, if you sell a house, the government takes a whopping 20%. I think part of the reason for this is an attempt to prevent wealthy people buying up large numbers of apartments, then charging exorbitant rents from poor tenants. The rich get richer while the poor get poorer. In the case of C2's family, they refused to pay. What happened next is most extraordinary.

I was shown their new house, walls partly constructed, with bricks and timber lying about. Apparently, the government sent a large number of thugs to pull the house down. When – naturally – C2's parents objected, they were manhandled, none too gently, resulting in knee and chest injuries. The father had not been well for some time, and in fact he died later in the year. I doubt if his treatment at the hands of this mob helped.

The son then intervened. The mob poured petrol over him and set him alight. Unbelievable, especially when you bear in mind that it is the government doing this, and in this country the CP is not under the law. Truly. Later I visited the brother, still in the burns unit of the local hospital. He has been guarded by the police, but thankfully there was no one on duty while I was there. He is recovering, probably due to his quick wit, in diving into a vat of water. I stayed a little time with him, wishing him well, praying for a solution to their problem, and giving him a blessing.

Why was C2 so insistent that I see this? I told her that I am not a reporter, and do not even know any reporters. Nevertheless, she wants her story to be known, so that is what I am doing. Subsequently, the government has offered 16,000 Yuan to cover medical expenses, so maybe they have a conscience after all. I do not know how far this will go. They have also offered 600,000 Yuan for the property, which I am told is worth 4 million Yuan.

Our return to Tongren was via a hired car, costing only 100 Yuan, compared with 30 Yuan for the bus. As there were four of us, we ended up in front. We were joined for our evening meal by yet more ex-students and one fiancé. We had a great night. You might say that this was indeed a mixed day.

78.   *Zaiying Village – 27ᵗʰ – 31ˢᵗ January 2013*

Next morning was spent with yet more of my former students. It has been really good to see them again and find out how they are doing.

In the afternoon we went to the home of yet another Cindy, some 2 ¼ hours away by bus in a village called Zai Ying, and what a ride it was. My seat was up front; great for seeing the view, not to mention hearing the noisy music and blaring horn. It is a rough road, yet so interesting to note how the driver negotiated it while smoking and using his mobile phone. Talk about multi-tasking. We arrived at 4.30 pm, time to stretch the legs with a walk.

The following day we walked to the home of Cindy's boyfriend, Wang Xing, about 45 minutes away. En route, we stopped off at a Buddhist shrine, situated about 40 metres up a small hill in this valley, in order to ask a blessing on their baby, not yet born. The rock type is limestone, with some evidence that perhaps this has been a glacial valley. These small mounts rise up sharply from the floor of the valley. At the foot of this mount is a small brick factory; the bricks, however, are not baked in a kiln, but simply made from pressed limestone. The village also boasts a large cement factory, again using the abundant supply of limestone in the area. We also saw a duck man feeding his ducks. When he appeared with his bag of feed, they came streaming across flooded paddy fields; it was quite a sight.

The girls decided that they would stay the night, so two returned by motor cycle to Cindy's house to collect our gear. Expect the unexpected. The families here are farmers, the small village surrounded by their fields. The house is made of wood, and is quite large, with a central courtyard. Heating comes from a fire in a hole in the floor, above which hangs pig's meat for curing.

You get used to sleeping in many different beds, and on this trip I would be doing just that, so I slept well. Next morning I went for a walk around the village. Even so early on this winter's morn, there were some people working in their fields, dim figures in the mist. The crops are vegetables – cabbages etc.; it is too early yet to be planting rice – that will be done in the spring. Most houses are wooden, though there are some of stone. Cement pathways lead hither and yon, a lot better than the muddy tracks I would find in other villages. Most of this day would be spent sitting around the fire, talking and doing puzzles. After lunch we packed our bags and went to the house of an aunt, before Cindy, Erica, Sonny and I went for another walk at a very leisurely pace, but very enjoyable spending time with them.

Back at the house I fell asleep, which is most unusual. I was actually a little dehydrated, not to mention coffee deprived. I had a headache. Later I went for another walk on my own to the end of the village, this one somewhat faster. I returned to find that Cindy's parents had arrived, so we shared an early 5.00 pm evening meal together. Cindy's father works in Guangzhou. C, E, S and I then walked back to Cindy's house.

What follows is a mystery – at least to me; for you, however, probably not, as I can imagine your diagnosis; "old age". You may be right. Cindy is getting married and it is customary to place money in little red envelopes. I decided to give her 3,000 Yuan, but this would not fit, so I put 2,000 in one envelope and 1,000 in another. We spent a day away at her fiancé's house, and when we returned, I checked the envelopes. One still had 2,000 but the other was empty. Now I know that at night-time, neighbours come to play mah-jongg, at which they gamble, and the room in which they play is next to where I sleep. I was certainly not going to cause any ruckus, so I slipped another 1,000 into the second envelope. Some days later, after I had left, C contacted me to thank for the gift – of 4,000 Yuan! What happened? Maybe they will really need that extra money.

On Wed., Jan. 30th, we left Cindy's place at 10.00 am, being driven down to the bus stop in the town for the 10.30 bus. He is a good driver, careful, though naturally he smokes and uses his mobile phone while driving, not to mention blowing the horn every 30 seconds – literally, as I actually timed him. By 12.40 pm we were back in Tongren. I booked into the same hotel as before, the Jim Carrey, but this time had a different room, one not facing the street. I think this was organized by the girls because of the noise. It is true that Tongren, small though it may be, is a very noisy town.

In the afternoon, the girls went shopping – naturally – so I did too, visiting a book shop, but they had no English books. I noticed that a major bridge over the river, the Jin Da Qiao, has been demolished and is being rebuilt. I think this is yet another example of built-in obsolescence. Much of the buildings currently being demolished to make way for new ones were constructed only in the 1980s. Our evening meal was not what I had expected, as the girls opted for KFC.

Next morning I saw something of the results of yesterday's shopping expedition; Sunny had bought me a new coat. She really wanted to buy me something. It is really warm too.

One of the former teachers from Tongren University has gone to Australia, so I called on her parents. Naturally we stayed for lunch; Chinese hospitality can be overwhelming. The Mum is also a very good cook!

Evening meal was spent at Kim's house; this trip I am doing a lot of eating. This was also a very special occasion, as a number of Kim's classmates came, people I had taught for three years. It was truly wonderful to see them.

After the meal we spent some time in a nearby park, San Jiang Gong Yuan (or Three Rivers Park). It is really beautiful to see the reflections off the water of lovely Chinese architecture. Here, unexpectedly, we met another former student of Tongren University, one who glories in the English name of Butterfly. She is a most capable young lady. Here I might add that I am so proud of Kim, who has decided to spend her life teaching English to poor primary school students in country areas. No chance of getting rich here. All the other girls there on this night are also teachers, except Nell who works in Tongren Government Complaints Department.

This trip back to Tongren has been truly delightful, and one I doubted I would make. Probably I will not be returning – but I said that last time. On the morrow we would be heading to Bijie.

79.   Bijie City – 1st – 3rd February 2013

On Friday, 1st February, we had an early start. My hotel cost me only 150 Yuan per night, and I am happy with that. We took a taxi to the intercity bus station, but then had to wait, not leaving till 8.30 am. It was a good trip, smooth, with not a concert being shown on TV – it was not bad either, certainly much better than the violent movies one usually gets on these buses. For some reason the windows were covered in black, making it difficult to see outside, not that there was much to see on this misty, wintry morning.

We reached Bijie at 7.00 pm, having travelled from the extreme eastern edge of Guizhou Province to its western extremity. It is much higher here in altitude, being over 1700 metres above sea level, compared with only 270 metres for Tongren. It was colder too in consequence.

We were met at the bus station by two other former students from Tongren, Amy, together with her niece and Andrea, who was with her boyfriend, whom I had met on my previous visit here, some 2 ½ years ago. It was good to see them again. We went to my hotel first to dump luggage. It is a good hotel, though sadly lacks a western toilet, which I much prefer, though I am fairly used to the Chinese squat variety. Then we all had a meal and a stroll in a beautiful park, Renmin Gong Yuan, or People's Park. I needed to supplement my coffee supply, so Andrea ducked away for a while, returning with a large jar of coffee plus a coffee cup; just too good.

Next morning, Amy and Erica did not turn up till 10.00 am, so I guess we all had a good sleep. We went to visit a cousin of Amy's up a narrow winding alley way, but he was not at home, probably studying at school, so we found a small family restaurant for lunch, consisting of a bowl of noodles. Nearby, workmen were carrying coal in baskets on their backs; they carry very heavy loads.

This night we would be eating at Amy's family home, so first we visited a supermarket to buy supplies. I too bought some goods and also had a rare success in actually paying for what we bought, amounting to more than 200 Yuan. This entitled us to some discounts. I bought chocolates for 1 Yuan instead 3, and a bottle of wine for 15 Yuan instead of 59. You really do have to know the system. There is a sequel to this – a sad one. I neglected to buy a corkscrew, the others assuring me that it would not be necessary. It was. That night one of the men, in attempting to open the bottle with his knife, only succeeded in breaking the bottle; no wine. I guess they are not wine drinkers. They told me that corkscrews do not work! Really? I also bought books for the girls and me; I would need them in the next couple of weeks.

Our university in Chongqing is situated in an area called Lieshimu, which means martyrs' tombs, since here are buried people killed by the Kuomintang. Bijie also has its Lieshimu, not far out of town, and here we were driven by Amy's cousin, who happens to be a government driver. I was impressed by the way he drove; slowly and carefully. Wow, taxi driver he is not. I guess these drivers are specially trained to protect their precious cargo. I have been shunted off a highway before when some government big wig was coming along. I guess some animals are more equal than others.

The park is lovely, occupying a hill site, with beautiful buildings at its base. The tombs are at the top. I do not know who killed these people, but presumably the Kuomintang, as the Japanese did not get this far. The climb to the top included some 300 steps. We took lots of photos.

From here we drove to Amy's house to meet her family and have dinner. The girls did the work – as usual – while the men sat around, but I wanted to make myself useful, so volunteered to cook chips. This I did, much to the amazement of the family to find their guest, a man at that, actually helping to prepare the meal. For the sake of those scoffers among you, I must add that the chips were not bad either, though possibly not up to the standard of the rest of the meal. Now a glass of wine would have gone down very well indeed… Actually we did have some sweet Chinese wine – I had bought Australian – and some *baijiu*, or white spirits, strong enough to blow your head off, so only to be sipped. I might add that it was the girls who also cleaned up after the meal, not surprisingly.

The girls also walked me back to my hotel, about a kilometre away. I probably would not have found my way back without them, but they were also thinking of my safety, as it was now 10.30 pm. It has been an interesting day. Tomorrow we would head off higher into the mountains to meet Erica's family and spend Spring Festival with them.

At midday, 3ʳᵈ Feb, I booked out of my hotel, wondering how we would travel to Erica's village. You never know what will happen next. It so happens that with Spring Festival nigh, some of Erica's relatives had come to town in order to buy provisions – and what provisions. We had a van and as I waited on the footpath, I looked in amazement at the boxes and so on piled on the roadway. They will never get all of that into this small van! They did, plus the people who were sitting two to a seat. Could this happen anywhere else? You've got to see it to believe it.

So off we went, with me wondering how this little van is going to manage climbing hills. The driver seemed quite composed, as he talked nonstop the whole way, puffing on cigarettes the meanwhile and blowing his horn – naturally. I was in the front seat next to him, surrounded by packages, but not nearly as squashed as those in the back. For the next 1 ¼ hours we jolted over some of the roughest roads you are ever likely to see, wending very slowly ever upwards.

As we progressed one could see the people going about their business, also preparing for Spring Festival. One woman, for example, was making tofu; she was at the mixing stage. Stage 1 is grinding the beans in a machine. Stage 2 is adding an appropriate amount of water. Stage 3 is stirring thoroughly, till a scum begins to form. Stage 4 is applying heat. Stage 5 is skimming off the scum, which can be used in several ways, as can the body of the tofu. Another family was making sausages, presumably using pig gut

Eventually we arrived at the house of Erica's grandmother, where it was planned that we would stay. After a meal with the grandmother, we went off to explore this beautiful valley, looking particularly attractive on this sunny day, especially with the blue sky, a phenomenon unknown in Chongqing. There is a creek running through it, with a man ploughing on the other side of it, but no, not using a tractor, but a buffalo. The buffalo walked or stopped on signals. A woman was collecting turnips from her field, so, cool as a cucumber, Erica walked up and asked her for some. We stood around talking with her while eating our turnips – very nice too. These turnips are not primarily for human consumption, however, but for the pigs. The people are very friendly, partly too I think, because I am probably the first Westerner ever to venture into this valley – at least that is what I was told.

Back at grandmother's house, we were informed that we would not be staying here after all, but in the house of one of Erica's uncles, a little way up the west side of the valley; whatever – you never what will happen next. This would be the sixth bed I have slept in since leaving Chongqing, with a least one other to come.

There are many relatives hereabouts, as Erica's mother has four brothers and two sisters, born – needless to say – before the One Child Policy came into effect in 1979. Another uncle has the house next to grandmother, occupied not only by humans, but also by a horse, a dog, 4 pigs, 4 rabbits and a couple of black and grey spotted chooks. What did happen next, after we had taken our luggage up the hill, was that the menfolk were in the process of killing a pig for Spring Festival, a practice being repeated at this time all over China. This particular pig was not too enamoured of the idea, its terrified squeals going on and on. Pork might taste very nice indeed, but the process of obtaining it can be most unpleasant – especially for the poor pig.

That night it was such a pleasure to gaze up at the stars. We are about 2,000 metres up here with the air much cleaner than in China's highly polluted cities. Interestingly, we see the constellations from a different angle than in the southern hemisphere. Orion, for instance, is more right way up here, whereas from Australia he is almost upside down. Sirius was fairly blazing, as was the planet Jupiter. At around 10.00 pm we had our meal, actually our second as we had eaten much earlier with the grandmother. The reason for this late repast is that the men had been too busy with the killing then cutting up of the pig. The meal indeed included blood from this freshly killed pig; I skipped this part. Dried blood, of several kinds of animals is a feature of some Chinese meals. As a sop to the stomachs of more squeamish Westerners, the locals say it is "chocolate". After the meal, we sat around for some time singing songs.

Next morning dawned bright and sunny, when the sun finally did appear over the eastern hills; remember too that here we are well west of Beijing – about one hour – and all time is set from the capital. China has only one time zone. The family was busy about domestic matters, especially in preparing the pig killed last night; its corpse was still lying in a downstairs room. To keep out of their way, I paced up and down on the roof as I said my office. I also walked behind the house to a little knoll overlooking the houses below. It is on this knoll that the pig was killed, wads of blood still thick on the ground. It reminded me of the knoll of Calvary where Christ shed his blood for the salvation of the world, so that we could inherit eternal life. The pig's blood was shed so that we could eat, so also so that we could have life – material life in this case. Further, the eating of the pig at Spring Festival is a powerful means of uniting the family. Similarly, Christ's death should be a powerful means of uniting the whole human family. This is what the Eucharist is meant to symbolise.

It was so nice sitting on the roof in the sunshine, that I continued to sit, reflect and jot down my thoughts, while four family members joined me and looked on, but of course, unable to understand my writing, which is not surprising, as I have trouble myself at times. On this occasion, however, my writing was good, and one of the boys was so impressed that he asked me if I could give him a sample, so I did. I wrote out for him Australia's national song, Waltzing Matilda, even though he would not understand it, both because there are so many Australian terms and because the whole spirit is so foreign to Chinese way of thinking; indeed it is quite revolutionary.

Next day we would climb a mountain; I could hardly wait.

81.   Mountain Views – 4th – 5th February 2013

You may know that I like climbing mountains; certainly Erica does, as we had climbed a number of mountains and hills around Tongren. She asked if I would like to climb a nearby mountain, probably rising about 400 metres above this valley, and guarding the eastern side. Would I ever!

So at 10.30 am on a bright, warm, sunny day, five of us headed off; Erica, Amy, Charles, Bernard, and I. You do have to know the routes, so a local guide is an essential. In this instance, the path to the top was picked up after finding our way between the houses on the other, eastern, side of the valley. It is not a difficult climb, but does provide stunning views of the surrounds.

A small stream runs through the centre of the valley, with fields on each side, while the houses cling to the lower slopes. Much of the hillsides are terraced, as one would expect, so that no arable land is wasted. Some of these have vegetables planted in them, while most are lying fallow, waiting for the spring before planting begins. From the top one overlooks the next valley to the east and as well one gets magnificent views of the surrounding mountain chain. We sat on the top for some time, at an altitude of about 2,300 metres – about the same height as Kosciusko – eating apples and listening to music. We were back at the house at 2.00 pm, after some 3 ½ hours in this delightful sunshine.

In the afternoon the pigs were fed smashed turnips; talk about manners. It was all in, not without the odd altercation. Isn't it interesting, that meals in common are such an important part of human culture? In sharing food we share each other. A "companion" is one with whom you eat, coming from "cum" (with) and "panis" (bread). The pig in the next pen was on its own. He dropped some food outside the bars and did he have fun trying to reach it! Repeatedly he tried to lift the gate – clever pig – but without success. He certainly knew what to do.

We humans ate something else: baked potatoes, cooked over a coal fire, something of a favourite in this neck of the woods, where so many potatoes are grown. We ate these down at grandma's house. You add a pinch of *lajiao*, but not too much, at least for me. The trick then is to keep the hot chilly at the front of the mouth; if it gets to the back of the throat I have problems.

That night I slept in a different bed, same house – plan F I think. I had a wash this night as well. Usually I shower every day, but not here, where there are no showers; you wash from a basin. I do not need to wash every day anyway, and none of you lot have to live with me, so what is the problem?

Next morning we were up at 8.30, or I was. I am getting so much sleep these holidays; marvellous. This is yet another bright, sunny day, with a gentle breeze. The weather has been so balmy; the locals have seen nothing like it. Where is the snow? It was so pleasant sitting up on the roof, with birds twittering, geese cackling and a man in his field instructing his buffalo. Meanwhile, the women were sitting in the courtyard below taking the shells off small round eggs; quail? They were bought, so are not produce from their own farm. The rubbish is not placed in bins, but simply dropped on the ground anywhere, to be swept up later and fed to the pigs, or to be used as fertilizer on their crops. Rice stalks are stacked in stoops. The dry outside is used to keep the farm animals warm, and when the inside rots it is used as fertilizer. Nothing is wasted. In one room I did notice two 50 kg bags of fertilizer – though at the moment they are holding corn – from Australia. There is a picture of the Sydney Opera House on the front. I did not know that the Opera House produced fertilizer. You learn something every day.

In the afternoon we visited another relative, whose house is on the eastern side of this valley. Her husband is crippled, while her two daughters are both unwell. They do have an adopted son, but apparently he is of little use. They are very poor, as you can imagine. Their house is wooden, with a dirt floor. I noticed too that it has quite a lean. Some people have such very hard lives, yet they were so cheerful and so grateful for our visit. I noticed Erica slip them some money.

It seems we spend about half the day eating. Lunch was very late, at 3.30 pm, while evening meal was at 7.00 pm. Many people – about 40 odd – were sitting down to eat, not only family, but also neighbours. One curious oddity about the menfolk around here is that it seems everybody smokes. Fireworks were let off during the meal, so Spring Festival is close. One man on another table kept staring at me during the entire meal. I gather I am the first Westerner he has ever seen. Erica's sister, Martha, arrived just in time for the meal. It was good to see her again. It is also wonderful to see the deep affection these two sisters have for each other.

This will do for this edition. Tomorrow we head further up into the mountains to Erica's family home, where I will be for the next nine days, so over Spring Festival.

82.   Shui Ting Village – 6th February 2013

On Wednesday I woke at 8.00 am, which is just before sunrise at this particular location. What this means is that with a range of mountains on the eastern side of the valley, the time the sun peeps above the horizon can differ by as much as an hour, depending upon where you are. If you are on the western slopes with a gap in the ranges opposite, then the sun rises early, but if you are on the eastern side in the shadow of one of the peaks, then you may have to wait a further hour before you see the sun. Interesting.

We left around 9.30 am to go further up into the mountains to Erica's village. We did not have to wait long before the girls hailed a passing van, the driver being a classmate of Martha. He agreed to give us a lift, but at the somewhat exorbitant rate of 100 Yuan; it is only a half hour journey. There is no plumbing in these mountains and no sealed roads either. The villagers simply allow their waste water to run onto the road, resulting in one very muddy road, which then gets rutted by passing vehicles. Some parts are rough stones while other parts are quagmires. The driver seemed to have no respect for his vehicle, being very heavy handed; no wonder he asked for so much money, as his van would not last long the way he was driving in these conditions. He was smoking – naturally – until Erica asked him not to. Well, yes, it is his vehicle, but we are paying for it. He agreed without demur, much to my surprise. This did not stop him from using his mobile while driving for one very long conversation. He actually stopped at one point at the precise location where another vehicle, coming from the opposite direction, also stopped, thus effectively blocking all other traffic. Were the two drivers talking to each other on their mobiles??? So we had this extraordinary situation of vehicles stopped in both directions, just stationary. Oh, did I mention the noise? You can take it for granted that he was blowing his horn at anything that moved or looked as if it might move, but as well, he had his music blaring loudly. Did I enjoy this trip? – not one little bit. But we got there.

"There" is a larger village, called Shui Ting. Erica had planned this trip carefully to coincide with market day, as the family wanted to buy many things for Spring Festival. The main road through the town, which is pretty much the only road, is narrow, with no footpath, and on this market day was crowded with stalls lining both sides. The traffic, as one might suspect was heavy, with barely room for vehicles to pass one another. Yet this did not stop vehicles from parking. At one point I counted five motorcycles side by side, leaving, as you may imagine, little space for traffic to squeeze through. Thoughtfulness for others is not exactly a character trait. Social consciousness extends only to one's inner circle, not to others. Did I mention the blaring of horns…? I watched as men fastened loads to their motorcycles; it is amazing how much can be carried, and not only luggage. Some were carrying as many as four people.

Some of the local minority people, (Miao, I think) added colour to the scene with their distinctive clothing, consisting of pleated skirts falling from a very low waistline. Indeed a pleasing aspect of this whole scene was the vivid colours of the produce lining the street, from fruit to spices. There was the green of vegetables, the red of tomatoes and *lajiao,* the orange of oranges, the white of garlic and *da bai cai* (literally big white vegetable; it is a cabbage), the ginger of ginger. One stall, selling hot chili peppers *(lajiao),* had a machine that was pounding the chilies into a powder while we watched. One man was selling colourful balloons. Supplies bought included fruit, vegetables and a carton of milk for me! They know I like milk on my cereal for breakfast each morning. They also had two iron cages. Now what could be their purpose? They were meant for the horse, but no, not to put the horse in, but to put on the horse on either side, so that it could carry loads, such as fertiliser. Poor horse; the cages were quite heavy, without even considering what they would be containing.

The family has relatives in this town, so our luggage was stored with one of them while all this shopping was going on. Erica and I would meet another aunt about a week later on one of our walks, a somewhat extended walk of about three hours, winding through the hills at the back, returning through Shui Ting along the road. On that occasion we stopped off in the town to eat some tofu, being cooked on the side of the road. The town also has a middle school, which Erica had attended in days of yore.

Normally, to get from Sui Ting to Erica's house, you walk. It takes about an hour. On this occasion, however, there was too much to carry, both in terms of personal luggage and supplies, so yet another van was brought into service. Just outside of Shui Ting there is a brick factory. On the right hand side, machines gouge limestone from the hillside. The rock is then immediately fed into crushers where eventually it is moulded into bricks. It is all done on site. We were able to drive all the way to the house, in about half an hour, although "bump" would be the more appropriate term, as the road is not exactly smooth. It is also quite muddy. The last time I was here, 2 ½ years ago, you could not drive all the way to the house, so there has been some improvement.

One very surprising feature was the weather. This is winter and we are in excess of 2,000 metres up in these mountains, yet there is no snow, except on the higher peaks. I was told that usually they experience heavy snowfalls, effectively cutting off Erica's village from vehicular access. At the end of my stay here, I would be heading back to Australia, and I really wanted to catch that plane. I had visions of hiking all the way to Bijie city, a distance of about 40 km away. Now that would have been fun in the snow! Thank goodness it would not be necessary. The locals were amazed at the warmth of the weather; global warming?

We had arrived, and I would be here for the next nine days, sharing Spring Festival with this remarkable family.

I have described Erica's house before, but that was 2 ½ years ago; so just on the off chance that you may have forgotten, I will describe it, briefly, again. It is constructed of solid wood, thick vertical posts and horizontal slats. This rests on a cement floor. The roof is partly tile and partly corrugated iron. There are two doors at the front. There is also a door at the back and one at the left side, but these have been blocked; I just hope they do not have a fire. The main door is on the right, leading into the central room, which really is the living room. There is a bed, a TV and a stove. This stove is basically a central tube into which coal is fed, with a box at the bottom to collect the ashes and a table at the top. This really is the family hearth, around which the main life of the family revolves. It is here that food preparation takes place. It is here that the food is cooked. It is here that meals are eaten, with people sitting either on benches or on the bed. It is here that the washing up is done. It is here that card games are played. And the family talks.

Around the room, hanging from the ceiling, you will find corn and meat. There is no refrigerator, so one must be careful that food supplies do not spoil. In Western history, this was often achieved through pickling or salting, practices that I have not noticed here. Instead two other main methods are employed. One is sun drying, but this is not often possible in this mountain region in winter. It is I think more of a summer method. Potatoes, for instance, are washed, cut into thin strips, then left out to dry. To cook, you simply drop them into boiling oil for about ten seconds, and hey presto, they are ready for eating. I will give more details on this in a later episode. The second method is smoking over the fire, wood fires in this case, as coal fires do not give off enough smoke. Smoked pork is simply delicious. A second reason for hanging food from the rafters is to keep them safe from rats.

Remember that Chinese society is closely knit, so it is not a problem to have many people in this room at the same time, even engaged in different activities. On one occasion, I went to sit on the bed to read my book, when I realised that there was a body in the bed; someone was catching up on some much needed sleep.

Meanwhile, people were preparing the meal, while junior – I will say more about him later – was watching television. I might add that I did a lot of reading, getting through four books during my stay here. This was partly due to my poor Chinese, making it difficult to communicate with the parents, who do not speak English. It was also largely due to the fact that they would not allow me to do anything. This is Chinese hospitality. They were horrified, for instance, at my suggestion that I might help in making dumplings, though just possibly there may have been some concern that I would make a right hash of it. The first time I made dumplings I certainly did; they kept falling to pieces; subsequent efforts, however, have been a little more successful.

One part of the room has lumps of coal. These are broken up with a small hammer, before being added to the fire. As these lumps burn they fall to the bottom. The ash is collected in a tray and placed in a pit just inside the front door. A word of caution here: do not fall into the pit as you come in, as it is only about 20 cm from the door! It is not deep, maybe 10 cm, and measures about 30 cm by 30 cm. Some mud is mixed with the ash, before this is added to the top of the stove. Its purpose is to slow down combustion- coal is expensive. In winter, the family really lives around this stove, but I wonder how healthy it is. Probably, not only carbon dioxide but also carbon monoxide is being given off, and I could smell sulphur as well.

Behind the living room, at the rear of the house, is a bedroom the one I would be using. The bed is quite comfortable and comes with a very heavy quilt, which I found quite warm enough in this cold weather. This is also a store room. Curiously, there is shelf running the length of the bed, on which are piled many items, creating noticeable sag. It did not collapse, thank goodness, at least not during my stay.

In the centre of the house is the largest room, also used as a store room, together with the loft. There is a ladder here leading up to this loft. The left hand side of the house has two other rooms, both bedrooms. The first room also has a stove. These stoves are used to dry clothes, as the outside line is not really suitable in inclement weather. It was not really suitable at night in winter, either, as I noticed that water dripping down from the clothes had frozen, while the clothes themselves were stiff with ice. Both rooms therefore, where these stoves are located, were festooned with drying clothes.

From the living room, there is another door leading to the animals. It is here that the pigs and horse are kept. You do not want them outside during winter. There is another reason for having them close at hand. When it is dry, there is more likelihood of animals being stolen. Some years ago, in fact, their horse was stolen, and it took a court case to get it back.

Next to the house is the barn, which looks really beautiful with its mossy green roof. Here the cow is housed. At end of the barn is a lean to, a thatch roof leaning against the side of the barn. This is the toilet. I refer you to chapter 33 for its description. The poles were rather too close together, so that I found it was better to move one of them, thus creating more space. When answering a call of nature in the middle of the night, it was necessary, in this cold climate, to dress warmly, before venturing outside.

Since I was here last, the family has acquired a washing machine, complete with spin dryer, so this makes life a little easier. In the attached photo you can see Erica doing the laundry. The pile out front is compost to be added to the fields in spring.

So this is where I lived for nine memorable days, enjoying the hospitality of these wonderful people.

84.   The Inhabitants – 6th – 15th February 2013

In the last episode I described the house, so now I propose to say something about the people who live here.

Mr and Mrs C have four children: two boys followed by two girls. Yes, I can sense your surprise: how can a couple have four children when there is a One Child Policy? Farmers, as you may know, are allowed to have a son, so they may have more than one child if the first is a girl, although there is a little more leniency in the countryside. In this case, however, the son came first – in fact two sons. I tell you, this couple is extraordinary, as is the family. In short, they had their children in defiance of the policy. Were there any repercussions to this? Indeed there were. The government was not very happy. In the episode on Songtau I gave an example of just how violent the government can be. In this case, however, they did not beat anybody up and nor did they set fire to somebody, but they did some damage to the house by pulling the doors off after Erica was born. Truly. Erica has only just found this out herself. It does explain, however, why the doors are askew and do not close properly. In addition the family had to pay a fine. One can but admire the parents.

There is another reason I admire these parents. Many parents wish to dominate the lives of their children, choosing their education, their careers and even their partners – all for the good of the children, of course. I may add that this tendency is not limited to Chinese society. Mr and Mrs C, however, have given considerable freedom to their children to choose their own paths in life. One of the outcomes of this is that it is the two girls, the youngest, who have gone on to university, not the two eldest boys. At one point I said to the parents; "You have two daughters, but I only have the one. How about if I take her to Australia?" They replied, "Fine – if that is what she wants to do." Amazing. Sometimes one gets the impression that parents have children for the sake of the parents – e.g. to look after them in their old age – rather than for the sake of the children, but that is not the case here.

Both daughters came home for Spring Festival. It is really heartwarming to see the great affection they have for each other, as I have noted before. In my book, God IS Love, and where you find love that is where God is, whether you believe in any systematic religion or not. God is definitely in this family. The two sons did not come home but remained in Shenzhen where they work. They have their own families and problems. Last year one lost a baby daughter, who died in hospital after a short illness. The hospital bills were crippling.

But their children were here, being looked after by the grandparents. This is common in China. There are hundreds of millions of migrant workers, who have shifted from the countryside to the big cities to find work. In the past, they would send a large part of the wages back home, but nowadays the cost of living has risen to the extent that they are themselves barely making ends meet. They work very long hours, so give their children to their own parents to raise, meaning that in many cases they rarely see them. Distances are vast in this huge country.

Dong, the eldest son, has his daughter here, a baby of about 10 months when I arrived. She gives no trouble, spending a lot of the day on grandma's back, as she goes about her daily chores. This is more than useful; for one thing, she will develop a great sense of balance, but more importantly she has that human contact, which will enhance her sense of self-worth; she is loved.

Shi, the second son, has his son is here also, a lad of just over two – and yes, the "terrible twos" have struck. Let me qualify this. I do not mean that he is throwing tantrums all the time. In fact he shows remarkable equanimity. If he does not get his own way, yes, he does throw a tantrum, but it does not last. No, the problem is he is a grabber. I put my coffee down for one moment, and he has it. I put my knife down and turn away – he has it. If you leave anything within his reach, he grabs it. Fortunately he was still too small to climb up on the beds – not for want of trying – so you could leave things out of his reach. He did climb up on a chair in my room; no big deal, except that I happened to by drying my towel over it, and his shoes were very muddy. One of his favourite areas was my rubbish bag, as he delighted in seeing what was in there, pulling things out and leaving them scattered over the floor. Great fun. When he was really naughty he would be chastised. This consisted in a severe tone of voice plus numerous spanks. I was very impressed by these spankings, as they carried no force whatsoever. The child was in no way hurt but still clearly got the message.

A very frequent visitor, who often slept over, was Martha's boyfriend, who is a carpenter, or more accurately a joiner. He is not only a very personable young man, but also a very responsible one as well. They should make a great couple. I say "visitor", though indeed he is very much part of the family already. Spring Festival is not only a time for family, but also for friends, so there were many visitors at this time, though especially the relatives. Reciprocally, the family would visit other families in the neighbourhood. Cards were also played from time to time, as a means of relaxation and entertaining guests.

Have I left anyone out? Oh yes – me! I was just, sorta … kinda … there. As honoured (truly) guest, I was not allowed to do anything. Hey, I am not used to this. I was not allowed to take part in any of the daily chores, be it food preparation, cooking, washing up afterwards, laundry or cleaning the house. Now I can understand the cooking part, as even my best efforts are barely passable, but the rest? About all I did was eat – and read. I would much have preferred to have done my share, but I guess the culture here is a little different.

It is a great group of people to share some time with. Next time we will look at the other residents.

85.   Other Residents – 6th – 15th February 2013

Other residents? What could this mean? Well we are talking about a farm, so there are animals.

The largest of these is the horse. His use is as a beast of burden, carrying goods; it is only occasionally that he carries people. In the Han Zuang Cun episode I mentioned the cage brought up from town, the purpose of which is to enable the horse to carry goods; it hangs down each side. In one of the photos, showing the front of the house, you will see a large pile of stalks from various crops, together with sundry other rubbish, like orange peels. This is carried by the horse in those panniers to be used in the fields as fertilizer. The horse was stabled in the room on the right of the house, next to the family room. This not only keeps him out of the weather, but also safe from thieves.

The next largest animal is the cow. No, she is not used to provide milk. Dairy products in general – milk, yoghurt, cream, cheese – have never been a traditional part of the Chinese diet. For some reason, they just did not investigate this line of foods, which may seem a little strange, given that the Chinese will eat anything that walks, crawls, swims, flies or slithers. Maybe they lack the gene necessary for digestion. The reason they have this cow is not for producing milk, nor for eating, but for ploughing. Both the horse and the cow do the heavy work. So on this farm, both the animals and the humans are very hard working.

Next, in order of size, are the two pigs. They share the same room as the horse, seemingly getting on quite amicably. One of the pigs was not well during my visit; he was not eating. The vet was called, producing an array of syringes. He seemed to know what he was doing, and it worked; within two days the pig was ok. Pigs are very important animals, not because of what they do but because of what they will become, to wit, pork. They will be the main source of protein for the family. When I left, they gave me a large side of smoke-cured ham. I tell you, this pork, even when treated by my inadequate culinary expertise, is simply delicious. Come and try some for yourself….

Continuing our downsizing, we have the chooks. When I was here last, 2 ½ years ago, there were five, but now there are only two, the other three having died. The elder of the two is an 8 year old, a lovely deep brown colour with black flecks; the other, smaller, is a couple of years younger. Their job is two-fold. Firstly they clean up. So you see them pecking away, head down, tail up around the house, on top of the fertilizer heap, in the house everywhere and at all times. Their second job is to provide eggs. Obviously two chooks are not enough to supply the family's needs, so most eggs are bought. I do not know why they do not acquire a few more chooks. Elsewhere in the district you will see roosters – and you hear them as well – and these are of a deep russet red with black tail feathers. They look beautiful. These chooks in the C household are remarkably tame. They wander around as if they own the place, and are little fazed by being kicked out of the house from time to time. They are most definitely, however, not allowed on the bed, nice, soft and warm though it be.

There is yet one more animal to be mentioned, one that has no role whatsoever be perform, except to exist in as comfortable a manner as possible; and that is the ginger cat. Now I am not sure whether the family adopted the cat or the cat adopted the family, but possibly the latter. During meals, or when reading, I would be sitting on the bed, my feet perched on a raised section at the stove, wearing slippers. The cat discovered that this too was a warm spot, and that slippers were very comfortable, so she would lie down on my feet. During meals I would drop wastes on the floor next to the cat for her to eat, but she never got them; the chook would grab them before the lazy cat could stir.

The family possesses a large wok, some 80 cm in diameter; this is used to prepare food for the animals. For the horse, stalks left over from harvesting are boiled and turnips added. For the cow, corn cobs are boiled for some time to soften them, when corn flour is added. For the pigs, boiled corn flour is prepared and also potato peals. In summer the pigs are given a plant which grows wild. I have seen Mrs C feeding it into a machine for mulching. Mind you, this is not all they eat. The horse and cow are still led out to graze on the hillsides. The families in the village take it in turn to watch the animals, to make sure they do not stray where they are not wanted. While I was there, it was C's family's turn. So Mr C rounded up all the animals from the village centre and headed off, assisted by his nephew.

Later in the afternoon, Erica and I joined them. I tell you, this is not a job I would want to do too often at least not in winter, as it is just so cold. They get over this slight problem by lighting a fire from the sticks which abound nearby and baking potatoes. They are really nice. And I do not mean a mere one or two each, but fifty, which the four of us nearly succeeded in devouring – and I only had four. You do have to watch the smoke, as the breeze can blow it around, and into your eyes.

86.   Walks – 6th – 15th February 2013

It is my custom to go for a walk each afternoon, definitely one I was keen to maintain while at Erica's house, for the twofold purpose of getting exercise and seeing the district. It was a good opportunity to get out of the house and warm up. Most afternoons I walked on my own, but sometimes Erica would join me; usually she was busy with household chores. I have mentioned that three hour walk we did on one afternoon, but most were not that long. Somewhere between one and two hours was fine. I found I could cover some distance in that time.

Invariably it was misty, meaning that we were up in the clouds, visibility reduced to a hundred metres or so. One's world was reduced in size, but without a sense of isolation, as this is China, and there are always people about. They would loom through the mists, shadowy forms, gradually materializing. As well, the sounds of human activity never ceased; a road grader and trucks were working on a new road; children were playing on the side of a hill; adult voices could be heard from a nearby village; dogs were barking; always something. Yet these sounds were never raucous, muffled as they were by the mist. They were gentle, pleasing, soothing sounds, aided by the absence of even a breeze, adding a sense of stillness. The people I met would usually remain silent, only one man asking me where I was going. How do you answer that? I am going nowhere – well, nowhere in particular. On one occasion I met a line of young people carrying immense loads on their backs, bent over, eyes on the path ahead. They too said nothing as they passed.

Just a word on the baskets they carry. One afternoon, we went to a local shop to buy some supplies, but were on the way home before we remembered that we had forgotten to buy beer, which – as I am sure you agree – is an essential commodity. Xiao Yan went back. I picked up his basket and attempted to carry it. Now a bag of rice was perched on the top, overhanging the sides. For one thing it was heavy, but my main problem was balance, as the load tended to sway way or the other. When Martha's boyfriend returned I was glad to hand it back to him. I do not know how they do it.

Villages are dotted throughout, mostly in valleys, the houses made of stone or wood, with roofs covered with tiles or thatch. There was little by way of modern conveniences that I could see. Satellite dishes attested to the presence of TVs. One sad sight is the prevalence of rubbish, simply thrown out anywhere. Quite apart from considerations of waste and the possibility of disease, it is so unsightly. I have already mentioned the dearth of plumbing, whereby waste water is simply poured outside, often on the road. Even in the big cities, plumbing is open to improvement. Sewerage pipes are too thin to allow paper to pass through, so are liable to blockage. Hence all papers must be disposed of separately. It is not uncommon for a Westerner, newly arrived in this country, to find sheir toilet blocked.

One more example of this is worth noting. In my bathroom, in Chongqing, both the sink and washing machine do not have permanent plumbing. A piece of plastic hose was affixed to the sink, linking with the washing machine and simply stuck in the drain. Naturally, it kept coming out, especially when the washing machine was in spin cycle, resulting in a flooded bathroom. This has since been rectified, with a new plastic hose inserted. This is fine, except that it now has an upward pointing u-turn, meaning that the waste water must run up hill before it can empty into the drain, resulting in stagnant water collecting in the hose. It is necessary to lift the hose manually to allow this water to drain. In the kitchen, the plastic hose running from the sink has a hole in it. Plumbing is definitely not a strong point. Life is fun, even though nothing is perfect – anywhere.

Getting back to my mountain walks, if there is one over-riding memory it is the mud. There had, apparently, been very little rain for some time, but everything was still muddy. People, who are dumping their waste water on the roads, obviously contribute to this, but as well, you have the mist. Each afternoon, when I returned, I would first spend some time scraping the mud off my boots. Inside, I wore slippers, though the cement floor was dirty enough. It would be hard to keep really clean. This mud was not in all respects bad. Gerard Manly Hopkins wrote a great poem called "God's Grandeur", in which he deplores the pollution people have caused;

"All is seared with trade; bleared, smeared with toil;
And wears man's smudge and shares man's smell; the soil
Is bare now, nor can foot feel, being shod."

We can treat the environment as just that – something around us, something apart from us. This is dangerous, allowing us to cause as much degradation as we feel like. It is especially dangerous when you add nationalism, with the desire to become, not AN, but THE economic superpower. There will be a huge environmental cost, meaning also a huge human cost, though short-sighted people cannot see this. We need to tap more into the wisdom of the world's oldest continuous culture, that of the Australian aborigines, for whom Nature is not something apart from themselves, but of which they form an integral part.

So how does mud fit into this? We city folk tend to keep ourselves clean, with the mud and dirt "out there". For me, walking through mud and having mud coating the bottom of my trousers somehow united me to the world in which I live. Country folk can be much closer to the earth. And this is good. Otherwise one can go to the ridiculous length of using bacterial wipes, a practice which is not only unnecessary but also dangerous. Is it any wonder our kids develop immune problems? Is it any wonder our antibacterial weapons against disease are becoming less effective, when we overuse them so?

As I go for my walks, not only is my body getting exercise, but so is my brain as I think about the countryside and its implications. Maybe your journeys take you to different destinations.

Martha, as her name implies, is the real busybody around the house. She is both hardworking and practical. She is the chief; the others are her assistants. I watch as the evening meal was being prepared; Martha was cutting up the meat; Erica was washing chopsticks; their mother was peeling potatoes. Me? I just had my head in a book while they did all the work. When I wash my chopsticks, I clean them one by one, but here they use a different technique, simply rubbing them together in a basin of water and detergent. It is effective.

Potatoes are a staple hereabouts, with the family growing their own. You may know that China is the world's biggest producer of potatoes. Sorry, Paddy. They originated, of course, in South America, brought to Europe by Drake, if I am not mistaken. They are a marvellous vegetable, full of nutrition. They can also be prepared in such a variety of ways. I have mentioned baking as one of the favourites here; another is crisps. First, you wash the potato thoroughly. Second, you cut it into thin slices. Third, boil some water, adding salt. Fourth, add the potatoes, boiling them for about ten minutes. Fifth, you take them outside to dry in the sun. Six, boil some oil in a wok. Finally, you drop the slices in for about ten seconds. Voila, you have crisps – very tasty if you do not overcook them, which is what I did first time.

Another common dish here is rice pasta. It is cooked in boiling water with sugar and eggs added. It is very nice. You can see that one of the advantages of being here in Erica's household is good meals, much better than I can manage for myself.

During Spring Festival week, we enjoyed a special dish for this time of the year, which we ate each day for breakfast: *jiaozi* or dumplings, but such as I had not had before. There is of course any number of different kinds of dumpling, depending both on what you use for the outside and on what you put inside. In this case the outside is made from buckwheat, which on its own tastes a bit flat and starchy, at least to me, but when you add sugar and sesame seeds to the inside, it is very nice indeed, quite sweet. Each morning the womenfolk (of course) would first add water to the buckwheat flour and roll it flat. A small portion would be broken off and shaped into a disc, the edges being turned up. Then the sugar and sesame seeds were added, before folding the disc shut, using water to glue the edges together. Next the whole was boiled in water for some time, the consequence of all this preparation being that we did not eat breakfast on these days till around 11.00 am. They were worth the wait.

The TV is on for most of the day, primarily to keep junior occupied and out of mischief. It does succeed in keeping him quiet, at least for some of the time, but he is extraordinarily inquisitive, so it does not take much to divert his attention. That is how he learns, of course.

There were also concerts for adult entertainment during this Spring Festival holiday. Some items were singing, some were comedy, some were contests. The singing items were accompanied by flashing lights, complex backdrops and noise. A pity, I thought, as the singer was lost. The special effects had taken over, instead of being an incidental accompaniment. This actually says a lot about this country, where the presentation, the show, is more important than the substance. The items were mostly pop music, but there were some minority group songs, some traditional Chinese songs, some from Africa and even O Sole Mio from Italy.

The contests were attempts by various people to break the Guinness Book of Records in some field or other, like climbing stairs on your head, or throwing basketballs into a basket using your feet, or seeing how many watermelons you can break within a specified period of time. Goodness, the things that people do! There was also a military concert. This country has the largest military machine in the world – and one might wonder why; what use will it be put to? – and it will be put to use; soldiers rarely just sit in their barracks. Moreover, the military is glorified and idolised. I do not think this is healthy, not for China and certainly not for China's neighbours.

Normally I shower every day, but not here. For one thing, there is no shower. You wash in a basin of water. A kettle is used to heat the water on the stove, and then it is poured into the basin. I did not do this every day, and indeed, I did not need to. Remember that I am not doing much here. So I washed every second day and changed clothes. There must be a real skill to this, which I have yet to master, as my bedroom, which is where I washed, would itself be awash. How do you stop splashing water everywhere?

I will finish this edition with an account of one book that I read during my stay – I actually read four altogether. This book was written by a French author/artist, Romain Rolland, and it gives three short biographies of Beethoven, Michelangelo and Tolstoy. The book was written around the beginning of the 20th century. What an interesting idea, to put together these three great men, geniuses within their own fields of music, art and literature. Each of them had gigantic personal struggles in their efforts to be real, to be true to themselves and to God. All three were purified, coming to love through suffering. For each of them it seems that beauty and truth came together only in love. There does come an ecstasy, but only after agony. It seems too that for these men at times the Church was less than helpful, which is a real pity, as this is precisely where the Church should be. Jesus went through his crucifixion before he could come to his Resurrection. As an institution, perhaps the Church is too much caught up with minutiae.

88.   Spring Festival – 10th February 2013

This, as you would know, is the most important festival in the Chinese calendar, and like all traditions, whether religious or otherwise, has become encased in ritual, beginning on the evening before. It began with the setting off of fireworks. These are so loud, that the door was shut in the adjacent room where Mr. C set them off, before hastily retreating to the family room. The idea is to drive away evil spirits – assuming they can hear, of course.

After the meal, four bowls were placed on the four corners of the stove, each containing a little rice and pork, plus one josh stick. After bowing to the fire, the head of the household, in this case Mr. C, placed a little of the rice and pork in the fire, followed by the josh sticks. The whole ceremony took about one minute. One can interpret the meaning as thanking God for the gift of food throughout the year.

The second ceremony caught me completely by surprise; gift giving. Mr C presented me with a pair of trousers, identical to the ones I had been wearing, and which by this time had their bottoms covered in mud. I could now wash them as I had brought only one pair of trousers with me, so had been wearing them unchanged for a couple of weeks. Mrs C gave me a pair of really nice walking shoes, presumably to offset my now very muddy boots. From Martha I received a jumper. Now I had only brought one jumper too, but I had others back in Chongqing and a whole stack back in Randwick, or so I thought, but after I had returned to Randwick a couple of weeks later, they were nowhere to be found, so I guess I do need this one. Erica gave me a pair of warm slippers, which I have since left at Randwick, to be used after I finish up here in China. All I gave them was a box of chocolates, some tea and some biscuits.

The third ceremony was playing cards, which the family continued till 2.00 am. I am not sure if this is just a family tradition or has a wider following. The cards were Western, but the game was Chinese. Meanwhile there was a four hour concert on TV. No, I did not stay up till 2.00 am, but went to bed considerably earlier. One must get one's beauty sleep, you know – especially if one needs either – the sleep that is or the beauty.

Not surprisingly, next morning was mostly gone before family members surfaced. Traditionally, apart from work needed to prepare meals, today is a day of rest, about the only one in the year. There would be no farm work today. And the weather is perfect, the mists had gone, and the sun was shining brightly. When the sun shines in Chongqing, it is never brightly.

This is also throughout China, a family day, so I am cognizant of the honour being afforded to me. Truly loving families are open, and indeed the same can be said for any society, including nations. Inward looking societies are selfish; love is essentially outgoing and all inclusive. Jesus did not come to found an exclusive group, but one that would be open – catholic – to all of humanity, irrespective of culture or nationality. I fear that at times, we have considered the "Catholic" Church to be more like a club.

At 11.00 am we had our breakfast of sweet sesame seed dumplings.

The afternoon would prove very interesting, as the whole family went for a walk, with a particular destination in mind, though Xiao Yan, Martha's boyfriend, kept ferrying people on his motorcycle; Mr C first, followed by Mrs C, then me, but by the time it was the turn of the girls, we had arrived; tough. The baby was carried on someone's back, the women taking turns.

Along the route, people were congregating, talking, playing mahjongg, enjoying the sunshine. My presence caused a bit of a stir, especially with some of the children, who had never seen a Westerner before. They ran off when I took a photo of them. Where did we go? We walked along the main road for about three kilometres or so, to the house of a relative. Mr. C had bought a tree and had gone to inspect it. What a surprise. It is an investment. He could use it to make furniture, especially as his future son-in-law is a carpenter, or resell it at a profit some years hence. While he was inspecting the tree, the rest of us ate turnips, freshly picked. And of course, we ate the ubiquitous sunflower seeds. I really enjoyed this brilliant sunshine, with clear blue skies.

By 4.00 pm we were back at the house; time for lunch. Truly! Back in Chongqing, some of our students have their evening meal about this time. We ate wheat dumplings, rice, tofu, pork and vegies. I spent the rest of the afternoon, sitting in the sun and reading Helen Keller's

"Three Days to See", which I thoroughly enjoyed. What an amazing person she was. I still do not understand how she learnt the alphabet and so mastered words, then ideas. Her teacher, too, was such an extraordinary woman. We really do need to appreciate what we have, and especially on a beautiful day like today to thank God for all Sheir gifts. To be able to see, to hear, to touch, to taste, to smell and so to speak and understand is all so wonderful.

When Helen wrote this book, the story of her life so far, she was only 22. It is full of appreciation for the beauty of nature surrounding us. She shows keen observations. She posits three hypothetical days, when she has the gift of sight, and tells us how she would spend them. On day 1 she would see the faces of her family, friends and animals. On day 2 she would look at human history at a museum, followed by a night at the theatre. On day 3 she would visit New York (she was American) to see how people live in a big city and in the evening would again visit the theatre, perhaps to see a comedy. What would you do, if you knew you would lose your sight in three days' time?

The essence of her thinking is not just learning, but appreciating. I completely agree, but would add that we also need to be grateful, thanking not only people, but the God who has given us so much.

89. Last Days in Han Zhuang Village – 11th – 15th February 2013

The village in which the C family live is called Han Zhuang – just in case you are wondering.

I have mentioned that the TV has been left on for much of the day, mostly to keep two year old junior out of mischief. One favourite programme is a daily cartoon concerning a black wolf trying to catch and eat white sheep. He never succeeds of course, in spite of many nefarious schemes, often ending up somewhat the worse for wear. This, however, never seems to deter him, as he returns to the chase with seemingly no ill effects.

When I was a boy, many cartoons – Tom and Jerry, for instance – contained a good deal of violence where the characters seemed to recover instantly with no ill effects. This is not real and I wonder what message is being given to young children. One particularly violent show was a pantomime, which I think dates back some centuries, called Punch and Judy. I never liked it and I wonder how on earth it got a G rating. It should be more like an R.

Another daily TV series is set in a previous dynasty – the Qing, I think, judging from the hair style, the forehead being shorn and a long queue at the back. These period productions are common in China. In this one, an elfin childish goddess falls in love with a soldier. He carries her half the time, or they ride on a dragon. When he gets wounded in some fight, she is able to heal him. On one occasion he even gets killed, whereupon she entreats the chief god to restore his life, which he does. What interesting mythology, with parallels in our Western mythology. Around the world, we are so much alike, with the same desires, even if expressed differently and within different settings.

One of the books I read at this time was on Greek mythology; it was good to refresh one's memory. Sisyphus was a tyrant king of Corinth, where later Paul would establish a Christian community. When he died he was punished for his cruelty by having to push a large rock up a mountain, only to have it roll back down to the bottom after he had nearly succeeded. He would be spending all eternity doing this. Now there is a bookstore in Shapingba, in Chongqing, called Sysiphe. What is the connection? I do not know, but one can speculate. Books represent freedom of thought and expression, which in this country is somewhat limited. Is this a subtle hint that the current tyrants will be severely punished???

This new semester, I have a student who glories in the English (Greek) name of Cassiopeia. Does she know the story of Cassiopeia in Greek mythology? I doubt it and I am not going to tell her. But this lady was the wife of the king of Egypt, and was very proud, boasting in particular of her numerous offspring; seven sons and seven daughters. This raised the ire of the gods who promptly slew them all, Apollo being the chief slayer. I am sure this girl is thinking of the constellation, which of course is named after the mythological character.

One of my favourite stories from Greek mythology is that of Eros and Psyche. There have been many paintings on this theme, my favourite being one I saw in the Louvre, Paris, painted by Francois Gerard in 1798. In the myth, Aphrodite, the goddess of love, is jealous of Psyche's beauty, so sends her son, Eros to shoot her heart with one of his arrows, so that she will fall in love with some unworthy beast, but instead, by mistake, Eros shoots himself. In the painting by Gerard, Eros is embracing her, but she does not notice; a butterfly hovers overhead, psyche also meaning butterfly, but I think it also stands for flightiness. We do not know who we are or our worth until we are loved. There is a lot more to this story, but this will suffice here.

On a completely different note, Spring Festival is a time for visiting other people's houses, especially relatives, and inviting them to visit you. Two relatives arrived to give a demonstration of this "inviting". Mr. C said "No". They insisted. "No". Was that the end of the matter? No, it was only the beginning. Quite literally they utterly refused to take "no" for an answer, even after seven quite definite refusals. The voices became a little raised, until it reached the stage when Mr C was grabbed by the arm and physically pushed out the door. I have never seen anything like it.

This relative returned on another day, and we ended up traipsing out at night time to join him and his wife for evening meal, even though we had already eaten. I ate a little and drank only a few sips of a most potent *baijiu.* They do make their own *baijiu* hereabouts, from fermented corn, but this particular bottle had been bought. Its taste was akin to kerosene. Next he wanted me to stay the night. Goodness. It was not very practical, so I graciously declined, more than once, as you can imagine. I noticed that his house was similar in construction and design to the C house.

Another book I have been reading is selected quotations. I like these, as we can tap into the insights of great people of past ages. Here are some examples:

1) The one who lives more seriously within, lives more simply without. Hemingway.
2) There is nothing noble in being superior to some other person. The true nobility is in being superior to your previous self.
3) The four freedoms are: freedom of speech, freedom of religion; freedom from want and freedom from fear. F D Roosevelt. As a comment on this, it seems China is hell bent on eliminating want, and incidentally they do not seem to care how they do it.
4) Peace comes from God, and is not the absence of war, but the harmony which comes from justice and consent, and is the absence of tyranny and force. This requires constant effort. F. W de Clerk

After nine days in Erica's house, the time came to say goodbye.

The night before we had some relatives join us for dinner, so that in all we had 17 people. In the West, this would be quite a drama; how do we cater for so many people? Here it is taken in one's stride. After eating, the cards were brought out, as were the cigarettes. Every single male smokes, in spite of the presence of two babies; awareness of the harmful effects of both active and passive smoking is just not present. I declined the cigarettes I was offered, saying simply that I do not smoke. This card playing continued till 2.00 am. Only four people left the house, meaning that 13 people needed to find somewhere to sleep. At least one bed accommodated three sleepers. I shared my bed with Shao Yan, who, I might add, slept like a log.

This final evening in Erica's house completed my stay here. On the following day I left to return to Chongqing.

90.   Han Zhuang to Chongqing – 15th – 17th February 2013

Next morning – or perhaps the same morning – we were up at 8.00 o'clock. I had breakfast and packed. With the family's generosity, I have so much stuff. This again was not going to be a problem, as a fleet of four motorcycles was brought into service to convey said luggage plus people to Shui Qing on the main road some 4 km away. In all 13 people set out at 11.30 am; what a procession! I, too, was given a lift for the last kilometre, though I would have been happy to have walked the whole way. As you can see, this is a close knit family.

In the town, my luggage was loaded onto a 20 seater bus for the trip to Bijie city. Our numbers were now reduced to four: Mrs C, Shao Yan, Erica and me. We left at 1.00 pm, arriving 2.00 pm in the city, nearly 40 km away. We took a different road from the one we had used coming up. This one was sealed for most of the way, though narrow and windy as we lost altitude, going around bends. It became very rough indeed for the last few kilometres. There are lovely views here of range upon range receding mistily, mysteriously into the distance. I love these views, so popular in Chinese paintings. I had seen them depicted in numerous paintings before I came to realise how authentic they are.

For some reason, you cannot get a taxi at the bus terminal, but must need walk about 200 metres to an intersection, where we did get one to convey us plus luggage to my hotel. Shao Yan headed back to Han Zhuang Cun, while Erica took her mother to the local hospital for a checkup.

Amy arrived to keep me company, so we went off window shopping. We had our evening meal with a colleague of hers, who then paid for the meal; I have paid for so little over the past few weeks. He was dining with his family, so we joined them. I was sitting next to a policeman – brother-in-law I think. Back at the hotel, Amy and I swapped photos.

Next morning I said goodbye to Mrs C, thanking her for her hospitality. I also told her to look after herself a little better, as her grandchildren now depend on her. She works hard, lives simply and loves deeply.

Amy, Erica and I then walked the 15 minutes to the bus station to catch my bus back to Chongqing. I was lucky that Amy had purchased my ticket two days previously, as I had landed the second last seat on the bus, right at the back. Actually somebody else was already occupying my seat – situation normal – so I took the window seat; better – I am happy.

Before we left the hotel, I slipped some money into Erica's bag while she was not looking, and I had been afraid she would find it before we left. I can just imagine the reaction; "My God..." – she might be a pagan, but I tell her she is a prayerful little pagan. Actually these girls are very fine people indeed, very close to God, whether they realise it or not. I had also left a little present with Amy, and she gave me two embroidered pillow cases, which are now on my sofa, as they are perfect for two cushions I already had.

The trip back to Chongqing was interesting. It was an overcast morning, the sun appearing weakly through the mist at around 9.00 am. For a long while, the sun was only faintly discernible, peeking in and out of the fog, with visibility reduced at times to about 100 metres, with the bus slowing to around 70 kph. The road is smooth, which is just as well as I was sitting down the back. At one point we crossed a deep limestone gorge, with a narrow ribbon-like river far below. I guess this limestone erodes readily. The bus TV was on, but thank goodness they were not showing the usual violent movies. Instead they showed a concert, with singing and comedy skits.

At 12.10 pm we stopped at a way station for lunch, after 3 ½ hours on the road. There was just room for seven large buses. People were selling foods; snacks, meals, mandarins. We hopped aboard again at 12.30 pm, but it was another 20 minutes before we left, as we were hemmed in by another bus, so had many tries, going back and forth, till we could get out. It took four attempts, but only after the other bus had moved.

In the afternoon the mist cleared and the sun shone. Our bus sped along this smooth highway, burrowing into mountains and dancing swiftly across valleys of streams and fields, villages and towns on long legs, while around us reared the pointed tops of limestone mountains. It was late afternoon by the time we arrived in Chongqing.

Now which bus station will we go to? There are quite a few. As luck would have it, we arrived at the south railway station; perfect, as from here I can get the 210 bus directly to our university. God is good.

It had truly been a wonderful, blessed time. I loved the scenery in the mountains, both the ranges and the valleys. I loved the way the farmers, over many generations, have terraced the hillsides, thus maximising their arable land. I loved the animals, watching them, hearing them. But on top of the list are the beautiful people I met and stayed with. May God bless and reward them.

In all I was away for 23 days. Now I have a full day tomorrow to organise myself for my trip back to Australia.

Chengdu Excursion, June 2013

91.   Chengdu – 21st – 22nd June 2013

Susan, director of the Lancaster/Robert Gordon Programme, invited David and I to go to Chengdu with her. Chengdu ("Perfect City") is the capital of Sichuan Province and is not far away, just over two hours by train – by fast train that is.

The normal trains that I have travelled on often are the K trains, which trundle along at 80 kph if you are lucky. Sometimes you just stop and wait as every other train flashes past. At the top of the range you have the very fast trains, which travel at over 300 kph. I have only been on one of these, going from the airport at Shanghai into the city. In between you have these fast trains, which travel at just under 200 kph, and wonderfully smooth and comfortable they are, too. There is a surprising amount of leg room. The attendants are dressed smartly like airline attendants. It is not expensive either, costing only 96.5 Yuan for the journey, much cheaper than the airline. The railway stations at both ends are very impressive, being more like airports than the usual run of the mill stations. It takes just over two hours to get to Chengdu.

Last Friday morning set off, returning on Saturday night, so staying only one night. Susan was meeting some of her classmates, whom she had not seen for 21 years. She was pretty excited and it became clear that they were equally thrilled to see her. We wined and dined most sumptuously, with us not being allowed to contribute anything, which is typical of Chinese hospitality. Now when they come to Australia, it will be my turn to host them, but when will that be? Unlikely, so we remain in their debt.

Chengdu is a most attractive city of some 8 million inhabitants. Unlike Chongqing, it is flat, so I suppose it is easier to plan. It is clean, with an abundance of parks and greenery. It also has more bikes, which are not all that practical in a hilly city. I left mine in Tongren. I also like the architecture, as it boasts some striking high rise buildings. It is really good to see some effort being made to beautify a city, and not just erect a jungle of concrete towers.

The city has quite a long history, dating from 316 BC during the Warring States period. That does make it just a little bit older than any city we have in Australia. Like so many of China's cities, it is built on a river, though some cities are built around more than one; Chongqing, for instance, has the Yangtze and the Jialing Jiang. Chengdu has the Jin Jiang. Jin means "brocade", a reference to the brocade industry which thrived here during the Eastern Han dynasty (A.D. 25 – 220). The province has in fact many rivers, though there are four main ones, and hence the name Si Chuan (four rivers).

We visited a fairly extensive park, called Jinli, with lovely ponds and lots of stalls selling everything from snacks to souvenirs. It is a kind of ancient town. It was most pleasant wandering around. We also visited Dragon Town, also known as Kuanzhaiguangzi Alley, for our evening meal. While the classmates chatted, David and I went for a stroll.

I had been here before, and in fact stayed here for about a week three years ago in a Youth Hostel, which is still here. It truly was delightful. So I know this area quite well. Dragon Town features old buildings, part historical, part touristy and part restaurants. One street, called Well Lane, has a wall composed of a collection of old bricks. There are photos of 20th century buildings where their architectural style is interesting, or perhaps they were constructed of bricks from previous dynasties. It is also interesting to note the different styles of brick and their patterns. Alternating the way the bricks are placed is not only pleasing to the eye, but also strengthens the wall in the event of earthquakes, which Sichuan is prone to. There was a Ming dynasty palace compound here, comparable to the Forbidden City in Beijing. There was a Manchu fortress here as well, beginning from 1718, with a circumference of some 5 km. There are bricks, too, dating back to the Qin dynasty (222 – 204 B.C.), when extensive walls were constructed around the city. This was a period for wall building, as the Great Wall itself began at this time.

China is developing rapidly and rebuilding itself; the amount of demolition and construction that has gone on even since I first came to China a decade ago has been unprecedented in human history. It has truly been an astonishing time and a rare privilege to be here. This country has, however, a long history, with much evidence of human endeavour stretching back thousands of years. The question arises, therefore, of what to destroy and what to protect. In the main, my opinion is that China has done an excellent job in maintaining this balance. There is a lot more I could say on this, but let us leave it at that for the time being; it is too big a topic.

Another park we visited is Wang Jiang Lou, or "River Viewing" as it is on the banks of the Jin Jiang, southeast of the city. I really liked it here, as it is both beautiful and peaceful. It boasts some 150 varieties of bamboo, some forming a canopy overhead as you walk along a path. There is even a horse and carriage made entirely of bamboo, very cleverly constructed.

This park is the retreat where a Tang dynasty poet, Xue Tao, lived. It was remarked to me that China's civilization reached its zenith in the Tang dynasty (A.D. 618- 907). I do not think I agree, as this supposes that China is unlikely to achieve much in the future. Certainly the Tang was extraordinary in many ways. This park illustrates two of these. Firstly its architecture was superb, so pleasing to the eye in its elegance and balance, yet not overly ornate. The house of the poet is here, simple yet sturdy. Secondly, the status of women reached its highest point at this time, with the greatest freedoms. Witness that this park is preserved in honour of a woman, one who loved nature and especially bamboo. I read recently that the nadir for women occurred during the time of Mao Zedong; possibly.

On the two afternoons we spent in Chengdu, we paused in our meanderings for tea, in typical Chinese tradition. Here it is green tea in its various forms; I chose rose tea on the first afternoon and jasmine on the second. It was so relaxing sitting on bamboo chairs, at a bamboo table, sipping tea, while other people did the same nearby or strolled about.

This is a fitting place to end this chapter – all so serene. The next chapter will be special.

92.   Li Bing – 22nd June 2013

On Saturday morning we sat down for breakfast, which I was expecting to be typically Chinese – i.e. boiled egg, steamed bread, green vegetables, tofu, rice porridge and spices but not so, as our thoughtful hostess provided Western style bread and, wonder of wonders, coffee. I do like my coffee in the morning.

After this welcome repast we climbed into a car belonging to one of Susan's classmates, and off we went, heading northwest for 60 km or so, about an hour and a half drive. We did not know where we were going, but this is normal, where information is rarely given in advance, but in this case it was deliberate; a surprise. I have mentioned that Chengdu sits on a plain, but as we travelled, both David and I noticed lee waves in the cloud formation. These can only come from mountains, so that we knew we were heading towards a mountain range, and we knew its orientation.

We arrived at a gravel car park, which we crunched our way across to a park entrance where we paid our dues – or most of us did, as David was free, being over 70 years old. For me it was half price; can't imagine why; maybe it's because I am so childlike! (Childish, some might say). We were also clutching umbrellas as it was a little damp, not raining heavily, but just a little. It did make it a little awkward for me to take photos, trying to manipulate the camera with one hand, while holding my umbrella with the other. It was worth it.

What we have come to is the Du Jiang Yang Irrigation Project. The Min River, which flows through this mountainous region, has variable flows, with low levels in winter, swelling to floods in the summer after snow melts on the higher peaks. It is also fast flowing. The problem was to mitigate the floods for the benefit of those people living along its banks and also to divert part of the river onto the plains below for irrigation. We are talking about the Warring States period (406 – 222 B.C.), when this region belonged to the Qin State and Li Bing was the local governor. Later the ruler of Qin State, Shi Huangdi, would conquer the other states to form the Qin dynasty. Military conquest has always been part of China's history – still is. After studying the problem for some time, Li Bing got to work in 270 B.C. What he did was nothing short of brilliant.

You could dam the river, but this river, being fast flowing, carries a lot of silt, and in time dams silt up. Basically he built an island in the centre of the river, rather than across it. Upstream of this island therefore, the river divides into two channels, the left hand side is deep water, while the right hand side is much shallower. Thus during times of normal flow 60% of the water goes to the left, 40% to the right. In times of drought, all the water goes left, while in times of flood, 40% of the water goes left, 60% goes right. Part of the reason for this plan was that the river had to be kept open for military use and this is more difficult if you build a dam.

The next step was to divert water from the left hand channel onto the Chengdu Plain for irrigation purposes. This meant blasting through a mountain, a somewhat difficult task when the rock type is particularly hard and before the invention of gunpowder. This was not insurmountable to a man of Li Bing's talents. He used the abundant wood supplies from the mountain to heat the rocks, before pouring cold water on them till they cracked. They could then be removed – by manual labour of course, but then again, this has never been a problem in this country. It took eight years to dig a 20 metre wide channel through Mount Yulei.

The entire project was completed in 256 B.C, after 14 years of effort, but it is still operating and successful today, more than 2,200 years later. The result mitigated flood damage, and ensured a reliable water supply for irrigation on the plain. Chengdu subsequently became very rich and productive. Li Bing was a genius.

We walked along the river towards the end of this man-made island. The method by which Li Bing dammed the water is illustrated in two models, using gabions, large stakes, bamboo and rocks. The levee used to divide the waters to the left and right is called Yuzui or fish mouth, since that is what it looks like. Opposite, on the other side of the river we could see the cliff face held together with many rock bolts. This is not Li Bing's work, however, but is modern, dating from the 2008 devastating earthquake which struck this region. In fact in the town nearby, 90% of buildings were destroyed, including schools where hundreds of children perished.

At the end of the levee is a swing bridge, modern in construction, but replacing a whole series of bridges over the centuries. It is called Anlan, or Couple Bridge, in honour of a husband and wife who were instrumental in constructing the 1803 version. This bridge we crossed was swaying so much that people had difficulty in keeping their balance. I was walking behind David, and noticed he had no trouble whatsoever, strolling along quite unperturbed. He is, after all, a sailor.

On the other side of the river is a temple, dedicated to Li Bing – and this was a revelation. Sometimes in life there are occasions when you realise something, as if a light suddenly goes on in your head. This was one such occasion. This temple appears almost identical to any other temple you can find, most of them Buddhist. Obviously this particular example is a religious shrine. It is not. It was built to honour Li Bing, and also his son, who took over his father's work. They are not gods, but people. Why is this so momentous?

When Catholic missionaries arrived in China in the 16th and 17th centuries, the problem arose as to what practices converts could continue to follow. If they worship in a temple, for instance, are they following a god other than the one true God? This was not a minor issue, but became a subject of heated debate, particularly between the Jesuits in China and the Dominicans in Europe. Can they continue to kowtow to the emperor? Can they honour their ancestors? A major blunder occurred – in my humble opinion – in trying to force Chinese away from their native customs. Christianity was seen as an alien, Western religion – and it is not. It is no more European than it is Arabian, or Chinese. It is the world's universal religion, without any cultural favour. This temple provides the proof, at least for me. Here, clearly, kowtowing, burning incense, even praying, are not religious acts, but cultural. It is the Chinese way of giving honour.

There is another aspect to this. China is the only country I know which has a department of religious affairs, whereas we in the West think that religion has nothing to do with the government. Why is this? Here religion is considered to be a purely social affair. If the vertical dimension – people to God – has been taken out of Chinese temples, then it may have no place in any temple, including Christian churches. One can see why the government lacks this vertical dimension: interesting, and worth pondering.

Enough. We returned to Chengdu, had another sumptuous meal and headed for the railway station for our return journey to Chongqing. What a wonderful two days. Thank you Susan, David, and Susan's friends.

Eileen's Wedding, Xiamen, Fujian Province, July 2013

93.   Eileen's Wedding – 1ˢᵗ July 2013

Over the years one teaches many students – thousands of them – but one keeps in touch with very few. Some students one might forget, but others never. Of course, from the student's perspective, they might be trying very hard to forget. One of my former students from Fuzhou invited me to her wedding. This does not happen very often, so when it does it is a privilege. I was also free for that time, so willingly accepted her invitation.

The wedding was to be held in her city of Xiamen (pronounced hsyamen, not ex-ee-a-men), a coastal port city on the Taiwan Strait, so on Friday afternoon I flew down. This time I used Shandong Airlines on the flight down and Xiamen Airlines for the flight back.

For those of you who may be thinking of flying in China, here is my ranking, just based on my own experience. Hainan Air is the best I have flown, followed by China Southern, Xiamen Air and Shandong. Other airlines come next, but avoid, if you can, Air China, Dragonair and China Eastern.

As we flew out of Chongqing at dusk, the plane needed to rise sharply to avoid the mountains (we did miss). As we rose we could see the brown pall of pollution which covers the city, so I delighted in soaring into the clear skies higher up. Chongqing is, I think, among the top ten most polluted cities in the world, though it has improved in recent years with the movement of factories and power plants elsewhere. Beijing gets the gong as the world's most polluted city. Someone asked me recently for advice on travelling to Beijing. My reply was curt; "Don't go". Recently a friend of mine did go there and reported that on the Great Wall all one could see was a few bricks, probably more modern than Ming, stretching away for only a few metres on each side, though this was due as much to the weather as the pollution.

Xiamen, on the other hand, having fewer factories and being a seaside city, has much cleaner air. Tina, another of my former students in the same class as the bride, met me at the airport. From a distance I did not recognise her, as the girl of six years ago has now filled out to be a beautiful young woman. Her hair style has also changed. One of her friends drove us in a Mercedes to a restaurant overlooking one of the waterways of this city. This man is in the import- export business and is doing very well – obviously. He wanted an English name, so he is now Michael. The meal was seafood, and was really delicious. I would be having quite a few seafood meals over the next week. What looked like a black omelette turned out to be *hai li* or oyster. After the meal we drove to the Di Le Hotel where I would be spending the night. It was really good to see Tina again, especially knowing that she is doing well.

The next morning I went down to breakfast, but did not fancy much, as I really wanted a coffee, which they did not have, but I had brought some with me, so had it in my room. Then Angel arrived. I have not seen her for six years. In class the other students called her "The Beauty"; she still is. She had her four year old daughter with her, and it was wonderful to see the affection they have for each other. We drove to her home, some distance from the city. It is a four storey structure, so she too is doing very well. Not far away lives Eileen, today's bride, so we next went around to see her, all dressed in red for her wedding, looking radiant. Red is the colour of good fortune. Her husband, an electrician, is a tall, quiet man. We had lunch, with many people already here, and the house decked out for the occasion.

After lunch we went shopping in Wanda Mall, spacious, modern, comfortable with top end shops and an underground car park, where each bay has an electronic indicator to tell you how many free spaces there are. Tina needed a wedding dress. Naturally, we went to shop after shop. My mother used to say; "Never buy anything in the first five shops". Then it was try-on time, with dress after dress. Eventually she settled on a beautiful white dress and it wasn't cheap. I decided to buy a belt while here, since the only one I had brought was rather too tattered for a wedding. I chose one just a little more quickly than it took to choose the dress, but then I looked at the price tag. "Oh my goodness – *tai gui le* – too expensive". As I was putting it back, Angel went off and paid for it! Just like that.

Then it was back to the hotel for a sleep, but a different hotel from last night, belonging to the 7 Days Inn chain, it being closer to Eileen's house. At 6.30 pm we went back to her house, where the first order of the day was photos. I then gave the traditional *hong bao* (red envelope containing money) to the groom. I knew that if I gave it to Eileen she would give it back. He promptly went looking for Eileen and gave it to her – not exactly what I had in mind. What followed was an interesting game, where I pretended to ignore her, while she chased me around a large round table. "I will be angry" she said. "Then we have a problem; you'll be angry if I give you this, and I'll be angry if I don't". She accepted it, eventually. Good.

Something like 150 people sat down to course after course, in true Chinese style, with about ten people to each round table. Our table was all former ACC (Anglo Chinese College) students. This is the college in Fuzhou where I had taught for more than four years.

At about 8.00 pm, Mendelssohn's Wedding March was played and the bride and groom walked up a red carpet flanked by lights to the stage, where they were met by the professional MC. Eileen was now wearing white, while the groom wore a suit. In China, they do not make vows to each other as is our custom in the West. At this ceremony, the groom knelt on one knee to declare; *"Wo ai ni"* – "I love you". The bride then took his hands, he got up and that was that. They next did the rounds of each table, to share toasts with the guests.

It was good for me to see some of my former students again, though I had forgotten some of their names. One young lady asked me. "What is my name?" I was not sure, but thought it may have been Susie. Maybe she misheard but she said, "No, guess again". This went on for some time. I hate this. Maybe I taught some fresh faced 14 year old boy many years ago, and you are approached at some reunion by a large 50 year old man, sporting both beard and paunch, who says, "Surely you remember me? Go on, guess, guess, guess." I am not into these guessing games. The first students I taught are indeed now well into their 50s. It turned out the young lady in this instance was in fact Susie. "But I said that first!" Most of those around the table are now married, and most have a child. An ACC photo was de rigueur – more memories.

By 9.30 pm all was over so it was back to the 7 Day Inn for sleep Tomorrow is another day.

94.   *Hui An – 3rd – 4th July 2013*

Next morning I slept late, and declined Tina's offer of breakfast, as I had my own coffee in my room. Her room was next to mine, so convenient. Eileen and Angel turned up and we went out for lunch. I was really not expecting to see Eileen the day after her wedding. We went to a very good restaurant, where, believe it or not, I had an

Australian steak, well done of course. If you order a steak anything less than well done, you still have the blood in it. They also use percentages; I said 80% done. The last time I had a steak, I sent it back to be heated a little more. This was heaven; sitting in a comfortable, air-conditioned restaurant, eating an Aussie steak, with an accomplished pianist playing classical music in the background, with these three beautiful people.

After lunch Eileen and I went for a walk in a park by the river, seeking what shade we could on this very hot day. Angel had to go and teach; she teaches Chinese. Later I would go for another walk on my own. Irrespective of the weather, I think it important to get one's daily exercise.

That night we went out for yet another meal, to the same place we had gone on Friday night, the seafood al fresco restaurant by the river, which leads into the Taiwan Strait. The menu included fish, prawns, pippies, soup, egg and vegetables, all washed down with copious amounts of beer. We were three men and two women, the men trying to get me drunk with *gan bei* after *gan bei* i.e. emptying your glass. There was also some wine, which I think was a port. These people are all Min, which is I think a subset of the Han, but they do have their own Min An Hua dialect, which they were speaking.

On Monday morning, Eileen, her husband and Angel turned up at the hotel to say goodbye. What a wonderful time we have had. We left at 9.00 am, Michael driving us to Tina's home town, Hui An, an hour or so further up the coast. Here I met Tina's husband, a burly man just out of the army where he served for twelve years. It is the government's responsibility to provide him with a job, but I gather there is no set time frame for this, so you wait – or find your own job. We went out to a restaurant for yet another large seafood meal, then to KTV; Tina likes to sing, which she does well. They had no English songs that I know, and I did not know the songs they did have.

We did a lot of driving around the district, including a nearby dam. I had actually been here about four years ago. We filled up with petrol at a service station owned by Tina's uncle, so that is handy. The rock type around here is granite, which seems to provide the backbone for the economy. Much of the buildings are made from granite blocks. There are also many statues, of Guan Yin, the goddess of mercy, of animals and other figures. Evening meal was yet another big seafood meal at a restaurant. Mind you, we do not get much seafood in Chongqing, situated as it is some 1,500 km from the sea.

That night, in a house near to Tina's, there was a funeral in process. We went to have a look, me feeling that I did not want to intrude, but Tina pushing me forward. I ended up at a room where opera was being performed, not the well-known Peking opera, but a local variety. It still looks much the same with painted faces, dancing, singing and musical accompaniment, including the discordant drums that I dislike so much. I felt very conspicuous standing there, with the dancer staring at me, so beat a hasty retreat. We walked back to Tina's house, where I turned in about 10.30 pm.

Next morning, we lazed around the house before going out for yet another big lunch; Lord knows what all this eating is doing to my girth. We drove to a beautiful park full of flowers, which, unfortunately, was closed. We still stood around in the shade taking photos, while Tina's nephew decided to pee on the grass; anywhere will do.

Another drive took us to a dam, where one could swim, so I bought a pair of togs – mine were back at the house – and did just that. The family was very concerned, absolutely insistent that I use a lifebuoy. Goodness, how can you swim? – but of course, very few Chinese can swim, and there have been quite a few deaths in this dam. I was equally insistent that I CAN swim. Actually I did not swim very far, no more than 500 metres, as I had not done much swimming of recent days, but I thoroughly enjoyed it, and in fact could have swum a lot more. The water was warm, heated by the sun, but underneath the surface may have been a different story. A sharp temperature gradient may be one reason for the deaths. None of the family swam with me; there were just a few young men in the water, none of whom was actually swimming, as they were clinging to a line of buoys.

We next went to Tina's parent's house to relax, eat some lychees and play with the kids, the baby joining in the fun by peeing over Tina's front! After that we went to hospital, not, I hasten to add, because having a baby pee on you is a particularly serious medical condition, but because a cousin had recently had a baby. Both proud parents were in the room, the baby a small three day old red bundle. I was actually surprised that they were still there, as in Australia they would have been discharged by now.

The next port of call was to the house of Tina's boss, working for an organisation called Anran. I really do not know much about what they do, but I was shown material which stretches to three times its length. When the fabric is burnt, it can be teased into fine thread, like spider web, before cooling into a smooth plastic like material. Anybody have any clues?

On Wednesday, I watched a video of Tina's wedding, on 23rd January, 2011. I was in Australia at the time. Here the essence was the procession of cars driving from Tina's parent's house to her husband's house, symbolic of leaving one family to join another. At her new house, she offered gifts at the household ancestral shrine, while her husband burnt incense. She then honoured her mother-in-law, before doing the rounds of the guests, offering tea, which each person drank, then gave her their *hong bao*, (red envelope with money) before she moved on to the next guest.

Surprise: Eileen, her husband, Angel, and Michael drove up from Xiamen to join us for lunch, so that altogether we had a party of eleven. We went to the best restaurant in Hui An, another seafood place, for a sumptuous feast. I was thrilled and amazed that they would go to all that trouble. You can see how wonderful the people are here. I left at 2.45 pm to take a bus to Fuzhou.

95. *Fuzhou – 4th – 7th July 2013*

The bus left Hui An at 2.45 pm, arriving in Fuzhou after a smooth ride at 5.00 pm. Vickie was waiting for me, but not at the bus depot; it was too hot, so she had sensibly elected to wait in McDonald's next door. She told me it was more convenient to stay in her house, rather than commute from a hotel, so that is where we went via taxi. She shares an apartment with her parents, sister, brother, sister-in-law and her baby. I might add that this family is U/G R.C.; Vickie came to Australia for World Youth Day in 2008, so she would be remembered in Australia.

There was also a religious sister joining us for the evening meal. The family asked me what I would like to eat. Well what could I say? Kangaroo steak? – hardly. But there is a Fujian specialty which I like very much, so I replied, "*Yu wan*", or fish balls. They went out and bought some; they really are very nice. But the surprises did not end there. It appears that the father likes to drink wine – as in grape wine – and he just happened to have a bottle of Penfolds bin 2, which is Australian for those not in the know. It was delicious. Ten years ago you would hardly find anybody drinking either wine or coffee, but now more and more Chinese are doing so.

After the meal, Vickie and I walked to Carrefour to buy some yoghurt, which the family likes. Then it was time to turn in. With a young baby on board, they like to retire around 10.00 pm.

Next day, Thursday July 6th, after a good sleep in, I left around 10.00 am to meet two good friends from Fuzhou days, Cathy and Grace. We were to meet at a large shopping mall, Wang Xiang Chen, actually at McDonald's first, as it is a good reference point. Incidentally, in Chinese it is Mai Dang Lao. The taxi journey was interesting, as I commented on the weather, saying it was hot. "Bloody hot, mate", was the reply. "I think it is going to be around 38." "Nah mate; over b… 40". Mind you, the conversation was in Chinese, but I thought you might like it translated into Strine.

As we hurtled along at close to the speed of sound I took a good look at the city, which was actually possible when we stopped at traffic lights, when within 0.000000000000001 seconds of them turning green, the taxi driver would blow his horn. I may be exaggerating here; perhaps I have one too many zeros. The city has changed. There are not as many bike lanes and not as many bikes. Ten years ago this was a bike city. Now it appears that those who used to ride bikes have progressed to e-bikes, when those who used to ride motorcycles have progressed to cars. There were then hardly any privately owned cars, but now the city is full of them. They are currently building a metro system, so that will be good. What used to be the heart of Fuzhou, Dong Jie Kou, is now a mess.

Both Cathy and Grace were looking wonderful; it is hard to believe it is six years since I have seen them. Cathy's baby son is now six years old (or 7 by Chinese reckoning). We had a wonderful meal together, catching up. Cathy then did some shopping for her son, Michael, who was to compete in an English contest the next day. She was looking for suitable clothes. Actually I did not like her choice of shorts, so when she asked for my advice I suggested another pair. So if he wins the contest – and in fact he did win – it is of course, entirely because of me! This is no mean achievement, coming first for his age group, putting him in the top 60 in the country. The top 20 were subsequently selected to go to Beijing and in that competition he came third. Well done indeed. Cathy is an English teacher and her own standard is excellent. She speaks English at home with her son, so no wonder he is so good.

After this I took another taxi to see Sunny, another former ACC student, at the school where she is working. It is a private English school and I sat in on a training session. Both of us then caught a bus for a 40 minute trip across town. I was surprised that the fare is only 1 Yuan, whereas ten years ago it was 2 Yuan. I did not know that prices went down – only up.

The meal was held in a very nice restaurant, very popular, situated on the 12th floor of a modern building. Daphne was already there, and we were later joined by Jane, who had been to Hua Nan College, and later still by Tina and her boss, who drove up especially from Hui An; what a surprise. I wanted to talk, but the talking of the other patrons was loud, as was the piped music, so I asked the manager if she could turn down the music. She did. We were late arriving, so as we talked and ate, the restaurant gradually emptied until we were the only ones left.

A number of these young ladies do not as yet have a boyfriend. Now in the West, this may not be such a big deal, but here it is, when every girl is expected to be married by late twenties. These girls can really get desperate. Outside on the street, I said to one of them; "Look at that young man; not bad looking. Shall I ask him if he has a girl friend?" Naturally the response was a look of horror. Yet there are at least 30 million young men who will never marry, because of the disparity in numbers between men and women.

It was late by the time I got back to Vickie's house, and she was waiting for me. Apologies. Next morning it was time to pack up. The family presented me with a pair of long shorts and a shirt, as if they had not already done enough. Nancy arrived, another of my former students, then Tina and Hong. Time for photos and a final meal, which included fish balls and was also washed down with wine. We finished with a prayer session, before Nancy drove Vickie and me to the station. It is always sad to say goodbye.

The train left at 2.30 pm, right on the dot, and arrived at Xiamen at 5.30 pm, with four or five stops in between. It is very smooth and comfortable, reaching speeds of 197 kph. For some reason this is as fast as they go, though they can go much faster. At Xiamen I had time and was thirsty so I had a mocha, then caught taxi to the airport. The taxi rank was quite long, taking half an hour to get to the front, but that was no problem as I had plenty of time, in fact more time than I had expected. When I got to the airport I realised that my flight was delayed by about 1 ½ hours, as were many other flights. The reason, I think, is that the skies are just so crowded. In this country, most of the airspace is prohibited to all but military aircraft, as I have stated before. This is a highly militarised country, due to a mixture of paranoia and aggression.

Naturally, by the time I got to Chongqing the last train had left at 11.15 pm, so that meant getting yet another taxi. The driver is practising for Formula One and I was soon home; he should do well. The first task was to turn on the hot water for a shower, but it does take

293

some time to heat up, so it was 2.30 am by the time I flopped into bed. What an extraordinary week. Thank you everyone for your amazing hospitality, and especially a big thank you to Eileen for inviting me to her wedding. May her marriage be happy and long.

Manchurian Series – the North East, July-August 2013

96. Manchuria -14th July 2013

This is the summer break, the longest of the year, at least for us mere teachers, though for the office staff it is another story. It appears that there has been a significant drop in enrolments for this coming semester, so they have been working hard, with not a single day off, to recruit new students. If they do not get them, I may not have a job!

But that is their worry; I decided to head off to Manchuria. To come to China for a holiday on an organised tour can be expensive, but not so if you are already here and simply join the local traffic. We planned to have four people in our group. Over the years I have seen a lot of China and in the process learnt a lot. Manchuria has been a lacuna. It is also called the North East, and is divided into the three provinces of Heilongjiang, Jilin and Liaoning, based loosely on the three major Manchurian tribal groupings. Let us have a look at some background.

Core China arose between the two rivers, the Yellow to the north and the Yangtze to the south (Huang He and Chang Jiang). This area was unified by the first emperor, Shi Huangdi in 220 BC. He was the one who first began construction of the Great Wall, firstly to control his population and secondly to serve as a protection against warlike tribes to the north and north east – the Mongols and Munchus, though they were not called that then. These areas were not countries in the way we understand that term, but were occupied by loosely federated tribes of people who were part nomad and part settlers.

One of the groups, called the Jurchen, put an end to the Northern Song dynasty in AD 1127, themselves ruling northern China from AD 1115 – 1234, being known as the Jin dynasty. These peoples later changed their name to Manchu. They in turn were conquered by the Mongols, who at the time conquered everybody in sight, and most people not in sight, setting up the Yuan dynasty in China from AD 1206 – 1368. Overlapping dates occur because it took time to subdue the entire country. The local Chinese finally began to rule themselves again; or rather they were ruled by a Chinese emperor, in the Ming dynasty, AD 1368 – 1644. Then they were conquered yet again by the Manchus, who set up the Qing dynasty AD 1644 – 1911.

During the Japanese occupation from 1931 – 45, Manchuria became Japanese, and they called it Manchukuo, setting up the last Qing emperor, Puyi, as their puppet. The Japanese were succeeded by the Russians who occupied the territory till the Chinese communist army arrived. The Russians had captured Japanese war material, which they then handed over to Chinese Communist Army. The civil war was particularly vicious here, especially with Mao's policy against civilians, where something like 200,000 died in Harbin and 300,000 in Jilin – far more than the Japanese killed in Nanjing.

This potted history does in part explain why today China is so paranoid about territory and claims suzerainty over as much land and sea as they can, no matter where it is geographically located, stating it has belonged to China "from ancient times". It would claim the North Pole, Antarctica and the moon, if it could get away with it. The country has been occupied and governed by outsiders for so much of their history that security is a huge issue. The irony is that while they hate being occupied by foreign powers, they have no compunction whatsoever about occupying other countries and claiming them as their own.

So what happened in Manchuria and Mongolia?

After 1644 and even before, there was widespread copying of Chinese ways and a good deal of assimilation. The Han and the Manchus simply intermingled. There are ethnic groups still in Manchuria today, but most of the population is Han. Thus we have the three provinces, which roughly correspond to three major divisions of Manchu tribes.

Thus Manchuria was assimilated into China. Mongolia was not; it was occupied. The Chinese simply took it over after the collapse of the Mongol empire. Thus Inner Mongolia, the southern section, is a Chinese province, while Mongolia, the northern section, is still an independent country for the time being, and this only after Russian intervention. One of my students told me that Mongolia belongs to China." Why?" "Because we conquered it." In other words, whatever China can conquer by military might is theirs by right. What a morality! – or lack of morality. I told him, "Well actually no; Mongolia conquered you." This was not to be countenanced.

On Sunday July 14th, early, I flew to Harbin, the capital and largest city in Heilongjiang. My flight left Chongqing at 8.15 am, meaning I had to get a taxi to the airport, as buses and trains do not operate so early. My taxi driver has absolutely no hope of winning Formula 1 this year, as he was being overtaken frequently by other vehicles. But he did drive safely.

Our flight had a stopover in Nanjin, where I got off the plane and walked around the terminal. I have been inside many airport terminals. At 11.00 am we took off again. In both cities, Chongqing and Nanjing, you can see the pall of pollution hanging over the cities. Once you climb high enough, you are into clear air with blue skies. On the flight, all announcements were made in Chinese and English, though the latter were not good; too staccato, with a lack of intonation and with Chinese expressions. Maybe I could get a job translating Chinglish into English. From the air one could see how green the countryside is, with lots of water, the rivers being flush with melted snow and recent rain, some land being inundated.

We got into Harbin at 1.30 pm, right on time, which is rather unusual, after a five hour flight; China is a big country. F1 met me at the airport, arriving just 40 minutes before me. I do not mind travelling on my own, but I much prefer to do so with others, especially when the company is really enjoyable. We took the airport bus to the railway station (20 Yuan), then a taxi to our hotel.

Whenever you arrive at a new place, you do not know the geography, the transport system or the costs. At the railway there is a taxi rank – but we did not know this, learning it later. From here there are set prices. Where we were, the first driver wanted 50 Yuan to take us to our hotel; they will charge whatever they can get away with. We eventually found another driver who charged 20 Yuan, still expensive, as our hotel was not that far away.

In the next edition, we can look at this city.

97. *Harbin Architecture – Hei Long Jiang Province – 14th – 18th, 21st, 26th July 2013*

Our first priority in Harbin was to check into our hotel, dump our bags, then go out to explore. We had chosen a very good hotel, but only for the first two nights of our holiday, after which we would switch to something more within our budgets. "Harbin" has an alternative spelling, "Ha'erbin", and both are to be seen. The word actually comes from a Manchu word, *alejin*, meaning "honour" or "fame". In group based, as opposed to more individual based, societies, where one takes one's value from the group, rather than from one's inner resources – or from God – honour and fame are very important attributes indeed.

In the hotel lobby we found a very helpful concierge who speaks English, so she was able to give us directions as to how to get downtown, not very clear directions, as we stumbled around for a while till we found the correct bus stop. We are on a major road here, Zhong Shan Lu, a very popular name in China, as it is also a name for Dr. Sun Yat-sen, the founder of the Chinese Republic in 1911. As we travelled we took in the scenery. At the bottom of this road is a roundabout – very common – with a large central ball – also very common. The city is clean with modern buildings and lovely architecture, as evidenced on a bridge we went over. The city, or at least this part of it, is decorated with plant sculptures, having different coloured plants, mostly green and brown, clipped into shapes. They are quite attractive.

The bus stops are not all that frequent, so that if you miss a stop, you may have a long way to walk back. We missed a stop. Suddenly we saw Hagia Sophia. Wow! At the very next stop – some distance off – we got off and walked back to explore this truly beautiful Russian church. It is called St. Sophia, though we do have a problem with languages here; are we using English, or Chinese, or Russian, or Latin or Greek? Since "*sophia*" is Greek for "wisdom", I'm sticking with the Greek and will use "*hagia*", meaning "holy".

There is a further historical reason. Christianity came to Russia in AD 999 after Russian ambassadors to Constantinople became so impressed, especially with the liturgies in the church of Hagia Sophia.

In 1890 the Russians got the contract to build the railway here. Many Russians came, setting up businesses and building a lot more than just the railway. Their architecture really makes this city both distinctive and beautiful. We would be seeing many examples of Russian buildings, but none is more beautiful than this church, built in 1907. We would spend some most pleasant hours here in Hagia Sophia Square, bathed in warm sunshine. Just look at the attached photograph to see how beautiful this church is.

On another day we bought a ticket to go inside, as it is no longer being used as a church – a pity – and instead is a museum to the city's past. The inside was extensively damaged by Mao Zedong and his Red Guards; one can still see what looks like bullet holes in the masonry. The walls are lined with photos of the city's past, plus some captions. I found one interesting; "Gradually a remote border town leaped into a modern city." "Gradually"… "leaped"…Was it fast or slow?

Also in this square is a steel outline of what looks like a church. One would see these steel frameworks elsewhere in the city and beyond. The square has small ponds, which give little reflections of the surrounding buildings. There is also a fountain, which was turned on for a short time, kids playing in the water. And there is a shop – naturally – this one Russian, selling many kinds of Russian goods, from dolls to samovars to paintings. Another pleasant experience was that one could actually walk around in a degree of comfort, without the enormous crowds one finds nearly everywhere. Everyone here, of course, was getting sheir photograph taken in front of the church. Pigeons are a feature, as indeed they are in many other squares around the world. Here they nest on the church, but not in the sun, preferring the cooler side. I imagine it will not be long before the reverse is true, as this city gets very cold in the winter, with temperatures getting as low as minus 40 degrees. Harbin is famous for its ice sculptures.

From Hagia Sophia Square we walked about a kilometre to what is called "Cobble St.", as it is paved with cobble stones and is a pedestrian avenue, vehicles being banned; great. In Chinese it is called; *Zhong Yang Da Jie*". This would become our favourite place in this city. It is really beautiful, flanked by many Russian buildings, well maintained, and reflecting different European styles, including Baroque and Renaissance. Some 25 of them have been classified and they bear plaques giving their history. There were many Jewish people here and there are plans to highlight their influence. The street is quite extensive, being nearly 1500 metres long and is a tourist area, so unfortunately it is thronged with people. One pastime was to sit and watch the people walk by, noticing what clothing they were wearing; some were very well dressed indeed. The women dress better than the men.

There is a shopping mall in one of the buildings, with a supermarket downstairs – a good place to buy supplies. It also has a Starbucks, complete with Wi-Fi. Another building is an up market hotel, which also has a tourist agency. We would be spending a few hours here over the next fortnight, planning our future trips. Du Bing spoke good English, thus making life much easier for us. She was marvellous; very helpful indeed.

The street ends at a park flanking the Songhua River, which flows through the city. This too provides recreation for the citizens, walking up and down this riverside park, or fishing, or boating or floating – kind of swimming with floaties around their waists. Very few people swim. Many people simply sit on the bank and talk. Or just sit.

It was around 6.00 pm when we arrived here, and we stayed till about 7.30 pm, it still being light at this latitude, some 45 degrees 45 minutes north. We were in time to witness a procession of women, dressed up and marching; there were no men and the women were of all ages. I do not know what the occasion was, but they were dressed like fairies or flowers. There were floats too.

After this we went off to have our evening meal – dumplings tonight – before returning to our hotel. But the day had not yet ended for us, as this hotel boasts a 25 metre swimming pool, so I did a few laps. It is an inside pool, on the 14th floor, yet it is called "Sunny Swimming Pool"; there is, of course, no sun, but the Chinese do like flowery language. Restaurants in this hotel are called "Mingshi Palace", "Princes' Abalone" and Jinjiang Palace". What is a palace? This hotel also boasts a "chessing room" – chess? Or where the boys chase the girls? You work it out.

What a wonderful first day. Stay tuned for day 2.

98.   Two Parks in Harbin – 15th – 18th July 2013

On Monday morning we were woken by the sunlight streaming into our room. Was it 6.00 am already? No it was not. Unbelievably we watched the sun peep above the horizon at 4.00 am! That is how far north we are. Of course we are also east of Beijing, so the sun rises earlier here by about 40 minutes, as Harbin's longitude is 126 degrees 39 minutes east, whereas Beijing is 116 degrees 23 minutes east. All times in China and its territories are determined by Beijing.

After breakfast we took a bus to the river bank and spent some time strolling along this riverside park, called Stalin Park. There is your Russian influence again. It took some time to get here, as we did not know which bus to catch and where. At this time of the year the Songhua River is at its highest, partly flooding its banks and flowing swiftly, bits of debris being carried along. In fact this park was built primarily for flood mitigation, but it has been made quite attractive with statues and plants. There is an island in the river called Taiyang Dao, or Sun Is. One way to get there is by cable car, which may be exciting as one dangles high above the river, but at 50 Yuan we deemed it too expensive, so opted for the more reasonable 10 Yuan boat crossing instead.

We spent most of the day wandering around the island, which is quite extensive. It has beautifully maintained gardens, a riot of colour with so many kinds of flowers blooming: fuchsias, marigolds, tiger lilies and many varieties of violets among others. There were also those plant sculptures they do so well here, including – not surprisingly – a giant dragon. And there are actually grass lawns. China is obsessed with laying paving stones everywhere in its parks, so to see some genuine grass was a real pleasure. There were the usual signs in flowery style, such as; "The foot steps gently; the green grass looks like shade". Like shade? – it is certainly restful on the eyes to look at green grass in blazing sunshine, rather than the glare from white paving stones. There was also the usual Chinglish, like; "To make the round of your road to remain the grass green". *Shenme?* One enclosure held around six deer. There were peaceful ponds, spanned by those elegant half-moon bridges, which I find so delightful, one of which forms the cover for this book.. Chipmunks and squirrels were cavorting around trees, butterflies flitted, while birds twitted. Idyllic really. There is a Russian style village, which we did not enter, but there are quite a few other Russian houses on the island. And there is a beer festival. Great – except that there was nothing on; disappointing, so we settled for an ice cream at KFC instead. Is KFC Russian???

In due course we hopped back on a boat to return to the other side, this time, for some unknown reason, it cost only 4 Yuan. Back on a bus, we headed to our favourite cobbled street, Zhong Yang Da Jie, where we ferreted out a Russian restaurant. "Ferreted" is the right expression, as it is underground. I had salmon and lamb on a skewer with a potato salad, washed down with Russian beer, much stronger and tastier than its Chinese counterpart. The quantities served were minute, but the price was high. I wish my Russian friends had have been with us.

Next day dawned rainy and dull. We checked out of our hotel and moved into a cheaper one, almost next door. It was a good day to rest up. In the afternoon we went for a walk up Dong Da Jie, the street we are on. We discovered no fewer than three churches. The first is Russian Orthodox, no longer in use. The second is Lutheran, and the third is Catholic, where the church itself is on the third floor, strangely.

The rain revealed a flaw in this otherwise beautiful city. It is only in recent years that the average citizen has been able to acquire a car, but as yet, the society does not know how to deal with them. Road rules, for instance, are virtually nonexistent. Another problem is parking. There are very few designated areas and not much segregation between cars and pedestrians. Footpaths, in consequence, are just as much for use of cars as for people. So cars drive on them and park on them any way they like and any how they like. The result is smashed up pavements. Now after this rain, pools of water were lying in depressions cause by cars on footpaths. It is a real pity. We were to see this time and again all over the north east. I hope the government wakes up soon and leaves footpaths exclusively for people.

The next day, Wednesday, dawned bright and sunny. We left our hotel around 9.00 am, endeavouring to get to Tiger Park. Getting around is not easy when one's knowledge of the language is so limited. We got a bus to Cobble Street, which we now know well, then after some difficulty got onto bus 29 which took us to Taiyang Park, where we were yesterday.

Here we were taken to a van which sold us tickets to the park for 90 Yuan – so not cheap. Our guide who conducted us there collected his commission – 15 Yuan. Next we got onto a minibus which took us a further 8 km to the park, where we arrived around 11.00 am. It had taken us two hours to bumble our way across town, via three buses. We now got onto yet another bus, complete with barred windows, which would drive us through this park. So what is the attraction?

This is the Siberian Tiger Park, dedicated to a species which is endangered. There are some 90 animals here, all big cats, most of them tigers. We would drive through a series of double gates from enclosure to enclosure. Within each enclosure the animals can wander free, while we were caged in our bus. Most of the tigers and other cats were too listless in the heat to be aggressive and were lolling around in whatever shade they could get. Only one tiger showed any spirit by biting one of the vehicles.

At one point we all got out and walked along a walkway over the animal pens, with wire mesh around us. In the cages below us were Siberian tigers, African lions, a white lion, a black panther, a leopard, a jaguar and a liger. Some were pacing up and down, obviously not happy with their confinement. So what is this about?

Ostensibly, this is all about protecting the Siberian tiger, which is an endangered species. Well, this is certainly partly correct, as we saw one pair doing their level best to preserve the species. There are certainly enough animals here to maintain a population, at least as far as the tigers and lions are concerned, but not the others, which are single individuals. These are here for the sake of the humans – and a plaque outside clearly states that this park is set up for tourism. The animals are fed, mainly live chickens, so they do not have to hunt. I am told that the idea is to release some tigers back into the wild; let us hope they can still successfully hunt for themselves.

I do not think this is the answer, as it does not address the central problems, namely 1) loss of habitat, and 2) poaching so that humans can increase their libido, or whatever. Re 1) there are simply too many humans; we are everywhere; we take nearly everything and leave very little. In my opinion, we need to set aside a reserve, a large reserve, say 10,000 sq. km, within which all human activity is completely barred. Re 2) we need to educate people against using tiger parts, or elephant parts, or rhinoceros parts or whatever, combined with much stricter penalties against poachers and their supporters.

We ate our lunch in the shade, sitting at tables, and no, we eschewed the live chickens. The next problem was how to return to our hotel. A taxi driver offered to do so for 50 Yuan, not surprising, but we noticed the return of the bus which had brought us here. This took us back to Taiyang Dao for no extra charge. From here we caught bus 29 back to Zhong Yang Da Jie, where we spent a couple of leisurely hours, before we headed back to our own street for an evening meal of noodles and beer at a Chinese restaurant.

It has been quite a day. Tomorrow we would rest up and organise our next adventure.

99. Yabuli – 19th – 21st July 2013

Now for something different; we decided to spend a couple of days at a small place called Yabuli, three hours away by train. It is a ski resort. Yes, this is summer and there is no skiing and no snow, but I wanted to look anyway. Skiing is a rich man's sport and has not been a feature of Chinese life. That could change, as China is now wealthy, many ski resorts are being developed and I can see China hosting a Winter Olympics in the not too distant future. Perhaps Yabuli would be the venue. It has already hosted an international youth competition in 2009.

Our train left Harbin at 7.50 am, with our compartment nearly full, but not for long, as many people got off after about an hour. During this time, however, a group of ladies played mah-jongg using cards, not tiles, and did so with much hilarity, obviously enjoying each other more than the game. Our trip was smooth if slow. The countryside was looking lush green, with row upon row of corn not far from harvesting, interspersed with rows of peanuts. I do not know what advantage there may be in this juxtaposition, but possibly peanuts are legumes, so return nitrogen to the soil. I imagine life here is pretty basic and indeed difficult during the long hard winters. At 11.00 am we arrived at our destination, which is the end of the line, to be met by a car to take us to our hotel, the Zhuangong.

This hotel is about 20 years old, somewhat neglected but majestic. It has a complicated design, with both high ceilings and mezzanine floors, so that you never really know what level you are on. The foyer is graced with a large globe entirely in English, which is a surprise. Outside is a lovely garden, full of flowers, except for large artificial cactuses, which add very little in my opinion, though they may add a touch of colour during the winter. There are also vegetable plots, so they do grow a lot of their own. Across the road is a small dam, the water very black, with hardly a ripple, reflecting hillsides and ski slopes.

We went for a walk to explore the surroundings. Nearby there appears to be a school, with a well maintained athletics track, and surprisingly, with people actually using it. We also noticed people being taught how to ski, so I imagine that in the winter this place is abuzz. Further up the mountain we found another hotel, the International Broadcast Hotel, whatever that means, but it is five star and very swank. It has a boardwalk threading its way through the forest for perhaps a kilometre, making for a very enjoyable walk amongst the trees. For the evening meal, we found that we were the only ones in the dining room, so there are currently not many guests. We had pork, rice, snow peas and beer. Time for bed – that is after we got the hot water going, as it took ages to come through.

The next day we decided to go for a walk, a long walk, which is one reason I wanted to come here. There is a park nearby with a 20 Yuan entrance fee, and a concrete road going through it. I had wanted walking tracks, but this would do. Conifers line both sides, with black-eyed suzies and snow grass. There were lots of butterflies, some flies and grasshoppers. One large black and blue butterfly is particularly beautiful.

The weather was perfect for hiking, at maybe 22 degrees, cool, overcast with some light rain. We had umbrellas, but were also able to seek shelter at small gazebos scattered along our route when the rain got a little heavier. There was a group of young people also walking, all wearing flimsy plastic raincoats, which slowly got ripped to pieces, the road becoming littered with them; yes, they just threw them on the ground. During one heavy shower, we all sheltered together, but no-one was curious enough to ask about us, and that is unusual. Soon a vehicle arrived to pick them up, and off they went. When the rain eased, we continued walking.

All the time we were walking upwards, mostly on our own, sometimes with others. After an hour or so, we came to a most delightful attraction; a long, three stage swing bridge. It was fun, with some of the men delighting in making it swing even more, much to the consternation of some of the ladies, who were shrieking in terror and shaking with fright. Nobody died.

At 12.00 noon we stopped for a rest at another gazebo, and talked with a young lady who spoke excellent English. We continued walking till we found a good place for lunch beside a stream, with tables and chairs. That group of young people we had seen earlier was already there. After lunch we approached their guide to find out where we were; she showed us on our map. She told us they came from the International Broadcast Hotel. I imagine rich parents can get rid of their kids during the holidays by letting hotel staff amuse them. We found we had three options; 1) return to our hotel the way we had come – about 9 km; 2) continue on this current road, which would eventually lead us back – about 12 km; 3) take up her offer of going back with them in their hotel bus. Perhaps you would like to guess which option we took?

Back at the hotel, I had a better look at this building. We are on the third floor, but there are many steps, due to the high ceilings and mezzanine floors. There is a number of dining rooms, including one "dining room". There is also a number of "proper" rooms; goodness, what is an "improper" room? There is scope for your imagination. Behind the hotel there are yet more vegetable gardens.

That night, at 12.15 am, we were woken by a new group arriving at our hotel, talking in loud voices, making no effort whatsoever to be considerate of others. This included a group occupying the room opposite ours. I got up, went across to them, said nothing, but closed their door. I hope they took the hint. It is the Great Wall operating again.

On Sunday morning, I walked up the mountain to examine one of the ski slopes. There is a road which goes part way up but then stops. The reason is that the usual method is to take the T-bar, especially with snow lying everywhere. Normally in China you find cement or stone paths are common, but not here. What is the point, when it is all covered in snow anyway? This particular run is for speed jumps, with a ramp to soar off, and a slope to slow you down after you have landed. There are seats for spectators and presumably judges. The ground is fairly smooth, so that you probably need only about 20 cm of snow for it to become usable.

It was time for us to head back. Is it likely that you will hear a lot more about Yabuli at some future Winter Olympics? I do not think so. It is far too remote, and China is currently building many more resorts much closer to Beijing. But China will host the games, I feel sure, in the not too distant future.

We were driven back to the railway station by a hotel staff member, and what a station it is. It is such a surprise to see this building out here. It is magnificent and very much resembles a church, both inside and out. It is also not crowded, and you cannot say that about many railway stations throughout China. Our train left right on time at 4.12 pm. It was so pleasant gliding through this lush countryside, farmers working in their fields. After two hours, we arrived at Mao Re Shan, the station where so many people had alighted on our outward journey. Well now they got on again; end of peace.

We arrived back in Harbin at 7.30 pm, eventually catching a taxi to our hotel. The driver, however, could not understand our Chinese, nor could he read the hotel card, so he took us to the wrong place. We got to the correct hotel eventually, then needed to convince the staff that we did indeed have a reservation, as we had turned up 45 minutes late. Goodness-the joys of travel – especially when one's command of the language is inadequate. Still we get by. Time for shower and bed.

Thank you, Yabuli. *Zaijian.*

100.   Hei He – 22nd – 23rd July 2013

You may gather that Harbin has become our home away from home, as we used it as our base for two excursions, the first to Yabuli and the second to Hei He. I was keen to go to this place as it is about as far north as one can get while still remaining in China. At a latitude of more than 50 degrees north it is further north than Beijing, further north than Inner Mongolia, and even further north than Mongolia, except for one small tip. It is even further north than parts of Russia. It is not, however, the furthest north that I have ever been before, as that occurred when I was in Northern Ireland, about 53 degrees north. It is about the same latitude as London.

The name of this town, Hei He, means Black Stream, and it is situated on the banks of what the Chinese call the Hei Long Jiang, or Black Dragon River. This province, Heilongjiang, is named for this river, which marks the border between China and Russia, and the Russians call it the Amur River, so from Hei He one can get a peek at Russia, which – as you will see – can be a cause of great excitement.

We arrived by overnight train, and that in itself was quite an experience, especially as we could not get a sleeper. This is holiday time. The traffic snarls and crowds of people milling around Harbin railway station have to be seen to be believed. We found our way to waiting room 3, which was wall to wall people plus luggage. This immense crowd is herded one by one through a race, so that a guard can check each ticket individually. The surge to get through is not without its pushing and shoving. Then it is a race to find your correct carriage and seat. We were in carriage 1, but just to ensure that life is not made too easy, there were two carriage 1s. Our carriage was not next to carriage 2, but next to carriage 10 – obviously – so back we trudged. Once aboard, we literally had to fight our way through in order to get to our seats, only to find that they were already occupied. Truly. Luckily a guard happened to be on hand, ensuring that the previous occupants went elsewhere – maybe to take someone else's seat. Surprisingly, we did find room on the overhead rack for our luggage.

The next hour was uncomfortable, as my seat was next to the aisle, with people moving nonstop one way or the other, causing those standing to lean inwards. One gentleman seemed to be constantly pushing me. And we have to sit up like this all night? But if you think it was uncomfortable for me, spare a thought for those poor sods who did not even have a seat, and perforce must stand all night. Need I say that it did not take long for the air to become somewhat foetid? You know, if you took away a billion people or so, this country could be quite pleasant – and would still be the second largest country on earth.

A guard came through and had a longish altercation with one of the gentlemen near me. Apparently he did not have a wedding garment on, so he was ushered out. At around 10.00 pm and then again at 11.00 pm large numbers of people got off, so that made life a little easier, meaning that there were now enough seats for everyone who was left, so no more people pushing into me.

By now it was getting somewhat chilly, so I got my tracksuit top out of my backpack. Opposite, six young people decided to play cards with great gusto. Don't worry about others trying to sleep. Later a railway employee came through sweeping up the rubbish – a veritable mountain, as it is customary to eat on trains and throw rubbish on the floor. Meanwhile our carriage was pervaded by the smell of cigarette smoke. Even though it is now illegal to smoke on trains, people take no notice.

Meanwhile some people – not me – were actually asleep, with their bodies contorted into all sorts of interesting shapes. One man had his head back, mouth agape, while others had their heads slumped forwards. Some were leaning on their comrades or on their arms placed on the trays, which separate the seats. Eventually our six young men finished their game and lay down where they were, either along the seats or simply on the floor. It was not a smooth ride, either, with the train jerking back and forth in fits and starts and rolling a little. I always travel with my office book, not just to pass the time, but to commune with the Almighty, who sometimes just has the right word that I need to hear at any particular time. The evening prayer for today read, in part, "…in quiet sleep our strength renew…" Obviously the writer has never travelled on an overnight Chinese K train.

But there was beauty, as outside one could see the full moon backlighting patterned clouds. By 3.15 am, the east was already lightening, such is our latitude. One could now see the countryside, mostly flat farmlands. Their growing season must be so short.

We arrived in Hei He at 6.30 am. Immediately we were accosted by hopeful rip-off merchants, offering to take us to our hotel for 50 Yuan. Hey, you do not find your way to this neck of the woods if you came down in the last shower. We found one man willing to take us for 6 Yuan, but had no idea where our hotel was. A lady taxi driver did, for 10 Yuan, and then took the trouble of actually getting out of her taxi to show us the building. You may have gathered that I do not have a lot of respect for taxi drivers, but some are really decent. People in general do not go out of their way like this in China, so that finding directions can be a challenge. The usual response is to wave a hand vaguely, "Over there". Thank you, but where exactly? How far is it? These are meaningless questions. Last year I found the Taiwanese to be so different; they would take me to where I wanted to go, or ensure that that I knew exactly where it was. The characters of the Chinese and Taiwanese seemed to me to be so different.

It turns out that our hotel, Hua Yuan Business Hotel, is located in a mall, so no traffic roaring past and no cars blowing their horns in the middle of the night. Good. I reckon I could do with a solid sleep tonight. I came to like this mall. The hotel is undoubtedly more used to Russian guests than Australian as the service directory was full of Chinglish. Herein are some examples;

"Guest is the god, service is the first."

"In order to increase our manage and service level, provide you comfortable and secure environment, we are eager to your valuable suggestions really."

"When leaving, close the door and especially put out the dog…"

Dipped into water; No matter if dip occurred, dial house call.

Maybe I could get a job wandering around China correcting Chinglish.

It turns out that the Hei Long Jiang is only a few hundred metres away. I like the mall and I like the buildings, so I think I am really going to enjoy my stay here. Have I spoken too soon? Wait.

101.   Oh My God! – 23rd – 25th July 2013

When one is travelling it is important to book ahead, especially in this country, where you cannot simply waltz up to a booking office and buy a ticket. Because of the massive population it is a good idea to do so in advance if you can. Hence, paradoxically, the first thing we had to do once we had arrived in this town was to get a ticket to leave again. Where is the nearest tourist agency? We hailed a taxi to take us to one, and ended up paying 10 Yuan for a very short trip. But you have to know these things. Even then it took us some time before we located the agency, again within a hotel. Today is Tuesday. We bought our return train ticket to Harbin for Thursday.

There is an esplanade beside the river, so we walked along for some distance. It is pleasantly decorated with bronze life-like sculptors, which have some meaning. For instance one shows a fat man and a small child on a see-saw, with the child easily lifting the man. How can this be? – because the child has beside her a pile of books. Knowledge is more important than brawn. One man was using a blow torch to whiten the paving stones; I have not seen this before. It makes them look nicer, of course, but somewhat glary in sunlight. Some men were "swimming"; a floaty tied behind.

The river itself is broad, swiftly flowing, and partly overflowing its banks. This is not due only to melted snow from last winter, but also from recent rains – it is carrying a lot of debris. We could see rain falling over distance hills; there has been a good deal of rain recently. The river's colour, incidentally, is not black, in spite of its name, but is a muddy brown.

On our way back to the town centre we noticed a large tent erected in a muddy field. Matting served as a floor, but it was still wet underfoot. The tent was packed with stalls selling everything from clothing to jewellery to food. From here we visited a Russian store – and there are many in this part of town – to buy some Russian goods: chocolate, coffee, and caviar. The latter would serve for our lunch tomorrow, spread on biscuits. The tin cost only 35 Yuan; I had thought it would be more expensive.

By now it was time for our evening meal, so – naturally – we went to a Russian restaurant. For some strange reason, the staff thought I was Russian, so began speaking to me in Russian. Do I look Russian? Certainly there are many Russian tourists here. We ordered "borsch", a soup made from celery, potatoes etc. I also had a Russian beer, which I found surprisingly light, not as good as the Russian beer I had sampled in Harbin. We would have our evening meal at this restaurant on the following two nights as well, sampling different Russian dishes. Don't ask me what they are called. We should have had some Russian friends with us. Really.

The night was cool and rainy. Boy, what must it be like in winter? In the morning we returned to the river and walked along. One of the things I wanted to do was take a boat trip. I was assuming that the actual border between the two countries lies half way between the two banks, so that we could hop on a tour boat that would remain on the Chinese side, and simply chug up river for a while, turn around, then chug down again: all very pleasant. So we paid our 50 Yuan and hopped aboard one such vessel. Much to my surprise – and consternation – it did not do that. Instead it headed straight for the Russian bank. "Oh My God!"

That is not what I actually said, but I am conscious of the finer sensibilities of some of my readers. My thought was; "We have got on the wrong boat! This is not a tourist trip, but a commuter trip. We are going to dock in Russia, and we have no visa." You cannot even get a visa in Hei He; you have to go back to Beijing to get that. We do not even have passports; they are still at our hotel. Oh my God! – You see, it is good to pray at such moments. We could be arrested as illegals. What does a Kalashnikov automatic rifle look like close up? Maybe we will find out. What does the inside of a Siberian gulag look like? We may find that out, too.

It soon transpired that all our fears were groundless. See God listens to our prayers. What is the Russian for "thank God"? We were in fact on a tourist boat that takes an interesting route, shooting straight across to the Russian side, so that we can wave to the Russians, while they wave back at us. It is all very friendly and makes for good international relations. We sailed merrily along for about 20 minutes, watching construction workers, before we crossed back to the Chinese side and then chugged our way back upstream. As I said, the river is flowing quite fast, so that it took us a further 50 minutes to arrive back at our dock. What an exciting boat ride!

As I said, I was assuming that the border between Russia and China lies in mid-stream. I have since found out that for some sections of the river that is indeed the case; but not here, where the border lies on the Chinese bank. In other words the entire river is in Russian territory, so we should be calling it the Amur River, not the Hei Long Jiang. If this seems strange, remember that we have done exactly the same thing in Australia, where the Murray River divides the two states of New South Wales and Victoria. The border is on the southern bank. In other words the river lies entirely within NSW, so it is not a Victorian river.

Technically therefore, we were in Russia. We had in fact crossed the border.

We returned to our mall. Yesterday we walked down one end, so today we walked down the other – very pleasant. It is lined with vendors selling jewellery, trinkets of one kind or another, and art works, one particular scroll painting I liked very much. Much of today was spent relaxing; sitting, yarning, enjoying the view of the river and its esplanade. We saw a couple of brides having their photos taken. We walked across a bridge to an island, but the flooded river means you would still have to wade through water to reach it.

The following day we found a tiny café where we could enjoy a mocha and watch the passing parade from a window seat. The rain had revealed the state of the footpaths, damaged by cars. We also explored an underground shopping complex, which is huge, extending for blocks. It is so easy to get lost down here. Such a complex would, however, be warm during the bitterly cold winters. We also found an above ground shopping mall, and here I bought something I have been wanting for some time; a small bag, just big enough to carry passport, camera, glasses, water bottle etc. I am happy.

We checked out of our hotel and returned to the railway station to catch the 8.36 pm back to Harbin. This time, however, we had a sleeper. Thank God for that. Goodbye Hei He and thanks we had a truly wonderful time. Dasvadenya.

102.   Harbin to Yanji, Jilin Province 26th – 27th July 2013

We returned to Harbin, our base, via sleeper, thus actually having a much more enjoyable journey than the outward one had been. We arrived at Harbin railway station at 7.30 am, joining the queue at the taxi rank; see, we are learning. Our taxi took us to another hotel, called Home Inn. It is a part of a nation-wide chain. The reason for choosing this particular hotel is that it is close to the airport bus station. We wish to go to Chang Bai Shan, but this just happens to be a popular destination, with every man and his dog wanting to go there. Hence, we cannot get a bus ticket and neither can we get a train ticket, so our trusty travel agent, Bu Ding, suggested, "Why don't you fly?" What a good idea.

This meant we had one final day to enjoy this beautiful city of Harbin. We revisited our favourite haunts, especially Hagia Sophia and Zhong Yang Da Jie, or the cobbled mall, which included Starbucks. I also went back to the Songhua River to sit and take it in. Some men were swimming, though that was an interesting phenomenon due to the swiftly flowing current. One man was doing his level best to swim upstream, only to find himself going backwards at a rate of knots. At least he was getting some exercise. We had our final Russian meal at an attractive restaurant, both in its architecture and inside furnishings, including a collection of antiques. It took us some time to find it, but was well worth the search. It is called "Russia Coffee and Food".

On our final morning, we had breakfast at 7.00 am, provided by the hotel, and – wonder of wonders – it included toast and coffee. This was the only hotel we came across in our travels which provided a western style breakfast, apart from our final hotel, which wanted to charge an extra 150 Yuan! No way. We checked out and walked to the end of the street – about five minutes – to board a bus for the airport. The ticket cost 20 Yuan. This left at 8.00 am for the 50 minute ride to the airport.

And there we waited – for five hours. Over the PA system we would hear again and again; "Ladies and gentlemen, could we have your attention please. We regret to announce that." Here we have a pause and a drop in the voice, obviously indicating the end of the sentence.

312

Why do they do that? It is so common here in China. Any pause should come **before** "that" and **not after.** So in due course the announcement would continue. "Flight XYZ has been delayed, due to ... airspace congestion." What does that mean? I have actually explained this before. This is a militaristic country, the like of which I have never seen before. Since no power is threatening China, one can only assume that China intends to threaten everybody else – and indeed has already started doing just that. The military controls the air space, with very little allowed for civilian use – hence congestion and hence flight delays.

Perhaps ironically, our carrier rejoices in the name of "OK Air". The delay, however, is not their fault. I went off to ask if they would supply us with lunch, and they said "yes". Great, but if I had not said anything, we would not have gotten anything. It was nice too- rice, meat, a vegie in a disposable container with disposable chopsticks. I wonder how many forests it takes to supply China with chopsticks.

We took off finally at 2.00 pm for a 90 minute flight. At Yanji airport, a small place, we eschewed the taxis for the local bus – much cheaper. At the railway station we hailed a taxi, only to find that we had actually driven past our hotel. We could have gotten straight off the bus, but of course you do not know these things.

Any thought that we had arrived in a sleepy, quiet backwater was dispelled very quickly indeed by the sound of military jets screaming overhead. I might add that here we are very close to the border with both Russia and North Korea. Incidentally, here in China, it is never referred to as "North Korea". It is always called "the DPRK". You do not know what that means? Well, I think it means "the Non Democratic, Authoritarian Regime of North Korea". China plays similar name games, calling some regions "autonomous", whereas in reality there is not a single autonomous region in all of China; all are governed by Beijing, although in recent days there have been signs that provinces have been showing more independence. Maybe this is one of the factors behind the trial of Bo Xilai, the erstwhile boss of Chongqing.

But let us return to our hotel, the Yanbian Zhou Ji Commercial Hotel; quite a mouthful. Oddly enough we were asked to photocopy our own documents, which is a first, as everywhere else the hotel does that. The service directory is in Korean as well as Chinese and English. Up until now we have got used to Russian everywhere. There were some interesting entries;

"You can always enjoy a hom – from – home feeling in cut restful and name arubience". I am sure you can express this a little better.

In the rules and regulations section, we are told; "Guns and firearms should be registered." Goodness, that is a surprise. I thought we were in China, not the U.S.

I liked their parting wish; "May fortune attend you and your understanding bear fruit." You do not get such sentiments in Western hotels that I am aware of.

After checking in, we went for a walk to explore the town. We are situated on the main street, Zhan Qian Jie, down which we walked for about 500 metres to the river, Bu Er Ha Tong He, which flows west to east. The street is quite broad, wide enough for six lanes of traffic, plus a footpath on each side about 10 metres wide. Naturally, this is where the cars park. The architectural style of the buildings is Western, and very attractive. At 7.15 pm the lights came on, and the effect was even more beautiful.

103.   Yanji to Chang Bai Shan – 28th – 29th July 2013

We did not come to Yanji because of its inherent charms, great though these may be. It is not as if I have had a fervent longing all my life to visit Yanji. It was a stopover, a means of getting to Chang Bai Shan. Yanji just happens to have the closest airport. Our first priority, therefore, was to get a bus ticket that would take us to where we wished to go. This we did, booking our ticket for the following day, Monday, except that this bus does not go to Chang Bai Shan either, but does go to the nearest town. We will get there – eventually. Meanwhile, we would spend an entire day here in Yanji. I have mentioned that this town is close to both North Korea and Russia, with Vladivostok not far away.

It was a good day for a rest, rainy and a little windy, making it more of a challenge to use umbrellas. One way to explore a town is to use public buses. We took bus 6 as far as it would go – only 14 stops – then got off, and took the next bus 6 back again. Great fun. It seems the town, a river town, is shaped more or less like the Chinese character for river, with one main road crossing the river, and two other roads at each end, parallel with this river – interesting. Then there are minor roads.

This is Sunday morning, and we did find a church, Protestant however, not Catholic, and with the people just coming out from their service.

There is not much to see here. At the top of Zhan Qian St. there is a park, which appeared to be the main attraction in town, with people congregating, mainly chatting it seems, as it is probably too wet to play games. We spent much of today in a hotel with Wi-Fi, so we could catch up on news and e-mails. In the afternoon, I did some running repairs to my shorts, the pockets of which had developed holes. I also did some reading, and maybe I will tell you about this later.

In late afternoon, we went for a longish walk, over the river before following it downstream for about a kilometre along an esplanade. For evening meal we went to a Korean restaurant. Just as Harbin has Russian influence, here there is a strong Korean presence. I imagine many of the people, or their parents, have escaped from North Korea, seeking refuge here. We had beef barbecued at the table. You place the meat on a lettuce leaf or a large mint-like leaf, add some spices, then roll it up and eat with your fingers. I liked it. The spices may include raw garlic, onion, cabbage, peppers and kimshi, which is, I think, radish plus something else. All this was washed down with Harbin beer. The waitress did the cooking, and when the meat was done, she cut it up using – would you believe – a pair of scissors. I understand that this is traditional Korean fare.

The next day we had breakfast in the hotel dining room, Chinese style, of course, and only a few people there. The dining room looks as if it has seen more grandiose days. In the afternoon we walked up to the bus station, next to the railway station, which is usually the case, conveniently so. Our bus left at 1.20 pm, for the 200 plus km journey to Bai He, our road roughly paralleling the border with North Korea. The countryside is lush green, bright yellow flowers growing beside the road, a lot of corn, with some rice and vegetables. We arrived at 5.20 pm. A taxi driver offered to take us to Chang Bai Shan, some 30 km further, charging us 60 Yuan. We agreed because there appears to be no other alternative. Interesting that we paid 46 Yuan for a 200 km bus trip, and 60 Yuan for a 30 km taxi ride.

We checked into the Shen Yuang Hot Springs Hotel, just outside the entrance to the national park we were interested in. Our tariff was 400 Yuan per night, compared with more than 1,000 Yuan per night at the second hotel here, just across the road. Ours was fine. Our hotel also had a travel agency, so we used it to book the next leg of our travels, a train trip to Dandong on Thursday night.

The concierge at this hotel was absolutely wonderful. He was so obliging in doing our bookings for us. The following day he even drove into the town in order to pick up our tickets from the railway station. When it came time for us to leave, he drove us to the station, and would not accept any more than 50 Yuan for his services. He spoke no English, so it was a struggle. You meet some truly wonderful people; may God bless him. Evening meal was at a nearby restaurant: fish, rice and eggplant, but what I particularly liked was the beer, called 12 Degrees; it is the best beer I tasted on this trip, with a tangy aftertaste.

We would therefore be spending only one full day here, and two nights. But that day, Tuesday would be something special. Till tomorrow.

104.   Chang Bai Shan – Heaven Lake – 30th July 2013

At 7.45 am on Tuesday we fronted up to the park gate to buy an entrance ticket, only to be told that there is another gate, 1 km further along the road, so we trudged along to that gate to find it crowded with people. Now what is the system? It took quite some time to find out, as it is complicated. We needed to ring Erica to get it all sorted out. So this is it;

You line up in a queue to buy an entrance ticket, which is very expensive at 215 Yuan. There are no concessions for age.

At the same time you buy a bus ticket for 80 Yuan, which is utterly exorbitant, as it only takes you about 12 km up the road to a place called Dao Zhan Kou. Even taxis are cheaper. Remember that it cost us 46 Yuan to travel 200 km by bus from Yanji.

You line up once more in a queue to buy yet another ticket, this time for 85 Yuan, which entitles you to get on another, smaller bus, to take you up the mountain.

Clutching said ticket in your hot little hand, you join yet another crowded throng to queue for a seat on one of the buses. The wait is one hour; just take a look at the accompanying photograph.

What is this all about? It is a rip off; the government is milking this for all it is worth. In my estimate, they are raking in about 15,000,000 Yuan per day maybe more.

Eventually our turn came and we boarded a mini bus for the ride up the mountain, the driver hurtling upwards, careering around corners; you needed to hang on. Soon we passed the 2,000 metre mark, the altitudes being signposted as we ascended, and just before the summit, the 2,500 metre mark came up, the temperature now noticeably cooler. I had brought my tracksuit for just such an eventuality; after all the average temperature here is a decidedly chilly -7 degrees. At 10.45 am, three hours after leaving our hotel, we finally made it to the top, considerably higher than Kosciusko. What is the big attraction?

This mountain is a volcano, which last erupted cataclysmically about 1,000 years ago, with subsequent smaller eruptions, the latest in AD 1702. It has a crater and this crater contains a lake, called Heaven Lake, or in Chinese "Tian Chi". There are many "heaven" lakes in China; in fact there are many "heaven" this and "heaven" that; it is a popular name, as is "dragon". The surface is some 2,194 metres above sea level, while the crater rim is formed by a ring of often jagged peaks, the highest of which is 2,749 metres ASL, meaning that as you stand on the rim, the lake surface is hundreds of metres below.

And it is beautiful, a serene cobalt blue, too cold for most life forms, barely rippled by soft breezes. White clouds covered part of the rim, the colour of which varies from yellow to ochre, from brown to black, with patches of green from vegetation. Much of the rock is unconsolidated, as it was blown into fragments by the force of volcanic explosions, before settling back down. You can see black basaltic rocks blasted into yellow tuff like sides.

This would be a great place to sit and ponder, gazing at all this majestic beauty, in peace and quiet – except for the people; thousands of people; tens of thousands of people. That was the case on our western side of the lake, but on the other side, the eastern, not a soul could be seen; it appeared utterly deserted. This, however, would not have been the case, as one third of the lake is in North Korea, the border a scant 2 km from our position. I am quite sure that the North Korean military would not have been far away, while the Chinese military are in evidence, with guards at the top and a base at the foot of the mountain.

This is not a place where you are left to yourselves to wander around as you please. Because of the vast crowds there are set pathways; you go up this way; you walk along the rim in this direction;

you come down that way – while all the time following the people in front. On the rim, you just wait, perhaps three or four deep, until it is your turn to have a look. Security guards – the soldiers – are there to keep order, and presumably to stop people stepping over the fences; it is a long way down.

We soaked it all in as best we could, then sat down to enjoy our lunch. We have developed the habit of taking our allocated boiled egg from breakfast plus steamed bread and keeping them for lunch, perhaps adding some fruit or yoghurt. While we sat, grey clouds started rolling up the mountain side, eerily. We spent about an hour at this beautiful lake before heading back down.

What does all this mean? China's population is just massive. With about a billion fewer people, it could be very pleasant. The Chinese, of course, are not as individualistic as Westerners, so they are used to following each other in droves. There is also government exploitation. But there is something else. There is something missing from their lives, and seeking economic prosperity and global dominance are not the answers, as they will find out. There is, I think, a spiritual lacuna. I feel like shouting; "Yes, enjoy this beautiful lake, but enjoy more the God who made it. First establish right relations with God, in thanksgiving for Sheir gifts and everything else will follow."

If you also would like to visit Chang Bai Shan you will see a vision of rare beauty. Just be prepared to be jostled and pummeled, squashed and squeezed, standing in queues for around two hours. Also be prepared to pay a lot of money. I have another idea; visit Mt. Gambier. In Australia, we too have a beautiful blue lake, which has the added attraction of changing colour. It too sits inside a volcanic crater. You will not have crowds and it is free. Enjoy. Of course, you will not see North Korea either.

In the next chapter I will describe what else this mountain has to offer.

105.   Chang Bai Waterfall – 30th July 2013

The fleet of mini buses, all 200 of them, kept ferrying people up and down the mountain, one after the other, loading and unloading. They do this all day. Thus we returned to Dao Zhan Kou, where we simply followed everyone else, and boarded a large bus for the next stage, only a couple of kilometres, to some hot springs. Here once again, the Chinese show their flair for entrepreneurial brilliance. People cook eggs and corn in the water from these springs. We bought a cob of cooked corn for 5 Yuan, which is double what one would normally pay. Whether the mineralized water made it healthier is probably a moot point, but it tasted okay.

Other souvenir stalls abound, as is usual. People were even collecting rocks. Since the population is so huge, it may not take long before this mountain all but disappears, to sit unnoticed in small bits on shelves all across the country. No, we did not take any; we have enough to lug around as it is. One small boy seemed to take great delight in knocking his sample against my water bottle.

The springs themselves are something to behold, with hot water giving off steam seeping right out of the ground, and in consequence providing an ideal habitat for plants, especially mosses. The green from the plants contrasts with the yellow of sulphur. I imagine these plants remain green and the ground snow free right throughout winter. You would not want to slip here, as this ground would be very slippery indeed. A walkway has been constructed over the top – very necessary. Trees are all around, absent from the summit, where it is too cold.

This walkway extends for about a kilometre, often including steps as one climbs upwards. You cross a river, the Songhua, which is also called here the Erdaobai, and get a glimpse of a waterfall in the distance. This is Changbai Falls, and it comes directly out of Heaven Lake. Three rivers trace their source to the lake; Songhua and Yalu, exiting from two different points.

I am not clear on the precise geography of these three rivers. The Songhua, of course, runs through Harbin and from there joins the Amur, a course of more than 1,400 km. The Yalu runs for nearly 800 km into the Yellow Sea, and for much of its length forms the boundary between China and North Korea. It has been a battle ground during three wars from 1894. The Tumen River also has its source near here, is about 500 km long and flows into the Sea of Japan, in part also forming a boundary between China and North Korea, and also with Russia.

The waterfall is impressive, thundering out of a gorge high above us, the river roaring down the valley. How can there be so much water? It appears the annual precipitation here is 1333 mm, but the loss through evaporation is only 450 mm, giving a net gain of almost 900 mm. When you spread this out over the 9.82 square kilometre surface of Heaven Lake, you get a lot of water. You do the Maths. It was cool and a little wet, the drizzle just heavy enough to necessitate using an umbrella. There is something compelling about a waterfall: majestic. I find myself wondering, with such a volume of continuous running water, when will it run out? – the Maths notwithstanding.

We spent a little time here, soaking it all up, before turning for home. We were soaking up the water too, as the rain was getting heavier and the bottoms of my tracksuit pants now thoroughly wet, with no way to dry them. Not to worry; it has been well worthwhile.

We had dinner at the same restaurant as last night; there is not a great deal of choice. It was more expensive than we had expected. Why? – Mushrooms. One must be careful here, as these can be very expensive; we should have enquired beforehand. They were nice, and so was that 12 degree beer. I wish I could get it elsewhere. I felt tired; we had walked no more than 6 km, but standing in queues for two hours is tiring.

The following morning the skies had cleared, so we put our wet clothes outside to dry in the sun. The other hotel looks interesting, so we wandered over to have a sticky; very nice. I wonder if they have coffee and Wi-Fi. The front desk said, *"Mei you"* But I found a pamphlet which said they did. We returned to the dining room and showed them the pamphlet. *"You."* Excellent. We settled down while they ground the coffee beans; this was real coffee.

At 11.30 am we checked out and our concierge drove us to Bai He, where we would spend only one night, another stage on our journey. It is a pretty little town, one main street, but with a lot of development going on. I do not know if they are building ordinary apartment blocks or hotels, to cater for the throngs going to Cheng Bai Shan, probably both. One building is huge, some 300 metres long.

The Erdaibao River runs through the town, and is particularly pretty. It has a green embankment, but I think it could be more user friendly, e.g. with the addition of some seating and shade. We sat on the grass to have our lunch. Nearby there are large reproductions of Transformers – nine of them. I have never seen the movies, so do not know much about them, but evidently someone here is a big fan.

For evening meal we found a restaurant just a few doors from our hotel, run by two ladies, probably sisters. We got on very well, so came here again the following night. The meal was cheap, with beer costing only 3 Yuan, and filling, the whole meal costing only 21 Yuan, or about $4. After the meal, we went to a nearby park, where a concert was in progress. The locals were celebrating 1st August, and had decked themselves out to dance, sing and play. The orchestra included both Chinese and Western instruments. Meanwhile, little children were running everywhere, with grandmothers in hot pursuit when they got too close to the performers. They were a performance in themselves.

Next morning I went for a longish walk to check out a museum of natural history, but there was little there. They even dug up an English teacher for me, but she did not know much. Her English was not so good either, so I do not know what her pupils are learning. We also visited another hotel, a little classier than ours, for Wi-Fi and coffee. Again, as in Cheng Bai Shan, they made the coffee especially for us, and charged only 10 Yuan. There is an interesting street market here, with many fungi being sold, plus ginseng and other substances which are used for medicinal purposes.

It is time to leave this pleasant town and continue our journey.

106.   Dandong, Liaoning Province – 1st – 2nd August 2013

The railway station at Bai He, for some unknown reason, is situated not in the town itself, which is usually the case, but some kilometres away, and there is no bus. The only way to get there is by taxi – or walk, which may not be ideal if one is carrying luggage. We got a taxi.

The train left at 8.15 pm. I crawled into my bunk on the upper tier (of three) and stayed there all night. I slept well. Next morning I woke refreshed, but cramped; there is not much space. These K trains have a small corridor table for those who have the upper bunks – like me – so this is where we had breakfast, the cereal we had brought with us. The train has hot water for our coffee, but you just have to find it, as it comes from a small boiler at the end of one of the carriages, hidden away in a cupboard. The train was slow, as are all K trains; it seems they give way to everything else.

This is of course a rural area, but the number of towns we passed through is amazing. If you come from dry Australia, you see a town maybe every 50 to 100 kilometres, but here in China it is town after town after town; hence the massive population. The predominant crop is corn. These days we seem to use corn for nearly everything. There is a mountain range on our left as we travel, which is, I think, the border with North Korea.

One mother on the train got her 4 year old to pee into a bottle. Well that is considerably better than getting him to pee on the floor, which I have seen. Then she simply dropped the bottle on the floor and left it there to roll around! Care for the environment has not yet penetrated peoples' consciousness, and nor has thoughtfulness for others. It is the Great Wall again.

We were supposed to arrive at Dandong at 1.30 pm, but it was about 3.00 pm by the time we pulled in. We had not booked any hotel in advance, so had to go looking for one. We got a taxi to drop us off at one from the Home Inn chain, but there was no room in the inn. They told us there was another hotel not all that far away, so we walked for about ten minutes till we found it. It is called the Yi Jiang and was very suitable, comfortable, and not expensive. Nearby we found a very good restaurant for our evening meal, again not expensive. The next priority was to have a shower and do laundry, since we had been in our clothes for two days; there are no showers on trains.

The weather was cool and showery. I have mentioned before the poor state of footpaths, damaged by cars, but here there is another problem; poor drainage. Drainpipes simply empty their water onto the footpaths, not into a proper drainage system. Here I must admit to prejudice against this city.

There is an advertisement for Dandong on TV, which I find most irritating. It goes something like this; **PORT** of **DAN-DONG, HUB** of **EAST ASIA**, and continues in the same vein. Maybe advertising executives should spend their Purgatory listening to their own ads. This is actually a travesty of what Purgatory is all about, but maybe I will leave this for another time.

The next morning, Saturday, our first priority was to find a travel agency, but without success: not at the railway, nor in any of the hotels. We did buy a bus ticket for Dalian for tomorrow. So we took a taxi instead to the Yalu River, which is not that far away; we could have walked.

Here there is a park alongside the river, and it is very popular. There are also two bridges. Why two? The first bridge was built by the Japanese in 1911, at a time when Japan was exercising overlordship in Korea. This river, the Yalu, is the border between China and North Korea. During the Korean War, China was pouring men and supplies across this bridge to fight against the United Nations' forces. Some three million Chinese soldiers took part, and nearly a third of them were killed. Mao remarked that he did not care if they all got killed; he would simply send in three million more…and three million more…"America can't do this", he said. True enough. Today, China can actually put some 500,000,000 soldiers into the field, when one factors in their compulsory military training.

Naturally, the United Nations forces bombed the bridge, but only the North Korean side; they were very careful about not encroaching on any Chinese territory. Today the North Korean side is still in ruins, while the Chinese side is intact. So it is a tourist attraction, and it is yet another way in which the government can make a lot of money, as people pay 27 Yuan to walk half way across. It is free if you are a soldier – Chinese, of course. We did not. The second bridge is the one in use today. From here you can take a train to Pyongyang. Just make sure you have all your travel documents.

There is an SPR coffee shop here which is very comfortable, so we spent some time here. Later we sat outside to eat our lunch, gazing across into North Korea. After lunch we walked the kilometre back to the bus station and for 7 Yuan bought a ticket to Tiger Mountain, 26 km to the north east. Here the admission price was 60 Yuan, a little steep; in fact it has doubled in the last five years. What is the attraction? This is the end of the Great Wall, and here forms the border with North Korea. You climb atop the wall about 150 metres elevation to the summit of a hill, where there is a tower, and below you is the river which forms the border, across which North Koreans can be seen labouring in their fields. There is a neat village here, with about 100 houses, all the same – and all made of ticky-tacky.

This section of the Wall is well worth a visit. Some of the steps are very steep, but the way it has been built to fit the contours of the land is ingenious. And it is not crowded – not like the Badaling section near Beijing. It was most pleasant being here, especially standing at the top gazing down at North Korea; so close. We could watch North Korean farmers toiling in their fields not far below us. We spent a couple of hours here, from 2.30 to 4.30 pm.

We caught a local bus to get back to town, for 4 Yuan, getting off at the railway station. Here we caught the 102 bus to get back to our hotel, except that it went in the opposite direction! We got off, crossed the road and got the next bus back. We told the driver where we wanted to go, and he shouted to us when we came to our stop. I thanked him. For evening meal we went to the same restaurant as last night; when you are on a good thing...

Dandong has a population of about a million people, but is not much of a city. The highlight was that riverside park and Tiger Mountain. Tomorrow we would head for Dalian.

107. Dalian – 4th – 5th August 2013

We checked out of our hotel in Dandong At 8.30 am on Sunday, and took a taxi to the bus station, where we boarded our bus for Dalian at 9.20 am, storing our luggage beneath. It was a smooth ride through the countryside, with just the one stop. The corn here is ripening. As usual we passed through many towns and villages

Just after 1.00 pm we arrived in Dalian and once again we had no advance hotel booking. Not far from the bus stop we noticed a Home Inn, so decided to stay there – if they had a vacancy. They did, though it was a bit pricey, at 429 Yuan a room (about $70), but we expected this as it is prime holiday season. After settling in, our first priority – as usual – was to find a travel agency so that we could book the next leg. Our travel bible has been Lonely Planet, so using this we tried to track down an agency. We found where it should have been, but alas, no longer. Not to fear as we found another, so were able to book a flight to Qingdao for Tuesday, plus accommodation once we got there. Good.

We spent the rest of the day exploring this city, on foot. We do a lot of walking when travelling, so it is good to be both healthy and fit, and of course, this helps to keep you so. There are so many beautiful buildings here, though the influence is neither Russian nor Korean, but is now German, as this used to be a German sphere of influence. One curious feature we noticed is that in one particular area, downtown, there is a plethora of banks – dozens of them. Why? Many of the old European buildings are now occupied by these banks. Is there are lot of money in Dalian?

As I write, Bo Xilai, the erstwhile boss of Chongqing, where I am now residing, is on trial for bribery, including a charge of accepting a whopping 20 Million Yuan from Dalian. Is he guilty? Well that is for the court to decide, but my guess is "Yes, very much so". I doubt if anybody does business here without bribes. So if the powers that be want to get rid of someone, they just accuse shem of bribery. Simple. So I doubt if they are too keen to stop the practice, all their posturing notwithstanding; it is just too convenient.

This is a flat city, so one would assume that it would be ideal for bikes, but surprisingly, not so. This is very much a car city. Pedestrians are not welcome. It can be difficult to cross roads, as there is not much in the way of pedestrian crossings or bridges. On one occasion a taxi driver did his level best to run me down, honking his horn, then giving me the finger sign (or so I am told – I did not see it), even though (a) he was turning right, and right turning traffic should give way to everything, (b) I was on a pedestrian crossing, and (c) I had a green light, while he had a red light. Aggression; might is right. Ironically, this occurred very close to Friendship Square! Really? – friendship with whom?

The main drag here is yet another Zhong Shan Lu, named after Dr. Sun Yat-sen. We found a bar selling German beer – on tap. Wonderful. It was great to get a full tasting strong beer. A little further on we came to an Italian restaurant, where we had our evening meal; expensive, but we do not do this very often. They also serve cocktails, so I had a mojito, which I had never had before. At 48 Yuan it was very expensive, but I thought it might be worth it. It wasn't; it was nothing more than glorified lemonade with a bit of mint.

The next day we headed for a beach, as I like to swim. There is one here called Xinhai Shatan, or "New Sea Beach". Bus 23 got us there, ten stops, so not all that far. I do not know why it has this name, but maybe there is some historical significance to "New Sea". It does not look very new, as the water is murky; you can see the muck, and also smell the sewerage. It is not a sandy beach but pebbly. All in all it is not a pretty beach, but nevertheless it was crowded. There are no waves, so no surf board riding. Very few Chinese know how to swim, and in fact I think I was the only one who swam. So what do the people do?

They eat. It is a favourite Chinese pastime, so there are lots of food stalls. There were people in the water, but just paddling around in the shallows, wearing life buoys. Speed boats take people for a spin. And then there is the tower. A line stretches from a tower at one end of the beach to the beach itself, forming a flying fox, along which people glide. Great fun. This tower also serves as a platform for bungee jumping. Now that would be even more fun. For some time we watched people jump off, then spring up and down for a while before being lowered into a waiting boat. Why don't I have a go? I tried, but they would not let me, saying that I was too old. Balderdash! Maybe I should not have told them my age? What do you think? I reckon I would have enjoyed it immensely.

If you are looking for a really good beach, might I suggest Coogee? It is much better than anything China has to offer. Do we in Australia really appreciate what we have?

Later we wandered around looking for Xinhua bookstore, as I was running out of reading matter. We found it eventually, and discovered that it has a number of good books, but too many to be carting around, so I settled for a book of short stories. It was only 30 Yuan. Dalian, for all that is a clean modern city, bright and shiny, especially on a day like today when the sun was shining. I particularly like the German influence. Tomorrow we leave for Qingdao; join us then.

108. Qingdao, Shandong Province – 6th – 8th August 2013

Tuesday in Dalian dawned overcast and a little rainy. We were lucky to get such a fine day yesterday. Our hotel is right next door to a major shopping mall, the New World; so convenient. Last night we had our evening meal here, in a tiny restaurant run by a lady whom I shall call Mrs. Pijiu. I asked her if she had any beer. *"You mei you pijiu ma?"* *"Mei you"*. What a pity. Then I saw someone drinking beer. Where did you get that? From their fridge. Closer inspection revealed the beer hidden down the bottom. *"Pijiu"* is beer. The mall also has a Starbucks, so after checking out of our hotel we were able to sit here drinking coffee.

At 10.30 am we crossed the road to catch the 710 bus to take us to the airport. After 12 stops we were there, or were we? We got off, but no airport in sight. We have landed in a suburban street. You walk to the next corner, only about 50 metres, then you turn right. Now you can see the airport, a further 400 metres away. To get there one must cross a road and walk up a ramp, then cross again. It is all so inconvenient and not well planned. This airport is so close to apartment buildings, which must be fun for the residents, watching planes take off and land, especially in a strong cross wind. Just imagine standing at your window watching a plane coming straight for you. On one occasion I was with a 17 year trainee pilot coming in to land on a country airstrip in Hamilton in Western Victoria. There was a strong cross wind and we were in a very small plane. I felt like yelling, "Hey mate, the airstrip is over there!" We made it.

On this occasion I would much have preferred to have travelled to Yantai by boat, and from there to Qingdao, but was outvoted. The land route is rather circuitous, going hundreds of kilometres out of our way around the Bohai Sea, at the top of the Yellow Sea, so that was out of the question.

Our flight was due to take off at 12.40 pm, but it did not. So we waited. There were no announcements made to explain the reason for the delay, but we all know why. China is the worst country in the world for airport delays. In recent days there have been instances of passengers rioting, so perhaps the authorities were afraid of that happening here. Our flight is just a short hop anyhow, so we were in Qingdao by 2.30 pm.

Now how do we get to our hotel, which we had booked in advance? We asked at the airport enquiry desk and were told local bus 702 would get us close. It did, so when we got off, we just kept asking people till we found it. That is what you do when you travel; ask and ask often. *"Qinwei, ni jidau zai nali...?"*

Having found our hotel we settled in. By 5.30 pm we were ready to explore. Conveniently, the 320 bus from just down the street goes downtown. It makes just one turn into Zhong Shan Lu, then straight down to the beach. It is only about 1.5 km, and over the next couple of days we would walk it a few times. You may notice that this is not the first Zhong Shan Lu we have come across. It is named after Dr. Sun Yat-sen and in fact there is a statue to him down near the beach. He was, of course, the first president of the republic, also famous for his three principles of democracy, civil rights and well-being (*ming zhu, ming quan, ming sheng*). I have a feeling that one day China will once again become a republic and be guided by these three principles. This road, and others we would come across, has some beautiful European style buildings, from 100 years ago, when the Germans were here.

The beaches I will describe in the next chapter. For our evening meal we went to the 8th floor of a shopping mall, but the food was not very good – just so-so. We walked back to our hotel, exploring some night markets en route. These are quite common in many places. People simply set up their stalls, on footpaths or anywhere, and sell clothing, jewellery, bags etc., and lots of food.

The next morning, we had breakfast in the hotel dining room as it is included in the tariff, and is the usual Chinese fare. Now we can explore this city in a way we have done many times before; just hop on a bus – any bus – and see where it goes. We found ourselves going through a long tunnel. Goodness, where are we? It was not a rounded tunnel, but square sided, so I concluded we were on the sea bottom, as this is the method used with the Sydney Harbour Tunnel. You prefabricate the tunnel sections, dig a trench on the sea floor, then just drop them in and bolt them together. Just make sure it does not leak. Qingdao has a harbour, and this tunnel goes under the entrance. There is not much on the other side so we came back again. Great fun.

Next we got on another bus going in the opposite direction. We found a large park so went to explore. The zoo is here. We did not go in, but enjoyed wandering around the rest of the park. The day was hot and muggy, so later we actually laid down on a shady park bench for a 40 minute rest. Wonderful.

This was an old German town, and has beautiful architecture. After two German missionaries were killed, the German Government pressured the Chinese Government into leasing Qingdao to them for 99 years, from 1898. As it turned out they were only here for about 15 years, as the First World War intervened and a combined British-Japanese force took the town. The Japanese remained till 1922, but then they returned in 1938. The best examples of architecture seem to have been taken over by the government, a few now being used as police stations. A hundred years ago, the Vincentians were here, and we found the old presbytery, now being used as a residence. Nearby there is a solid Protestant church. I do not know if it is still in use, but if so, then only on Sundays, as for the rest of the week, it is a tourist venue, with the government making money out it by charging people 10 Yuan to go in and have a sticky. It has granite foundations and a wavy pattern on its ochre coloured outside walls. Visitors seem to enjoy climbing the bell tower, on the top of which is a clock. The lavish mansion built by the German governor is also close by.

The following day we found a German castle, reminding me of St Mary's Towers at Douglas Park, not far from Sydney. Here too visitors like to climb up the tower – for 8.5 Yuan. Now there's a thought; we could have Chinese tourists pay heaps of money to stroll through SMT; we could make a mint!

Nearby we walked through what is called "The Eight Passes" area, Badaguan. There are eight streets here named after eight passes famous in Chinese history; famous to the Chinese, that is. The area has lots of greenery, especially pine trees, beeches, myrtles, cedars and peach trees, interspersed with well-built German houses. Lonely Planet suggests this is a good place for a pleasant stroll; hardly, with the area jammed packed with cars; cars on the pedestrian crossings; cars lining the roads; cars packing the footpaths; and cars simply abandoned in the middle of the road.

On our bus back, I witnessed a little scene which may provide food for thought. People got onto the bus, with the usual rushing for the doorway, then rushing for seats. One young girl acted particularly selfishly, in diving for a seat, even though many older people were standing. Her brother also got a seat, but after a while he offered it to his rather harassed looking mother. I commended him for his unselfishness, whereupon his sister hung her head, evidently feeling ashamed of herself. I am assuming they were brother and sister, even though this is rare with the One Child Policy.

Let me finish this episode with another incident. We had our evening meal at McDonald's – the only time we did. It tastes the same. I wanted a small ice-cream. "Sorry, you can't have a small ice-cream; if you want small then you have to have two." What? Why is that? I had a large instead.

Enough for now. Stay tuned for more exciting stories about Qingdao in the next edition.

109. Qingdao Beaches – 6th – 8th August 2013

On one of our jaunts we travelled to the eastern, more commercial and more modern section of the city, a cityscape of tall shiny new buildings. A large red sculpture by the harbour stands out. The pollution, however, is a drawback, with a brown haze casting a pall over what would otherwise have been a beautiful scene. It was hot as we wandered around, so to cool off, we went into the atrium of one of these modern buildings and simply sat there, on the edge of a fish pond while we rested and cooled down. The girl at the reception desk took no notice of us.

This city has a number of beaches and each has its own character. We wanted a beach where I could swim. On Thursday we hopped on a bus which travelled along the shoreline so that I could have a look. Beach No. 3 looked good, so here we stopped, finding a shady place under some trees. There were two hammocks slung between trees, with a woman resting in one of them. We tried the other; very comfortable; then the lady came over; "30 Yuan". It was her private business. They will try anything to make money. "No thanks."

I liked this beach, and spent some time here swimming, following a line of buoys, which mark out an area. The beach is so shallow, even at its deepest, that people scared of deep water would have the security of knowing that for most of it all they have to do is put a foot down. Of course there is no surf. The water was a little dirty, but not too bad. There were a lot of people here of course, mostly just paddling in the shallows, rubber duckies around their waists.

There were lots of brides having their photos taken by the seaside, even at times with the groom. This must be the season for weddings, as we have seen so many couples. Isn't it interesting how the focus is on the bride rather than the groom? I once performed a wedding ceremony at Randwick, with everyone lining up afterwards to have photos taken outside the church. When the photographer had finished, a young man came up to him and said, "What about me?" "Who are you?" "I'm the groom!"

After our swim we walked around the coastline. There is a walkway extending for more than 40 km, part cement, part wood, and no, we did not walk all of it – in fact very little, but the section we did walk was quite pleasant. We came across one intriguing scene; row upon row of young men, sitting on the beach, all wearing black bathing caps, seemingly doing nothing. At beach 3 I had noticed a group of young men in the water, also doing nothing, but these had been wearing yellow bathing caps. What is this? They are soldiers. With the world's largest army, it is not surprising that one comes across them everywhere. There is a military base near beach 2, where the black caps were, and it seems this beach is reserved for them, as we saw nobody else there.

As we walked we saw yet more bridal couples having their photos taken, the grooms all handsome of course in their Western style suits, and the brides all beautiful in their flowing white dresses, though on this hot day, some of them were looking a little dishevelled and decidedly grumpy. Isn't your wedding day supposed to be the happiest day of your life? I thought some of the photographers were a little far-fetched. One groom, for instance, was asked to twiddle a twig under his beloved's nose, while she was supposed to look coy. Another couple was supposed to be walking, but instead they were standing stock still, one leg raised in the air. Goodness. What is wrong with walking? In China much is made of the wedding photos, which can be taken up to a year before the actual wedding, and cost thousands of Yuan. They are heavily airbrushed so that all brides look much the same and ditto for the grooms. See one set of wedding photos and you pretty well see them all. A pity.

Now let us return to the No. 6 beach, the one closest to where we are staying, at the bottom of Zhong Shan Lu. If you look at the photo you will see why I did not wish to swim here. The water is not very clean, and in fact we saw men throwing nets into the water, not to catch fish, but to collect rubbish. This beach is just so narrow, only a few metres wide, yet is lined with stalls selling beach ware, shells, souvenirs, and food – whatever. These stalls are set up right on the sand; truly amazing. You would never see this on an Australian beach. Do the vendors pay a fee to the government? At high tide the water can be seen lapping at the supports. And it is just so crowded, not only on the beach, but on the promenade above it, where it is a popular pastime to hang over the railing and watch the people below. On the beach people mostly stand or sit as there is not enough room to lie down.

Speed boats and jet boats were also for hire, with people whizzing out over the bay for a five minute spin. At the end of the bay is a lighthouse, perched on a green promontory. Maybe this is where the name of the city comes from, but that is just a surmise. *"Qingdao"* means "Green Island". There is also a pavilion perched on the end of a causeway, so maybe the name comes from here. This, incidentally, is depicted on the Tsingdao beer bottles. In the main harbour, you can even go yachting. Qingdao was the site of the boating events at the Beijing Olympics.

The footpaths, too, were filled with parked cars, except in some places where they were protected by flower pots or bollards. The presence of the latter is a surprise, as it does show that the authorities are conscious of the problem and the need to keep cars off footpaths. Maybe they should put these bollards all over the city to protect the footpaths and the pedestrians.

We also found another coffee place, called "Tommyboy's Coffee". You may have gathered by now that I like coffee shops, places where one can relax in air conditioned comfort, plug into the internet and watch the passing parade, all while enjoying a cup of coffee.

110.   Qingdao; St Michael's Cathedral 7th – 8th August 2013

There is one other attraction in this city that we were anxious to see; the Catholic cathedral of St. Michael's. And it is beautiful. Not surprisingly it is a German building, with German SVDs here a century ago. It was built in 1908. Outside the cathedral there is a photo of Fr. Joseph Freinademeitz, who was sent here by Arnold Janssen, the SVD founder.

There is a square in front of the cathedral, in which I counted no fewer than 13 bridal couples having their photos taken, with this beautiful church as backdrop. One side of the square is a large building, which used to be the administrative centre, but is now an art gallery, closed. At one end is a bar, downstairs in a dirty, musty cellar, but the beer was good. We chose Belgian; a very good, back palate wheat beer. The local brew is Tsingdao, reputed to be the best in China, but it is a little weak. This is also China's first beer, another gift from Germany.

The church itself was blocked off, the access gate being padlocked and guarded. I asked the priest at the gate if I could come in and pray, telling him who I was. No problems, as he shook my hand. And I did pray; it is so beautiful, in white with orange-gold trim, basilica style (row of columns on each side). There are statues to St. Francis, St. Anthony of Padua, the baptism of Jesus, and St. Joseph, and Mary outside, plus paintings. An organist was playing softly in the background. The church was not always like this, as it was wrecked by Mao and his Red Guards during the Cultural Revolution.

In my view churches should be open all day for people to come and pray, but this one is open only for daily morning Mass and then on Sundays. But in this case I agree that it should not be open. What would happen? Tourists, with no sense of the sacred, would come flocking in, having their photos taken, talking loudly. "It is written in the Scriptures that God said; My temple will be called a house of prayer, but you have turned it into a den of thieves." Mt. 21/13. They would not be treating it as a house of prayer.

Later we were talking with a seminarian, studying in Beijing, now home for the holidays. He told us there are 200 studying altogether, both male and female. The diocese of Qingdao has three churches and 12 priests, four of them here, including the bishop. The Church will survive, but in a Chinese way, and with Chinese personnel. At the moment, in my opinion, it is still too European, but I am sure that in time that will change, not only in China, but throughout the world. It is wonderful to note that the faith planted here by the Germans is deeply rooted and will survive. In Guizhou province, where I worked previously, it was the MSCs who planted the faith, and they, too, were Germans, and there, too, it is deeply rooted.

Let me clarify my vision. I am not just talking about "plant", about buildings. Nor am I only talking about what goes on in those buildings, whether worship, or teaching or healing the sick, since wherever the Church has gone, education and health care have been priorities, important those these may be. I am talking about relationships, firstly with God, then with each other, in a way that breaks down the barriers between peoples worldwide. I am talking about universal brother/sister hood, with God as our Parent. I am talking about something wider than nationalism.

This seminarian also expressed deep appreciation to the Germans for what they had done for China. Given that they were here for such a short length of time, they certainly gave China a lot, in terms of architecture, institutions, technology, beer, and some knowledge of God in Jesus. They also took a sleepy fishing village and turned it into what is now the fourth largest port in China. Praising overseas powers, however, is not the usual position taken, where instead they are hated for taking over sacred Chinese territory, so I was very surprised. Hypocritically, the Chinese have no qualms about taking over other people's territories, and then acclaim the good that they may do, while conveniently ignoring the atrocities.

I could have spent more time here, as there is so much more to explore, but we had already booked our ticket out. That is always a problem with buying tickets early; it precludes extending one's stay. Maybe next time; but one does not have to see everything, and in any event, this is an impossibility. What is important is enjoying what one does see and learning from it. We would leave the next day, Saturday.

For our final evening meal in Qingdao, we went to one of the many restaurants just up from the beach. Many people were dining al fresco. We chose one and I decided to have pork, which I had not had for a while, as here by the sea we had been having seafoods. Mistake – I think the pork had passed its used-by date, especially considering the heat, about 34 degrees. I also have doubts about the cleanliness of many of these restaurants. In any event, I had an upset stomach for a while; this is one of the dangers in eating strange food. Not to worry, as I was OK in a couple of days.

Next morning we checked out of our hotel and headed for the railway station, where we boarded a fast train to Shanghai, a G train. These are wonderful, and I have been on a few of them now. There is no standing, everybody being allocated a seat. Furthermore, there is so much space, with 56 seats in this first class carriage, and 90 seats in second class – which we were unable to procure. This compares with a K train, where 150 people cram into a carriage. This high speed carriage is more like an aircraft. There are four seats across, with a central aisle, rather than the usual six seats across. With fewer people, there was none of the usual bun rush to get on; everything was orderly. The train ride is also so smooth, with none of the clickety-clack of other trains, yet it is so fast, reaching a speed of 299 kph; they always keep it just under the 300 kph mark, I think for safety reasons, after one train ploughed into the back of another last year. Hence we got to Hong Qiao station in Shanghai in seven hours, arriving at 4.30 pm.

There is only one more stage in our journey remaining: tomorrow.

111. Shanghai to Chongqing – 10th – 12th August 2013

Hong Qiao is truly amazing in its vastness yet also its convenience, if you do not mind walking. Literally *"hong qiao"* means "rainbow bridge", which is quite apt, given that it is a transport hub; rainbow is a symbol of hope. Here, as we have noted, is the terminus for the fast G trains. From here one can connect with a suburban train, as two metro lines converge, 2 and 10. Shanghai's metro system is huge; on another occasion it took me two hours just to travel across town. Here too is the airport – or one of them – with two separate terminals. Close by is the long distance bus station. This city is so huge – as populous as all Australia – that there are two major airports, the other one, Pudong, also being a major transport hub. From here one can catch another very fast train from the terminal to downtown.

I find it a little amusing that there has been such rapid development here in China while in my own country very little gets done; lots of talk but very little action. There has, for example, been talk for years about building a second airport for Sydney yet nothing has happened. There has been talk, talk, talk about extending Sydney's suburban rail network to the North West and along the northern beaches, but again, no action. Recently I read that Australia will build one – one only – fast train, linking Sydney with Canberra, in – wait for it – **17 years!** Here in China they just do it. New metro lines open every year, as do new fast train routes. In Qingdao, their metro system is currently being extended out to the western part of the city. We can learn a lot from China.

Since we are separating here, each returning home, we decided to stay at an airport hotel, something I have never done before. It may be a little expensive, but so convenient. It is such a pleasant place, with everything so clean, neat and new. It was a little strange in that airports have always been places to rush to, so that one does not miss a flight, or depart from quickly, but on this occasion the airport itself became my home – at least temporarily. In the summer, Shanghai gets very hot, but here, it is all comfortably air-conditioned. Exercise is not a problem, as one can – and we did – walk kilometres around the terminal. Eating is also not a problem as there are so many eateries to choose from.

I have a friend here in Shanghai, but unfortunately we were not able to meet. I will probably only come to Shanghai once more, and that for a brief layover on my return to Australia in one year's time. Maybe she will come to Australia.

Our hotel, Bo Yue, is owned by Air China. We stayed two nights and on the first we were given a complimentary drink at the hotel bar. I had a chocolate martini – very nice. We were the only patrons, sitting, chatting, reminiscing and listening to good background music. Mind you, one drink was enough, especially at those prices. Our room looked out over the runways, so we could watch planes take off and land, seeing a little over the roof of the departure section, which is between our room and the runways. Surprisingly it was quiet. We were also able to watch some movies on TV. What a wonderful way to finish our holiday.

On our final morning, we had breakfast in our room. Now we could have paid an extra 150 Yuan to have a hotel breakfast, Western style, but that is just a little too steep. Instead, I wandered down to McDonald's for some milk, which I used with my cereal. After that we spent some time at Costa Coffee for coffee and muffin, while waiting to board my flight to Chongqing. It was delayed, of course, but only a little. Our flight left about 11.30 am, getting into Chongqing just after 2.00 pm. Using the metro system, it takes two hours from the airport to my apartment, so that I was back home about 4.30 pm. Wow! What a holiday!

Packing and unpacking is something I have done many times over the past month, but now it is done for the last time. Then you turn on the hot water system before going out to buy supplies, as there is very little in my fridge.

For the next two weeks I would be on my own, before everyone else returns, giving me time to do some writing. Unfortunately, I found I had no internet connection, so that my daily routine settled into a pattern of writing in the morning, then going across to Café Liberthe on campus to get on line, while enjoying a milkshake, not to mention the comfort of air-conditioning. It was hot, with the temperature close to 40 degrees most days.

The university pool was operating, so I made use of it, attempting to do laps. I say "attempting" as there have been a lot of people in the pool and most just splash around or go from side to side. Maybe 50 metre is too far for most of them to swim. One day an army squad arrived, all dressed in black shorts and khaki T-shirts. They could not swim either, but just paddled around. I may have mentioned that there is an army base close by; in fact there are two. Unfortunately, the pool is only open from 5.30 pm to 7.00 pm. I found this out when everyone else got out of the pool and I was still doing laps.

Down the road in Lieshimu there is a wet market – selling fruit and vegetables, but also fish. The fish arrive in a sealed water tanker. The lid is taken off and the fish are scooped up in a net before being dumped into a large blue bucket, which is then manhandled into the market. One afternoon three fish escaped and went flapping off down the hill. Unfortunately for them the nearest river is a good 20 minute walk away. They didn't make it. The man picked them up and dumped back into the blue bucket, none too gently, I might add. Poor fish. You see them still alive – barely – in supermarket tanks, some of them floating upside down.

One night, the 21st, I walked up to the upper campus to watch the full moon rise over the city. It was a beautiful sight, the moon seemingly enlarged close to the horizon, and a little orange in colour due to the polluted atmosphere.

I have had a most amazing holiday. Thank you, Lord. I hope you too have enjoyed it, at least vicariously.

Conclusion

This book only concerns my travels between from 2008 to 2013. Maybe the earlier travels from 2002 to 2007 will form the subject of another volume. Also this book says nothing about my life in China as a teacher. Perhaps this too can be treated in another volume.

What is important, however, with regard to travel, is not how much territory has been traversed, but how much I have learnt and how much I have changed. As I said earlier a traveller should be a pilgrim and not just a tourist.

The second point that should be made is that the journey is just as important as the destination. Too often in life we are so busy with rushing into the future that we forget about the present. If we enjoy the present then the future will take care of itself. Travel is not an inconvenient but painful necessity that must be born before we arrive. Rather it is of itself of great value. Each moment in fact has an eternal value.

To have been in China over the past ten years has been a rare privilege, one that I have enjoyed very much. I have been fortunate enough to have enjoyed my travels as part of this, in spite of any inconveniences along the way. In consequence I have enjoyed my life, which is in itself a journey. I do hope that you are enjoying yours, and maybe – just maybe – this book will also have been enjoyable for you.